I0975294

BEYOND SHYNESS

HOW TO CONQUER SOCIAL ANXIETIES

Jonathan Berent, A.C.S.W.,

WITH AMY LEMLEY

SIMON & SCHUSTER

New York London Toronto Sydney Tokyo Singapore

SIMON & SCHUSTER
Simon & Schuster Building
Rockefeller Center
1230 Avenue of the Americas
New York, New York 10020

Designed by Irving Perkins Associates
Manufactured in the United States of America
1 2 3 4 5 6 7 8 9 10

Library of Congress Cataloging-in-Publication Data
Berent, Jonathan.
Beyond shyness : how to conquer social anxieties /
Jonathan Berent with Amy Lemley.
p.   cm.
Includes index.
1. Anxiety.   2. Bashfulness.   I. Lemley, Amy.   II. Title.
BF575.A6B47   1993
155.2'32—dc20   92-35206
CIP

ISBN: 0-671-74137-3

Acknowledgments

Although names and identifying details have been changed, the essence of the stories contained here is true. The authors would like to thank the many individuals whose stories became the basis of this book.

We also wish to thank our agent, Jane Dystel, for her tireless effort in helping to shape this book and finding it a home.

Alice Mayhew and George Hodgman of Simon & Schuster are committed professionals, and we are grateful for their enthusiastic guidance.

Many thanks also to Eliran Eliaz, Ph.D., the world's first Ph.D. in drama therapy, for his expertise, and to anthropologist Robert Vetter for his research.

Jonathan Berent wishes to thank Marcia Cohen for her true friendship and support.

Amy Lemley wishes to thank Sarah Bruce, Katie Chester, Jonathan Coleman, Jay Fennell, Norman, Laura, and Jane Lemley, and Julie Speasmaker for their support and encouragement during the writing of this book.

Contents

CHAPTER ONE

Anxiety: Friend or Foe?

Shyness. We've heard this word a lot. At one time or another, all of us have probably thought of ourselves as shy. Indeed, research shows that 93 percent of all people have experienced shyness. What does it mean to be "shy"? For some, it may mean being quiet, reserved, or timid. For others, shyness is a catch-all word to describe what may at first seem like a personality trait, but is in fact a fear response that pervades their lives and prevents them from doing things that they would like to do, such as finding personal fulfillment and achieving career goals.

Over the years, in working with thousands of people who call themselves "shy," I have come to realize that this word is too general to be of much help in identifying a problem and solving it. The actual response to the stress of interaction is called *social anxiety*. Of course, just as one person might say he is "a little shy around women" and another might say she is "extremely shy about speaking in front of a group," it is also true that there is a wide spectrum of social anxiety, from mild nervousness all the way to *social phobia*, in which interaction-related anxiety is so extreme that a person actually avoids the specific situations that cause it. Avoidance, too, has its degrees, and can mean anything from being characteristically reserved at work, even though you have an idea or solution to propose, to refusing to attend social gatherings. Social phobia—commonly defined as performance anxiety in which the individual fears humiliation, embarrassment, or being evaluated—is quite common, and, according to a November 1991 article in the *Journal of Clinical Psychiatry*, is an emerging problem that is just beginning to receive attention: "If the 1980s were considered to be the 'decade of anxiety,' most would agree that panic disorder and obsessive-compulsive disorder received the most attention. The 1990s are sure to be another decade of anxiety, but we can expect other anxiety disorders to take the limelight, particularly social phobia." Until now, the article states, social phobia has been "overlooked" as a disorder, and I believe that mental health professionals have often looked at it as part of a general anxiety problem, lumping it together with other conditions. But social anxiety is a very specific problem. As a psychotherapist with more than thirteen years of experience in developing a program for individuals with social anxiety, I have observed that by nature, people with social anxiety are extremely resistant to getting help, so there is much about this population that has not been fully understood or studied. As for the increased aware-ness of social anxiety, I see it as an indication that technological advances and an increasingly competitive workplace are taking their toll on society. Further, I think families today are less able to "hide" or protect their socially anxious members. People with social anx-iety can only benefit from this increased awareness. For some, a little information about how they respond to stress may be enough to minimize the anxiety response; for others, a more detailed appli-cation of overall strategies is in order. Whatever your social func-tioning level, this book can help you to work through your anxiety to be a more productive and fulfilled human being.

As you begin your exploration of social anxiety, it is important to grasp some basic concepts. First, understand that *"shyness"* and *social anxiety* are two closely related dynamics: Both terms describe a *learned response* to social interaction. In unfamiliar situations, or even familiar situations whose outcome may be unknown—meeting new people, giving a speech, asking someone for a date, negotiating a raise—a "shy" or socially anxious person may hesitate to pursue the things he or she is interested in, or even begin to avoid situa-tions that cause nervousness or anxiety. For example, if you fear that asking your supervisor to explain a basic point at work will make you appear stupid and you therefore avoid asking questions, you are allowing your social anxiety—your fear of humiliation or embarrassment—to control your actions and inhibit your career success. In your personal life, feeling out of place at parties because of anxiety might lead you to decline many social invitations. When you fear rejection, the interactions you do have can become unsatisfying. Your anxiety can prevent you from giving all you can to a conversation and can prevent others from responding fully to all you have to offer.

I call this fear response *interactive inhibition.* How does interactive inhibition affect you? At work, you may stay in a "safe" job, in which all duties are clear and manageable although no longer challenging, rather than ask for more responsibility or look outside your company for a change. In your personal life, you might hesitate to get close to people, although you have friends to socialize with. Your inhibited emotion may inhibit the quality of intimacy.

When your interactions are inhibited by social anxiety, you are unable to get as much out of life as possible, and so a "harmless personality trait" can become a major obstacle that stands in the way of fulfillment and productivity. But this doesn't have to be the case. *Social anxiety is a learned response—a habit that can be broken.* This book will show you, step by step, how to break the social anxiety cycle that may have caused loneliness in your personal life, decreased productivity in the workplace, and an overall lack of fulfillment. As you begin to understand that social anxiety is a combination of attitudinal, emotional, behavioral, and physical responses, you will see that *there is actually no such thing as shyness.* Rather, what you may refer to as "shyness" is actually social anxiety, a psychophysiological response that you can learn to control. To recognize social anxiety is to give yourself permission to resolve the issues that cause your symptoms. In working through this self-help program, learn to substitute the phrase "social anxiety" for the vague term "shyness" and you will start to see your response pattern in a different light: as a way of reacting that you have chosen, not some unchangeable instinct that has chosen you.

In more than a decade of psychotherapy practice, I have met

thousands of people who refer to themselves as "shy." Often, these people believe shyness is a fait accompli, a matter of genetic predisposition that they must deal with as a fact of life. They say they were "born shy"—their parents, grandparents, or other relatives are shy too, and it's just in their blood to be timid. Of course, behavior also can be handed down through conditioning—perhaps your mom always got nervous before a party so you learned to react the same way. Believing that "shyness" is an indelible component of the personality can be a real stumbling block to overcoming social fears. "That's just the way I am" becomes an excuse for not taking responsibility for individual well-being. In order to change this mindset, it is important to understand that because shyness is learned, it can be unlearned. Anxiety can be controlled.

But there is no pill to cure the problem. As with all aspects of life, if you really want to get the most out of your social interactions on the job and after hours, you have to put a good deal into them. It takes hard work and a genuine commitment to change. If you sit there waiting passively for the day when your "shyness" will disappear, you will miss out on all the things that, deep down, you really want. And I am not just talking about having fun. In our ever-changing economic climate, your job security and career growth depend on your ability to interact productively, to initiate dialogue, stand up for your ideas, and negotiate compromise. Your ability to evaluate the social chemistry of the workplace and to establish and maintain your position on the team may well determine your career success. Not everyone rises to the top, outshining colleagues, but not everyone wants to and that is not always what is required. But most people must work with others, and cooperation demands social skills and confidence.

This reminds me of David, a brilliant young computer programmer whose difficulty in interacting almost cost him an important promotion. Right out of college, he landed an excellent entry-level job with a growing firm. Within nine months, he was promoted to a managerial position—a real success story. But it was after his promotion that his troubles began.

Although he was fine in front of a computer terminal, David had great difficulty coordinating his work with other members of his department, whether they were his superiors or people who reported to him. Poor communication skills and a tendency to be a perfectionist combined to create a management nightmare: Though it was clear David knew exactly what needed to be done to keep things running smoothly, it seemed he had trouble delegating his duties to subordinates. When a problem arose, he preferred to solve it himself—even when it took twice as much time—rather than ask his superiors to jump in and help. At his quarterly review, his boss addressed the department's concerns and offered to extend David's probationary period if he would try harder to interact with others. In working with me, David became aware that he was uncomfortable turning over any aspect of his responsibilities for fear of seeming unable to accomplish his job on his own. After exploring these doubts, he was able to fully utilize his superiors' knowledge, and to rely on his co-workers to get the job done in the most productive and efficient manner. As David learned, if you accept the challenge and take responsibility for your reactions, you will begin to see that you can learn to manage your anxiety and have a healthy, rewarding social life, as well as a more fulfilling career.

The first step in overcoming your problem is to acknowledge that what you call shyness *is* anxiety, a very specific kind of anxiety. As you begin to understand this concept, you will be able to make use of the strategies and techniques I have developed to solve the problem. Remember, to use the word "shy" to describe yourself is to give up control of your life and your ability to improve it. Call yourself "shy," and that's the end of the story. Admit you have social anxiety, however, and you are on your way to a more relaxed, fulfilling life in which you are in control. Shyness, after all, means many things to many people. But anxiety is more concrete—I usually describe it as an attitudinal, emotional, behavioral, and physical response to stress, although not necessarily a negative response.

Picture the athlete at the starting line of a race—adrenaline pumping, energy flowing, muscles tightening, skin aglow with anticipatory perspiration, heart beating faster and faster, the mind focused on only one thing: the starter's gun and the race. Now, picture the person about to enter a social gathering. He or she approaches the door, behind which a number of people are talking, laughing, having fun—adrenaline pumping, energy flowing, pulse beginning to quicken, the mind focused on anticipation: "What will happen when I enter the room?" "Will I see anyone I know?" "What will they think of me?"

What do these situations have in common? The answer is anxiety. For the athlete, anxiety is channeled into energy that just may win the race. By allowing the anxiety to play a role in gearing him or her up for the race, the athlete is making good use of the natural fight-or-flight response. For the partygoer, it is not so clear. If that person is willing to let being "keyed up" or "excited" be a positive kind of energy flow, then any initial nervousness or uncertainty will remain manageable and nonthreatening. But if the physical sensations of anxiety become distracting and the thoughts obsessive, the party guest is in for a difficult time. Similarly, a person who prepares for an important meeting may feel a kind of nervous energy in gearing up for negotiations. But if that same person, although well prepared, allows interactive inhibition to keep him from suggesting a solution, questioning a point, or voicing an opinion, he will feel a real letdown. When holding back becomes a habit, the pervasive feeling of "Oh no, I did it again" may lead to a lack of enthusiasm that interferes with productivity and job satisfaction. The truth is, we all want to be heard without—if we can reasonably avoid it— being rejected or embarrassed. How to resolve this dilemma? First, by understanding anxiety in its simplest terms. The more you understand about anxiety, the more you will be able to control it. Remember, social anxiety is not some abstract phenomenon or indelible personality trait. It is an explainable dynamic that you can choose to control.

Let's look more closely at the athlete. For that person, in that situation, anxiety is normal and appropriate. In fact, it is crucial to effective performance. Without it, the physiological workings of the body would fall short of what is required. In the second example, anxiety is also appropriate. But it can become negative if the person begins to worry about what is going on inside the room: "What are they laughing about?" "Will anyone talk to me?" "Am I dressed right?" "Will I seem nervous?" At that point it's the degree of incapacity—the extent to which the anxious feelings and thoughts prevent interacting—that becomes the most important issue. (In the workplace, these thoughts may run to "Have I done enough research?" "What if I can't answer my boss's questions?" "Can they tell I'm anxious?")

Anxiety is a fact of life! Everyone experiences it. It began in our cave-dweller days as a *fight-or-flight response*. Think of it this way: If you were walking through the woods and you ran into a bear, it would be normal for your body to activate the fight-or-flight response. Your heart would race, your muscles would tense up, your pupils would dilate, you would breathe more rapidly. The same thing would happen today if you were walking down the street and ran into a mugger. There is a simple, scientific explanation of this response: Your mind and body are preparing to protect you— whether you can feel it happening or not.

Let us briefly examine this process. Your nervous system is divided into two basic parts: The *voluntary nervous system* controls actions that require thought, such as using the different parts of your body to drive a car; the *autonomic nervous system*, among its many functions, suspends all nonessential activity of the body and increases the physiological activity needed to confront the situation—either by *fighting* or by *fleeing* the external threat. Here is what it is responsible for:

- increased muscle tension
- accelerated heartbeat
- rapid breathing
- constriction of peripheral blood vessels (this is what causes cold hands)
- dilation of the pupils
- suspension of the digestive process
- dry mouth
- a voiding of bladder and bowels

In addition, the fight-or-flight response causes a marked increase in the flow of adrenaline through the bloodstream and therefore added strength.

What does running from a bear have to do with social anxiety? Everything. *An anxiety reaction is your fight-or-flight response.* If you see a bear, it's okay to run, and in fact your physical symptoms of anxiety will probably be the least of your problems. But if you have those same symptoms when you go to a party or speak in front of a group, you are almost certainly overreacting to a stressful but relatively safe situation. It is a question of degree, and there are many degrees of anxiety. Some nervousness is all right, but not so much that you begin to run from interacting with other people.

I am well versed in relaxation techniques and have served as a stress management consultant to numerous corporations. Yet even I experience anxiety symptoms on occasion. During the past several years, I have had the opportunity to appear on many television and radio shows and have given countless lectures. Never have I made an appearance without my hands being cold! What does this mean? When your hands are dry and warm, you are relaxed. When your hands become cool and sweaty, it's a safe bet that stress and anxiety are present. And yet I enjoy public speaking! I have gotten to the point where these appearances are fun, and I look forward to doing these shows. When I do them, I am concentrating intensely and working very hard to channel my energy. The cold hands are merely a physiological manifestation of this hard work. My mind and body are gearing up to perform, and the result is *positive anxiety.*

Anxiety becomes negative when you start to avoid the situation that causes it. For example, if I were to stop making public appearances because I didn't like the physical manifestations of my stress response, or even to make the appearances but allow myself to be distracted by my cold hands or other symptoms—perhaps thinking, "Can they tell my hands are clammy?" "Am I making sense?"—that would be counterproductive. It's important to me to make these appearances, so I channel my gearing-up anxiety into positive energy.

Anxiety does not exist to control you. You exist to control it. It is, as I said, a simple fact of life that can be managed. In fact, used properly, it can actually give you an extra boost by heightening your energy and awareness. If you have social anxiety about such things as giving a presentation, speaking up at a meeting, attending a social gathering, initiating plans, developing intimacy in friendships and dating, then learning to manage your anxiety will help. This book will teach you how to *channel* your anxiety—not how to eliminate it. The twelve chapters delineate a five-step program that essentially works like this:

Step 1: *Identify your anxiety symptoms and recognize the ways in which they interfere with your life.* Your social fears prevent you from doing things you would like to do (pursue friendships, date, achieve career success). Pinpointing your stress responses and noting what causes them give you the information you need to move on to Step 2.

Step 2: *Set short- and long-term social goals.* Having identified the situations you have trouble confronting, you can identify immediate goals to work toward, and start to form a vision of your ideal social self. Goal-setting is a valuable way of letting your imagination offer a reward for your hard work. Next, you will begin to learn skills that can make your dream a reality.

Step 3: *Learn stress management and self-awareness.* The techniques outlined in this book will allow you to control your anxiety response and tune in to your own desires and strong points, giving you more to share as you become more comfortable interacting. With your anxiety in check and your self-awareness guiding you toward fulfillment, anxiety becomes positive energy and will be the base of your self-empowerment. Now you are ready to polish your social skills.

Step 4: *Learn or refine social skills.* Your fear has diminished, making it possible to refine social skills and enhance your interactive productivity, which will make the difference between social success and failure. Good conversation, active listening, an awareness of what behavior is appropriate—all of these skills will add to your overall social ability and self-empowerment.

Step 5: Expand and refine your social network. At this point, you are ready to roll. You understand your anxiety, your stress is manageable, and you have learned the finer points of interacting in a positive, productive manner. The final step is to use your community's resources to create, expand, or refine your social network to best meet your interactive goals. No matter who you are, you can improve your social network to better suit your needs. From here, anything is possible!

As you follow this program, you will learn to accept that *it is okay to have anxiety. What is not okay is to let your anxiety control you.*

Alan, a young man of twenty-two, is typical of the people who have come to me for treatment. Outwardly, he seemed well adjusted and likable. His sense of humor added fun to our sessions, and he was an active conversationalist who was well liked by his peers. If you met him in an informal setting, you would have no idea that an attractive, articulate person like Alan could get nervous or anxious about any social situation. But Alan suffered from the most common social anxiety today: fear of public speaking. He was afraid to stand up in front of a group and talk. For almost four years, he put off taking the public-speaking class that was required for college graduation. By his last semester, however, he knew there was no more avoiding it. He had to take the class or miss out on receiving his degree. Although he was scared, he was also highly motivated to confront his fear and finish his course load.

At first, Alan experienced a typical anxiety reaction or panic response: His hands got clammy, his heart raced, and he experienced every stutter, every verbal misstep as a huge blunder that no one would ever forget. He would blush, or imagine he was blushing, and then worry about what his classmates thought of him. Sometimes, he would feel a little short of breath and then worry that he would hyperventilate and need to rush from the room. He was intensely aware of all these symptoms of nervousness, though his audience of classmates thought little of it—they too were nervous about their speaking assignments, and were sympathetic. Alan's symptoms diminished as he gave more speeches, and watched others make the same mistakes without losing face.

The sensations that troubled Alan are typical of anxiety sufferers. Also typical is the tendency to avoid what you fear. The possibility of blushing or hyperventilating had become as scary to Alan as giving a speech, and in putting off the class, he was avoiding all these things.

Alan was not alone. Far from it: *Millions of people feel some panic or anxiety symptoms regularly.* Sometimes they are mild reactions that are easily connected to a particular situation or event. But in other instances they are more pervasive and more debilitating. The physical sensations may even be severe enough to warrant a visit to the emergency room, where a frustrated anxiety sufferer may be told that there is nothing wrong but stress. But panic symptoms are indeed real. Their cause? An internal mishandling of stress or emotions. What occurs with a panic or anxiety attack is a *psychophysiological reaction:* a mind-body response. While the body is preparing itself to confront the stressor, the mind is filled with fear and apprehension, with thoughts like "I'm losing control" or "I know I'm going to fail." Together, the body and mind are overreacting to their own fight-or-flight instincts.

Let's consider situations you may be avoiding because they cause a fight-or-flight anxiety reaction. Below are some possibilities:

Interaction with an authority figure
Giving a presentation at work
Eating in public
Speaking in front of a group
Taking interactive responsibility at work
Signing a check or other document in front of someone
Talking on the telephone
Talking to someone you don't know
Talking to someone you do know (outside the family)
Making social plans with someone (outside the family)
Going on a date
Using a public bathroom

Going to a party
Going to a singles-oriented event or program
Interacting with people at work
Waiting in line
Sitting in a doctor's or dentist's waiting room
Being examined by a doctor or dentist
Going to the theater
Going to a restaurant
Maintaining eye contact when talking to someone
Going to any public place
Taking public transportation
Other

Are some of these situations stressful for you? Go back over the list, checking off the ones that apply to you. As you check them off, think about the degree to which your fear hampers your social life. And if you recognize a situation that you actively avoid because you find it too stressful—say, you never use a public bathroom at all because you're "too shy" or it makes you anxious—make note of that, too.

Now that you've given some thought to the situations that cause anxiety, let's examine the particular symptoms of your anxiety. We will look at physical symptoms—what your body does when you feel anxious—and thought patterns—what thoughts bother you when you feel anxious. Use Charts 1 and 2 (pp. 23 and 24) to rank these symptoms in terms of frequency (whether they occur twice a month or as often as once a day), severity (whether they cause you minor discomfort or absolute panic), and the degree to which they interfere with your social life (not at all or significantly). The last category is very important, since it will help you to determine to just what extent your social anxiety disables you. The rankings in that category should be interpreted as follows:

1. *Not at all.* If you choose this answer, you usually experience no discomfort whatsoever when the thought or feeling in question arises. You may experience the symptom, but you are fully able to continue what you are doing (talking to an acquaintance, addressing a group, working with your supervisor,

and so on) without becoming distracted or trying to leave the situation.

2. *A little.* If a symptom interferes a little, it may occasionally cause you to lose your train of thought, or to falter or hesitate during conversation. Still, you find ways to compensate, and your interaction is not inhibited to a noticeable extent. You continue to interact with others on a regular basis, and none of your symptoms causes you to avoid interacting completely.

3. *Moderately.* A symptom that moderately interferes with interaction would be one that occasionally keeps you from doing something you would like to do (such as approach and speak to a stranger at a party) or are required to do (make a cold sales call on a prospective client). You are uncomfortable enough with the symptom at least to consider whether encountering it is worth the anxiety involved.

4. *Significantly.* For social anxiety symptoms to affect significantly the degree to which you interact, they must have caused you to develop the habit of avoiding the situations that cause them, whether by procrastination or merely by passive participation (such as attending a meeting without contributing anything). While you don't avoid all interaction, you probably try to stay out of it when you can, and spend a great deal of time negatively evaluating those interactions you do have. This may cause others to view you as aloof or distracted in conversation.

5. *Severe to the point of incapacity.* This is where social phobia comes in. We'll talk more about that in Chapter 4, but for now, understand that for social anxiety to become a phobia, it must be so severe that you avoid the situation that causes the anxiety whenever possible, even when it means forgoing a promotion or spending all your free time in total solitude. At this stage, you fear your symptoms just as much as you fear the interaction.

Now take several minutes to go through each list of symptoms, using the rankings to determine how much each plays a role in your current daily life.

Chart 1: Physical Anxiety Profile

What does your body do when you feel anxious or nervous?

Frequency	Severity	Social Life Interference
1 = Never	1 = No problem at all	1 = Not at all
2 = 2 times a month or less	2 = Minor discomfort but you can manage it	2 = A little
3 = 1 or 2 times a week	3 = Noticeably uncomfortable	3 = Moderately
4 = 3 times a week but not daily	4 = Severe	4 = Significantly
5 = 1 or more times daily	5 = Absolute panic; feels out of control	5 = Severe to the point of incapacity

a) Shortness of breath
b) Accelerated heartbeat
c) Sweating
d) Dizziness or faintness
e) Nausea or abdominal stress
f) Choking
g) Depersonalization—feeling of unreality, being "outside yourself"
h) Tingling or numbness

i) Flushes or chills
j) Voice quivering or shaking
k) Sweaty palms
l) Cold hands
m) Your mind going blank
n) Twitches, tics, or spasms
o) Lump in throat
p) Stuttering
q) Difficulty concentrating
r) Other

Total Scores:

Remember, there is a wide range of what is considered normal, and even feeling slightly nervous or keyed up is within that normal range. The goal is not avoiding anxiety but *managing* it, getting it under control. Whatever your anxiety level, by following the steps in this self-help plan and adapting them to your needs, you can empower yourself to interact more effectively. Later, you will do these indexes again. It is important to realize that your progress will be based on relativity. As you compare previous indexes to the most

Chart 2: Mental Anxiety Profile

What thoughts recur when you are anxious or nervous?

Frequency	Severity	Social Life Interference
1 = Never	1 = No problem at all	1 = Not at all
2 = 2 times a month or less	2 = Minor discomfort but you can manage it	2 = A little
3 = 1 or 2 times a week	3 = Noticeably uncomfortable	3 = Moderately
4 = 3 times a week but not daily	4 = Severe	4 = Significantly
5 = 1 or more times daily	5 = Absolute panic; feels out of control	5 = Severe to the point of incapacity

a) What will people think of me?
b) Am I good enough?
c) Am I dressed okay?
d) How do I look?
e) I'm going to embarrass myself.
f) People can tell I'm nervous.
g) People can tell what I'm thinking.
h) I'm going to lose control.
i) I'm going to have to run from the room.
j) What will I say?
k) I'm ugly.
l) If they knew me, they wouldn't like me.
m) I always do the wrong thing.
n) They can see I'm different.
o) They can see I'm lonely.
p) They can see I don't belong.
q) I can't.
r) They all have more than I do.
s) I always screw up.
t) I don't know what to say.
u) Other

Total Scores:

current one, look not only at totals but also at the individual categories and their frequency, severity, and degree of interactive interference.

To help you make general sense of your ratings, let me use as examples two people who have come to me for treatment. Each experienced different extremes of anxiety—Shelly was highly functioning but unfulfilled professionally, while Adam was incapacitated by fear on all fronts. Whereas Alan, our earlier example, a relatively high-functioning person with severe anxiety about a specific situation (public speaking), was somewhere in the middle, the two people introduced here were at opposite poles when compared to the norm: Shelly was high-functioning, and Adam was low-functioning. Understanding their perspectives may help you to gauge your own level of anxiety.

Shelly: At thirty-five, Shelly was an associate with a small law firm. She and her husband enjoyed socializing with friends and neighbors in the suburb where they lived, and often entertained at home. Shelly was not anxious or inhibited in purely social situations, and often hosted gatherings herself. At work, however, she did experience a slight degree of anxiety when it came to initiating projects or accepting responsibility. Her *interactive inhibition*—resistance to asking for help or doing things on her own—was preventing her from being made partner. How did social anxiety interfere with productivity at work? For Shelly, the safety of her position, with its predictable duties and conservative style of dress, was reassuring when she joined the firm right out of law school. But in order to get ahead at the firm, Shelly needed to do more than conform to the social system that existed at work. She had to go beyond meeting assignments and seek out new solutions and challenges.

Instead, though, Shelly waited for her supervisor to give his opinion on the cases assigned to her. Usually, her hesitancy to make decisions or take action on her own caused her to procrastinate—a bad habit that was hard to conceal as deadlines came and went. She didn't realize that action relieves anxiety. Instead, she feared the outcome of the risks she had to take in speaking her mind. She was unwilling to endure the pain of anxiety these risks would entail. Even when she had ideas of her own, she was extremely hesitant to express them, assuming that they were off-base or, as she said, "Somebody else would have made the same points already." Shelly's thinking was skewed: The firm hired her because they recognized capability and potential. Her training and experience were valuable to them, so some more initiative on her part would only have increased her value and could have netted her the partnership she hardly dared dream about. Perhaps more important, even if her ideas were rejected, the outcome would not have been devastating. No one is right 100 percent of the time or always says or does exactly the right thing. Shelly would not have been fired for thinking aloud as part of a problem-solving team.

Shelly's interactive inhibition had another cost as well. In performing the same duties the same way, without the experience of taking a risk that might pay off, of following a case start to finish, of meeting new challenges, she had dug herself into a rut. Her limited self-esteem was self-perpetuating, and the result was a lack of fulfillment. It's true she was successful in many ways, but without the confidence to move forward without being anxious about interacting, she did not *feel* successful.

How did Shelly score on the anxiety profile? The types of situations that caused Shelly anxiety were not that easy to identify—and after all, she did manage to get through the day with no physical symptoms of anxiety. At home, when she thought about work, she did tend to go over and over the same situations again, wondering what would have happened if she had done things differently. Occasionally, this led to a tension headache. Shelly did well in most situations, and she usually was willing to attend social events. But when she thought she must measure up by being assertive, she felt pressured and feared humiliating herself. Shelly's physical symptoms registered as minimal because none inhibited her interaction on a daily basis. She may have experienced minor symptoms such as cold hands or sweating, but she was not aware of them and they had no effect on her ability to interact. If she got a headache, it occurred at home—not during an interaction—and therefore it did not interfere with social interchange.

For thought patterns, Shelly's overall score was in the moderate range—not surprising, since it was her thought patterns that made her uncomfortable enough to clam up, taking direction instead of initiative. Recurring thoughts, such as "Am I good enough?," "I don't have anything to add," and "I don't know what to say," had a moderately inhibiting effect on Shelly's interactions, particularly on the job. These recurring thoughts, by reinforcing her low self-esteem, played a role in keeping her from advancing up the career ladder.

Adam: Adam was a young man whose anxiety turned into a monster. Where Shelly had a very mild case of social anxiety, Adam's case could only be called severe. Over a period of several years, his underlying social fears developed into a full-blown school phobia. A quiet, unassuming person, Adam had never stood out in the classroom. Through elementary school and on into high school, he neither excelled nor failed his subjects. By no means a discipline problem, the "shy" Adam kept to himself and seldom talked in class, whether to answer a teacher's question or chat with his buddies. In fact, he really had no friends, and the only peers he socialized with were his cousins, whom he saw at weekly family gatherings.

Though he watched the other kids working together on projects or playing sports together, Adam never approached them to join in. Maybe they wouldn't let him, he thought. Maybe he wasn't good enough. Being rejected was not a chance he was willing to take.

Adam never tried hard in school either. If he didn't understand something, he kept quiet, fearful that raising his hand would bring ridicule. When he did poorly on an exam or paper, it only confirmed to him what he was sure was true: He didn't measure up. He became so apprehensive about his tests that he began to feel physically ill at the thought of each approaching reminder of his inadequacy. Even though he had studied hard for a math test, for example, he could barely bring himself to get out of bed on the morning it was to take place. His parents, who thought of their child as a reserved but obedient boy who would eventually grow out of this awkward adolescent stage, did not pressure him. Adam was defensive and withdrawn, overwrought by the looming possibility that he would fail.

For the two class periods preceding the math test, Adam's mind was awash with geometry theorems, and his stomach churning. As waves of nausea washed over him, he began to salivate and swallowed hard. His eyes burned and he closed them, wishing he could block the test from his mind. When his head started to feel heavy and he became short of breath, he asked for a hall pass and headed for the bathroom.

Alone, he let his anxiety overtake him as he stared into the mirror, letting the cool water flow from the faucet and onto his sweaty palms. He would feel better, he thought, if he could just throw up. But even when he forced his finger down his throat, there was no relief. His dry heaves made him feel even weaker. He slumped to the cold tile and began to cry. Adam never went back to math class that day; instead, he got a pass from the nurse and went straight home.

Of course, the pressure Adam was feeling was not just related to the math test. The roots of his anxiety went much deeper. Still, the physical symptoms of anxiety became so debilitating that he eventually quit going to school altogether. Naturally, his parents were extremely concerned but also uncertain what to do. It took almost a year before Adam was sufficiently in control of his symptoms to return to school.

Clearly, he was working to avoid the pain of any kind of interaction, because he was so afraid of rejection or humiliation. His social anxiety became so extreme that he feared the symptoms as much as the stressor itself; in fact, his fear of interaction developed into a full-blown phobia. Adam's anxiety profile obviously featured all the physical symptoms on the list (especially shortness of breath, accelerated heartbeat, dizziness, and depersonalization). They surfaced almost daily and were extremely incapacitating, affecting him to a high degree *whenever he was actually in the situation that caused them.* Of course, when Adam avoided these situations, their frequency and severity diminished, but their degree of interactive interference increased until it was at level 5. The symptoms were so bad that they were preventing him from interacting, all the way to the point of incapacity. Obsessive thought patterns were a contributing factor as well: "Am I good enough?" "Will they like me?" Adam even had these recurring thoughts when he was alone in his room, looking out on the street at the neighborhood kids playing below.

To gauge the median, let's look again at Alan's situation. His physical symptoms, though fairly noticeable, were limited to specific situations in which he had to address a group; these symptoms included a lump in the throat, difficulty concentrating, accelerated heartbeat, a quavering voice, sweaty palms. But they only appeared during public-speaking situations. Otherwise, Alan handled himself with relative ease. The same was true of the obsessive thought patterns, which were limited to a specific situation: "I'm going to embarrass myself," "People can tell I'm nervous," "I'm going to lose control." The frequency was isolated, and therefore low, but the severity when the situation did arise was moderate. As for interactive interference, Alan places in the moderate range: He was high-functioning, but he did in fact actively avoid the stressor for a time.

Identifying your symptoms is the first step in creating a map for change. In order for change to occur, you need specific information to work from. This anxiety profile provides those specifics. Knowing what you're afraid of means you know *why* your pulse is racing, and that knowledge provides you with a choice: Handle the anxiety in a healthy way by identifying the cause and managing the symptoms, or handle it in an unhealthy way by running from the situation you fear.

Changing your responses may sound like a tall order, but it gets easier step by step. You can monitor your progress by referring back to these indexes, gauging once again the frequency and severity of your symptoms and considering the degree to which the various situations are still inhibiting your social life. Keep your initial responses handy (and leave room in the margin for later retesting) so that you can chart your progress from beginning to end.

As you work through this self-help program, you will teach yourself a new attitude and a new way to recognize and respond to anxiety. I've often heard it said that everything new starts with a thought. Here is yours: My *social anxiety symptoms are temporary and eventually they will diminish significantly and may well disappear altogether.* This sentence must become part of your daily routine. To ensure progress, you have to develop what I call PMA—Positive Mental Attitude. A positive outlook is one of the strongest and most powerful strategies of this self-help program. What you are doing is self-coaching, and a vital part of being a good coach is boosting morale. How? Through PMA, of course!

A negative mental attitude has no doubt been a contributing factor to your social anxiety. Here is a diagram of the sequence in which social anxiety develops:

The individual makes mistakes

- This causes feelings of confusion
- Which cause feelings of rejection
- Fear builds
- Which leads to avoidance of the threatening situation
- Which lowers self-confidence
- Which decreases the chances of success
- Which in turn creates more potential for confusion, rejection
- And brings on anxiety, lack of fulfillment, and possibly depression

I have found this cause-and-effect sequence to apply to most people who call themselves "shy." The key element, of course, is the degree of avoidance. In looking at social anxiety as a series of events—essentially social failure leading to a fear of rejection leading to avoidance of the situation that *causes* the bad feelings—a simple premise presents itself: Social anxiety syndrome is learned. This is good news. Why? *What is learned can be unlearned, relearned, or reprogrammed.* It may be true that people are genetically predisposed to certain characteristics, but the bottom line is that the problems discussed here can be controlled, reduced, or even eliminated. If your NMA (Negative Mental Attitude) is winning out right now, you may be saying that it's too late for you, that old habits die hard. But try to turn your thinking around—use that PMA. Yes, it is true that the earlier in life you interrupt this anxiety cycle, the better your chance of controlling the problem. But no matter how old you are, if you allow yourself to step in as coach and work your way through your symptoms and fears, you'll meet with success.

During a recent radio program I took a call from the mother of an eleven-year-old girl who told me her daughter was having trouble with some girls who teased her on the playground at school. When her class played open games such as kickball outside, she was almost

always chosen last. And on field trips, while other kids would partner up as instructed, this girl was usually left to be "partners" with
the teacher or teacher's aide. This child was obviously upset, so
much so in fact that she was faking illness in order to stay home
from school. The mother told me that she had allowed her daughter
to talk about her feelings, but insisted that she go to school anyway,
and tried to find other ways in the community for her daughter to
make friends, such as afterschool classes and a church youth group.
I told this mother she was right on: She supported her daughter by
letting her express how she felt and tell what she was afraid of, but
she also gave her the message that it is unhealthy to simply avoid
the situations you find unpleasant. The little girl had to learn to deal
with her problem by identifying her fears, expressing them, and
then confronting the situation that caused them. This mother did
the right thing.

As an adult, you can do this for yourself. Be your own coach,
using PMA to boost "team spirit." Let the coaching part of you be
the part that develops the objective perspective of your situation.
Do not deny the reality of your current outlook. Be honest with
yourself as you examine and reexamine the indexes in this chapter
and subsequent ones. And keep in mind that your success graph will
not be a straight line headed up and off the page: There will be ups
and downs, many successes but some failures too.

Here is what your success graph may look like:

Use this graph to gauge your own experience. There is no such thing
as straight-up progress. There is no success without failure. And it

has to be a step at a time. The key is not to let the little downs become one big down that leads to an extreme degree of avoidance. When setbacks occur, don't be discouraged. Remind yourself of your long-term goals. There is a path to follow. Think of it as your map for change:

1. Develop PMA—Positive Mental Attitude.
2. Identify your symptoms.
3. Set realistic goals.
4. Learn to control your anxiety and its symptoms.
5. Refine your social skills.
6. Apply what you know.
7. Keep applying it!

As you master each component, you will be able to see your progress by looking back at the charts in this chapter. This is an ongoing process—once you attain one goal, you must *maintain* it: Continue trying to understand your symptoms, to work on making PMA a part of your personality. I am hopeful that you've already come that far in this chapter alone. Keep at it! Ultimately, you will be moving forward—an occasional backstep is merely part of the overall advancement to a new level of sociability. Give yourself credit for meeting little goals, and don't be threatened by your long-term ones. It has taken a long time to develop your social responses—and it will take some time to relearn them. But with the right attitude—and adhering carefully to the steps of this program—you can get beyond "shyness."

CHAPTER TWO

The Truth About Social Expectations and Loneliness

Human beings are social animals. They thrive in community with other human beings. From the toddler stage onward, they seek to interact with their fellows, first as playmates, then as classmates, and later as club members, sports opponents, even neighbors and colleagues. Why all this togetherness? On the surface are the obvious reasons: We join clubs because we have mutual interests (books, travel, stamp collecting, bird watching, and so on), we play sports for exercise, we are neighbors because we live near one another, we are colleagues because we have to make a living. But there are other reasons too. We interact—one-on-one and in small or large groups—because we desire companionship, a sense of belonging, of shared experience.

Within any group of people, whether a family, a neighborhood community, a club membership, or a workplace, there is a social system in place, with customs and protocol to be followed. The people who are most successful at negotiating this social system are those who best understand it and are most capable of working within it. Does this mean taking only a passive role, remaining quiet and reserved and always looking to others for initiative and leadership? Absolutely not. Successful people are able to make active contributions, alone or as part of a team, within a given social system. By developing good communication skills—giving and receiving accurate social signals—you too can perfect your skills of negotiation and compromise in all situations.

Healthy interaction, free of the burdens of anxiety and avoidance, is an essential component of what esteemed psychologist and author Abraham Maslow calls "self-actualization." A self-actualized person is someone who feels content and fulfilled: in his social life, his career, his family, and his interpersonal relationships. Think of self-actualization as your definition of success—not material success, as in how much money you earn or what kind of car you drive, but personal success, as in the way you feel about yourself and your accomplishments. By controlling your social anxiety you will allow yourself to channel your personal energy into the kind of self-growth that will maximize your potential. *When you make self-actualization your long-range goal, you are taking responsibility for seeking the life you want.*

Let's begin by exploring the way we learn to behave. As we grow up, we acquire social skills by interacting first with parents and family members, then with playmates, teachers, and later employers and colleagues. Television is another place where we observe socialization, and we may take many of our cues—good and bad—from what we see represented on the screen.

Socialization is a vital part of our development throughout our lives, but its roots can be traced to infancy and early childhood, when the foundation of the personality is formed. It is through human contact that we learn patterns of thought and behavior (including our language, skills, beliefs, and values). Through human contact, we acquire cognitive skills such as reasoning, thinking, remembering, and using language. Human contact also accounts for our "affective" development, that is, the process of learning emotions and feelings.

Without effective socialization, a person becomes incapable of facing life's challenges. Because we don't live on instinct—the human world is too complex for that—we rely on each other, not just for survival, but for support. Even if our physical needs—for food and shelter—are met, human needs go beyond basic survival.

In the thirteenth century, Frederick II conducted an experiment that demonstrated the difference between surviving and thriving. A medieval historian documented his actions: "His . . . folly was that he wanted to find out what kind of speech and what manner of speech children would have when they grew up, if they spoke to no one beforehand. So he bade foster mothers to bathe and wash them, but in no way to prattle with them or speak to them, for he wanted to learn whether they would speak the Hebrew language, which was the oldest, or Greek, or Latin, or Arabic, or perhaps the language of their parents, of whom they had been born. But he laboured in vain, because the children died. For they could not live without the petting and joyful faces and loving words of their foster mothers." Children need more than physical care to survive; social contact is essential to normal development. Without an emotional bond, socialization is inhibited, and irreversible damage is done to the personality. For adults, however, there is a way to reverse the damage done by delayed social development.

An adult is capable of meeting his or her own survival needs. But again, there is a difference between surviving and thriving. And that difference means a healthy, rewarding life that includes a productive career and a number of close friends with whom to share good times and bad. What can make that difference? A positive mental attitude—a can-do outlook—will send you on your way. Stamp out the negative thinking that has been party to your interactive inhibition, and commit to overcoming your social anxiety.

WHAT IS SOCIAL INTERACTION?

When people talk about "socializing," they often refer to scheduled social events such as parties or dates. But socialization occurs on many levels, both at school or work, and after hours. Throughout the day, we interact with people—asking and answering questions, initiating conversations, responding to others' conversational openers. Buying popcorn in a movie theater involves social interaction. So does participating in a business presentation. Borrowing your neighbor's hedge clippers involves social interaction. So does asking for a raise. *Social interaction* is any situation in which you talk to someone else, especially someone outside your family.

Often, the quality of your relationship depends on how well you and the other person communicate with each other. Some people call it "chemistry." Others call it "being on the same wavelength" or "speaking the same language." However you choose to think of it, remember this: *Good communication is an essential part of successful interaction,* whether with your colleagues or in your friendships. What is the essence of good communication? People want to feel understood. They want to feel comfortable. They want to feel respected. It is easy to forget that these three rules hold as true in work situations as they do in more personal relationships. How can you best make people feel understood, comfortable, and respected in the workplace? By adapting yourself to whatever hierarchy exists there and participating fully within the existing social framework. You can't change your boss, but, if you approach him or her appropriately, in a way that makes your boss feel understood, comfortable, and respected, you can make yourself heard.

Communication depends in part on the degree of *intimacy* in the relationship—on how well you and the other person know each other. In close relationships with romantic partners and good friends, a sense of acceptance is an essential component. Without it, no true sharing can take place, and the relationships you do have are not only likely to be unsatisfying but may even become filled with conflict if emotions are repressed. So a high level of intimacy is important. I remember discussing levels of intimacy with Brad, a client who came to me to talk about some problems he was having with his girlfriend of eight months. Brad, a white-collar government employee, came from a very different background from Justine, a hair stylist. Although he enjoyed spending time one-on-one with Justine, Brad had no interest in introducing her to his colleagues or other acquaintances. In talking with me, he admitted that though he found Justine sexy, and appreciated the time she took to make herself attractive to him, he worried that other people would see her as "flashy" or "trampy," as he put it. Obviously, there was a measure of honesty missing from the relationship. Brad could tell there was a lack of intimacy—of true closeness and a sharing of feelings—but he stayed with it because, as he said, "It's better than not having anyone to be with at all."

What I explained to Brad was that he seemed to be hanging on to this relationship in order to avoid the unknown, to avoid the lack of control he might encounter in another, new relationship. It was clear to me that Brad liked the control he had over Justine. She doted on him, making almost no demands of her own and conforming to his schedule and his desires without complaint. For Brad to end the relationship and move on to one in which both partners were equal would mean taking responsibility for sharing his feelings honestly and responding to the woman's feelings as well. To get past his problems with Justine, Brad had to look closely at his expectations of the relationship, and then at his needs, in order to decide whether to stay and try to work things out, or to break it off in hopes of finding someone with whom he was more comfortable and could express himself on a more intimate level. In the end, he left.

In any interaction, being able to gauge the comfort level is important. Assessing the other person's comfort accurately means understanding the underlying boundaries inherent in any relationship. As you work to overcome your social anxiety and build a social network, you will begin to identify two basic categories of people you interact with:

Acquaintances: These are the people we have contact with in the course of the day or week—neighbors whom we know "over the fence" or down the hall, shopkeepers we see frequently, classmates with whom we meet for a study group, co-workers we say hello to on the job, or might join for a coffee break or even an occasional lunch. With acquaintances, your conversation probably stays fairly light; you might talk about what you're doing that day or you might discuss current events, but you wouldn't get too personal or offer up the intimate details of your life.

Friends: These are the people to whom you turn in bad times as well as good. You probably share some of the details of your lives—things that you are proud of, things that make you worry. A friend is someone you confide in, whom you could call with good news, or to discuss something that is bothering you. You see a friend fairly regularly if possible, or at least manage to stay in touch by telephone or letter.

There aren't strict boundaries when it comes to interacting, but it is important to be able to distinguish between acquaintances and friends. One is not better than the other, just different. As you follow this program, learning to overcome your anxiety and develop a social network, you will be able to pursue relationships more easily. In time, you will have both acquaintances and friends to share your time with.

"But I prefer to be alone. Isn't that okay?" you may ask. Yes, solitude is okay. Enjoying your own company is okay. In fact, it can be very valuable to be able to spend a certain amount of time alone, so long as you are content. Time alone, spent productively in relaxation or recreation, can heighten self-awareness. It is loneliness that is unhealthy.

Jack was a nice-looking twenty-one-year-old college graduate whose parents asked him to come to me for individual therapy. Jack had no friends to spend time with, and his only social interaction was with family members. Yet somehow, despite his deep-rooted social anxiety, he was able to hold a job as a department store sales manager, working with others on a daily basis. Jack poured all his energy into work, and talked about almost nothing else during our first meetings. As he related tale after tale of his ability to get things done, it became clear that his involvement with work was so intense that it had caused more than a few personality conflicts on the job. He may have been respected, but he was not well liked. For several weeks after his parents contacted me, Jack resisted the idea of therapy, saying there was nothing wrong with him, that he liked his life just as it was.

When he finally met with me, Jack expressed these same feelings. "I don't need friends," he said, and he seemed, on the surface, to believe that. "I am happy without them." As we talked, Jack revealed that he had spent seven hours the previous day shopping for a Mother's Day present. I remember thinking that it would be nice if Jack could put as much energy into a girlfriend. But in order to get him to see things my way—and admit that there were some social fears that had caused him to become overly dependent on his family relationships—I had to break through his initial denial of any desire for friendship or romance.

As I said, loneliness is not healthy. And that is not just a figure of speech. *Studies have in fact shown that loneliness can be dangerous to your health.* A recent report from the Institute of Social Research at the University of Michigan indicates that being cut off from friends and family actually doubles a person's chances of sickness and even death. A lack of social relationships in itself heightens a person's susceptibility to illness. This study summarizes data gathered from research conducted in the United States, Finland, and Sweden during the past twenty years, drawing on interviews with some 37,000 people over periods of up to twelve years. Social isolation, the study concludes, "is as significant to mortality rates as smoking, high blood pressure, high cholesterol, obesity, and lack of physical exercise. In fact, when age is adjusted for, social isolation is as great or greater a mortality risk than smoking." This is bad news if you have a limited social life.

Now for some good news: *You do not have to be lonely.* Does the Michigan study mean that we must constantly be surrounded by people to be well? No. As I said, there is nothing wrong with *enjoying* time by yourself. And after all, even people who have a very busy social life can suffer from bad health. Clearly, social relationships involve more than just being physically present with other people. Interacting involves negotiation and compromise. When we interact, it is because we want to share, we want to be understood, and we want to be accepted. The opposite of loneliness is a sense of belonging.

PERFORMANCE ANXIETY

If it is indeed human nature to seek social relationships, then why would someone choose not to socialize? As we discussed in the first chapter, fear is usually the motivating factor that causes people to avoid socializing. We fear failing, being rejected, being humiliated, being made to feel that we don't belong. This fear is commonly referred to as *performance anxiety*. How does performance anxiety interfere with a fulfilling, productive life? When you fear being judged harshly by others, you may hesitate to take risks that could ultimately benefit you, whether personally (such as asking someone out) or professionally (applying for a new job). Norman, a fifty-year-old advertising executive, came to me to discuss just this problem. He had worked for the same firm for almost ten years, and found himself intimidated by some of the young people who had recently come on board. Although he had kept up with the computer design technology and trends in advertising, he felt somehow out of touch but was too embarrassed to approach any of the "new kids" and allow himself to learn from them. Nor would he talk with his more seasoned colleagues or his superiors about his concerns. He found that his feelings were interfering with his ability to contribute ideas in creative meetings, and that he had come to dislike going to work because he didn't like the way being there made him feel about himself. Eventually, he quit his job, venturing out on his own to do, in his words, "a little consulting here and there." In fact, he was what I'd call "semiretired." His self-esteem suffered. His income suffered. His family life suffered. All because he was afraid of what his colleagues would think of him for wanting to learn a few things he felt he didn't know.

Norman tried to correct his negative self-image by avoiding the situation that caused it. But avoiding what we fear—staying away from social situations because we are unsure of how we will be perceived—is not the answer. As you explore ways to manage your anxiety, you will become more comfortable taking risks to get what you want: a healthy social life.

Expectations are another factor that causes social anxiety. Sometimes, a person will place undue pressure on himself, setting expectations that are simply out of reach for his social skill level at the time. Two of my clients come to mind, both of whom let unrealistic expectations keep them from finding companionship at all.

Charlie, twenty-five, was coming to me for individual therapy. He worked for a landscaping firm, and spent a lot of time alone, planting trees and shrubs on the job site. One of the things that struck me right away was that Charlie made little effort with his appearance. Although our evening sessions took place a few hours after Charlie got off work, he usually came in wearing his dirty work clothes and didn't seem to have combed his hair since morning; he was not averse to going a day or two without shaving, either. One of the things he often talked about was his desire for female companionship. One afternoon, after a therapy session, I accompanied him down in the elevator to get a cup of coffee. As we walked out of the building, he pointed across the street. "There's the kind of woman I want," he said. "She's hot." He was referring to an attractive, sophisticated woman in her late twenties who was getting into a black sports car. I found myself thinking that Charlie was setting himself up for rejection. To have such high expectations when appropriate social behavior was still such a struggle for him would inevitably lead to the very disappointment and rejection he feared most.

Unrealistic expectations can actually keep socially anxious people from seeking out relationships that are within their reach. A few years ago, as part of my friendship network program, I introduced two thirty-year-old baseball fans to each other for the purpose of friendship. Ben was attractive and athletic but possessed limited intellectual ability, and Jim was a bookish college graduate with a slight hearing problem. Neither one had any friends. The two attended a baseball game together, and both reported enjoying the evening. But Ben said he didn't want to get together with Jim again. I questioned him further and the truth came out: He didn't want to be seen with someone who wore a hearing aid.

Appearances. Some people get so caught up in them that they actually let appearances perpetuate their loneliness, and keep them from having the friendships that they so desire. They let what other people think—or worse, what they *think* other people think—keep them from even making an initial foray into the social world. In order to set realistic social goals, it is essential that you hone your expectations down to what is realistic. *Of course* Charlie found that sophisticated young woman attractive; but to hold out for someone of her apparent social standing would mean forgoing the possibility of other, more attainable, relationships. For Ben, although he had no friends at all, association with someone who had a visible handicap, however manageable, made him fear that others would see him as handicapped. To act on this fear—a fear of being evaluated then dismissed by others—was to forgo a friendship that actually had some possibilities. *In many instances, a preoccupation with appearances—unrealistic social expectations, impossible standards—can be the single largest barrier to a satisfying social life.*

When I talk about social expectations, I use the term "pecking order" to describe a kind of hierarchy of sociability that exists in the minds of the people who suffer social difficulties. Generally, people who are well adjusted aren't giving much thought to that guy whose friend is wearing a hearing aid, or how that guy could date that unattractive woman. But people who fear judgment are inevitably far harsher judges of themselves than any outsider could ever be. And yet, at the same time, they deny that there is a problem in need of attention.

In fact, *denial* can be the largest stumbling block in overcoming social anxiety. I see denial at every level. Those in deep denial make statements such as "I don't want a social life." Those whose denial is less ingrained make excuses such as "Sure, I'd like to socialize, but I'm too busy with work" or they say offhandedly, "I really prefer to spend time by myself." But these comments may not tell the whole story. To deny the reality of the social situation is to ensure that the problem will go unaddressed. Denying that loneliness exists allows loneliness to remain. Denying that social anxiety exists can only mean that the anxiety will continue to control your life.

Having worked with thousands of people whose social fears got in the way of their general health—emotional as well as physical—I have come to believe that the person whose denial is so severe that it results in perpetuating the social problem is sick. And the person who avoids social interaction solely out of fear is also sick. But this sickness is temporary—and entirely curable! All it takes—though this is a big "all"—is for the individual to *stop* denying, *stop* avoiding, and begin to take responsibility for his or her choices. Even those highly functioning individuals who feel that the quality of their relationships falls short of their ideal will find that abandoning their bad habit of denying their desire for intimacy and fulfillment will lead to the self-actualization they truly desire.

In order to make reasonable progress toward a rewarding social life, you must set reasonable goals. You must keep your expectations in line with what is possible for you at the time. As you become more comfortable with your social self—by managing your anxiety, increasing your self-awareness, and developing your social skills— you will be able to expand your expectations accordingly.

To reach these goals, it is essential to determine your degree of social anxiety, to understand the factors that have created it, and then take steps to correct it through anxiety management and social skills education. Socialization, as we have established in this chapter, is learned behavior, and learning takes practice.

YOUR SOCIAL FUNCTIONING LEVEL

In the previous chapter, you identified the ways in which your fears have kept you from socializing. Now, let's examine the degree to which you are affected. Below, I have defined five different levels of social functioning. Use these as a general guideline for evaluating how well you manage your social interaction. At different times in your life, you may cope better or worse with your social fears, so you may recognize your capabilities in two or more of the lists. In any event, as you follow this program, you will be able to track your sociability by referring back to these lists and charting your progress. If you wish, jot down your thoughts on your functioning level in a notebook; make a note of the date, and then refer back to it later, adding any changes in functioning level or self-image.

Level 5—Fully functioning

Seldom feels social anxiety; does not avoid social interaction.

Seeks social relationships; is comfortable with strangers; looks forward to meeting new people.

Often initiates social events; is frequently invited to socialize.

Member of clubs or organizations; can take leadership role.

Comfortable asking favors, volunteering to help.

Aware of physical appearance, but comfortable and not overly concerned with it.

Level 4—Highly functioning

Is aware of social anxiety, but able to manage when interacting, without thought patterns interfering.

Has several close friends, plus larger circle of acquaintances developed from different areas of life—workplace, neighborhood, club memberships.

Occasionally initiates social events; usually responds to social invitations.

Seeks friendships and pursues dating relationships.

Performs well on the job, and can handle well-defined social interactions with ease.

Can overcome anxiety most of the time; aware of it, but in control of it.

Able to ask favors, offer to help.

Level 3—Functioning

Feels a significant degree of social anxiety; will sometimes cancel social plans because of anxiety.

Has a few close friends, several acquaintances.

Feels anxious when talking to others, but can overcome when necessary.

Occasionally responds to social invitations, but seldom initiates social events.

Can hold a job and perform well when duties are well defined, but doesn't seek attention; more a follower than a leader.

Avoids asking favors, volunteering to help.

May be overly concerned with physical appearance.

Level 2—Moderately functioning

Anxious about socializing; usually avoids social situations.

Depends heavily on family members for most social life, and all emotional support.

Seldom initiates or responds to invitations to socialize outside the family.

One or two acquaintances, but no close friends to turn to for emotional support.

Uncomfortable approaching store clerks, talking to waiters, etc.

Can hold a job, but has difficulty relating to co-workers, asking for help, increasing responsibility.

Unaware of physical appearance and how it factors into social situations.

Level 1—Low functioning

Extremely anxious about socializing; avoids social situations altogether.

Relies solely on family members for all social life, emotional support.

Never initiates or responds to invitations to socialize outside the family.

No meaningful relationships outside the family.

Unable to approach store clerks, talk to waiters, etc.

Difficulty seeking employment, performing job duties, keeping a job.

Poor attention to physical appearance.

As you consider these categories, you might start to note some goals that you would like to work toward. Would you like to feel more comfortable initiating a particular conversation—say, proposing a new system at work or asking someone for a date? Would you like to feel more confident or comfortable about your appearance? We'll talk more about goal setting in later chapters, but it helps to be aware not only of where you are now, but of where you'd like to be.

Now that you have a general understanding of the levels of social ability, let's concentrate on establishing your *social ability level*—focusing once again on where you are at present. No definitive test exists to measure how well a person functions socially, so to close this diagnostic gap, and make it easier for people who have trouble socializing to get the help they need, social anthropologist Robert Vetter and psychologist-statistician Richard Evangelista helped me to develop the Social Ability Questionnaire. This index of social skills is designed to help determine how well you function socially. Using a true-false format, this test is built around six categories connected with socialization:

1. *Concept of self:* How do you feel about yourself? How do you see yourself in relation to others?
2. *Social anxiety:* To what extent do social situations make you uncomfortable?
3. *Feelings toward parents:* Do you rely on family for social context?
4. *Degree of independence:* How well do you cope with day-to-day living on your own?
5. *Knowledge of social etiquette:* Do you know how to behave around others?
6. *Empathy:* How easily can you see things from another's point of view?

In addressing these issues, you will begin to take a careful look at yourself as a social person. A key is included on p. 49. But there are no right or wrong answers. Think of the test as a series of statements that are true or false for you and you alone. Be as honest as you can.

The Social Ability Questionnaire: An Index of Basic Skills

Directions: Please read each statement carefully, and decide whether or not it describes you. Circle "T" for true, if the statement applies to you, and "F" for false, if it does not.

T   F   1. I listen patiently to others, and try to see things from their points of view.

T   F   2. I often think about my physical appearance and what kind of an impression I make on others.

T   F   3. I am very uncomfortable talking about myself.

T F 4. I am good at knowing how much to share about myself: I know when to keep emotional distance, and when to speak intimately.

T F 5. I try to emphasize the positive in others when I confront them, rather than the negative, or things they do wrong.

T F 6. I am able to discuss openly the quality of my relationship to someone else in my conversations with him or her.

T F 7. I am prone to attacks of anxiety and don't know how to control them.

T F 8. My values are unclear, and I often have difficulty in deciding which course of action is right and which is wrong.

T F 9. I sometimes think I'd be happier if I could exist all by myself.

T F 10. I don't know how I will be able to survive after my parents die.

T F 11. I often feel that life is not worth living.

T F 12. I'm good at interacting with other people.

T F 13. I understand all the different roles I play in life.

T F 14. I'm uncomfortable at parties and large, noisy events.

T F 15. I have plenty of self-confidence.

T F 16. I am secure on my own, and don't need any money from my parents.

T F 17. When I look at how things are going in my life, it's hard to imagine that I will ever amount to anything.

T F 18. I have frequent bouts of nausea and vomiting, especially when I am forced to interact with people I'd prefer not to talk to.

T F 19. There is nothing that I think I do very well.

T F 20. I can place myself in someone else's shoes and ask, "What would I do if I were him or her?"

T F 21. Before I challenge someone, I first try to understand him or her.

T F 22. When I'm in public, I often feel confused about how to act.

T F 23. I'm good at starting conversations with people I don't know.

T F 24. I'm good at both speaking and listening to others.

T   F   25. I'm good at knowing what to do in familiar surroundings, but the idea of doing something around people I don't know terrifies me.

T   F   26. When I meet someone new, after the first sentence or so, I don't know what else to say.

T   F   27. I am only able to get from place to place because my parents are willing to drive me.

T   F   28. I like sharing: communicating thoughts and feelings to others.

T   F   29. I understand the difference between a friend and an acquaintance.

T   F   30. I understand what people are saying to me, but I'm often confused about their intentions and motivations.

T   F   31. I have no significant friendships or relationships outside my family.

T   F   32. I often feel frustrated about my parents. They love me and protect me, but I get angry when they are overly protective of me.

T   F   33. I would never admit it, but my parents give me the only strength and support I receive.

T   F   34. Sometimes I think I know someone, then all of a sudden I realize I don't.

T   F   35. If an opportunity came up for a date, I'm sure I could think of a place to go and a way to get there.

THE RESULTS

Only you know whether the answers you gave reflect your true self or a projection of the person you would like to be. Consider whether you have answered each question truthfully. Are your answers colored by your expectations of yourself? If you think you may not have been honest with yourself, then take the test again. When you are ready, check your responses against the key at the end of this chapter to gauge your level of sociability. To determine your rating, give yourself one point for each answer that corresponds with the key. Then add the points together to determine your final rating. The average score for individuals who have moderate social anxiety problems is 22.5.

Interpreting Test Scores:

Social Ability Level	Score
Low	17 or below
Medium	18–27
High	28 or above

A Note for Parents

For people such as Jack, whose family was concerned that he depended excessively on his family relationships, it may take parental intervention to bring about healthy change. As I've said, there are many different levels of social functioning. In the case of adults with severe social anxiety problems, parental intervention is quite common (see Chapter 3 for more discussion of the parents' role in social anxiety). For adolescents, parental involvement is also essential. In my clinical experience, highly to fully functioning people (levels four and five in this chapter) generally take the initiative to improve their interactive ability and stress management skills on their own, while low- to moderately functioning people (levels one and two) characteristically rely on a relative to facilitate healthy change. For those who function adequately (level three), there is a less defined pattern of behavior.

If you have obtained this book for your adult child, please follow these guidelines in working with your son or daughter. As a parent, you have three roles in utilizing this test. First, take the test yourself, answering the questions as though you were your adult child. Second, administer the test to your son or daughter, explaining the directions and providing general guidelines. Emphasize that he or she is free to ask you to explain anything that is unclear. Third, and most important, you should use the test as a basis for a dialogue between the two of you. For example, look again at the questions that the two of you answered differently. Is your son or daughter ignoring a deficit in his or her social knowledge or ability? Are you? How does that particular question relate to a specific skill or attribute?

ANSWER KEY TO THE SOCIAL ABILITY QUESTIONNAIRE

1. T	13. T	25. F
2. T	14. F	26. F
3. F	15. T	27. F
4. T	16. T	28. T
5. T	17. F	29. T
6. T	18. F	30. F
7. F	19. F	31. F
8. F	20. T	32. F
9. F	21. T	33. F
10. F	22. F	34. F
11. F	23. T	35. T
12. T	24. T	

CHAPTER THREE

Good Intentions: The Parents' Role in Social Avoidance

Over the years, I have encountered resistance and confusion when I talk about the role that parents play in the lives of socially anxious children and adults. But my clinical experience has confirmed that when social anxiety results in avoidance, dependence on others—usually parents or other relatives—is almost inevitable. What follows is aimed primarily at parents who are seeking help for a low- to moderately functioning child, adolescent, or adult. But adults on the higher end of the interactive spectrum who are seeking help on their own will also benefit from reading this chapter, which offers background information on how social anxiety develops. If you are a functioning to highly functioning adult in search of self-help, reflect back on the ways your parents may have helped to perpetuate your social avoidance, rescuing you from the situations that made you anxious instead of empowering you to confront them on your own.

Over the past decades, Twelve-Step addiction programs and other treatment options have used the term *enabling* to describe the situation in which a relative or spouse helps to perpetuate an addiction. How does this concept apply to social anxiety? Avoiding the situations that cause anxiety is a kind of addiction—a habit almost too hard to break. How can parents and others enable an avoidance addict? Here is an example: A high school student feels ostracized on the school bus, so she persuades her mother to drive her to school every day. Her mother consents, knowing of her daughter's anxiety but rationalizing that "the bus ride is awfully long, and it's not out of my way to drive her." Here is another example: A twenty-seven-year-old hotel catering executive becomes anxious when he has to write proposals to present to prospective clients. His assistant writes the proposals for him, allowing him to use her notes and take all the credit when the presentation rolls around. It's easy to see from these examples the way in which avoidance and dependence go hand in hand. If you avoid doing something that must be done, someone else must necessarily step in and do it for you. (More on this in Chapter 4.)

Parents in particular often confuse nurturing with rescuing. To nurture is to *empower*—to provide the skills and information that will eventually allow for independent, productive living. To rescue is to *enable*—to perpetuate avoidance of the situation that caused the anxiety in the first place. Empowering should be the overriding goal of every parent. Empowerment allows a child of whatever age to face fears and take responsibility for his or her life.

Shannon, forty, was a prime example of someone whose parents were enabling her social avoidance and encouraging her dependence. Until three years earlier, Shannon had lived in an apartment a few blocks from her parents. But when her mother died, she and her father, who was sixty-three and in excellent health, agreed it would be "best" if she moved back home to help him run the household. Shannon had little time to date those days, spending her free hours entertaining her father's friends or attending plays or concerts with him. She sometimes missed the companionship of her peers, but at other times said she had enough social contact at her job as a receptionist. It was true Shannon hadn't been asked out in a while, and that injured her self-esteem. In fact, that was why she came to me, seeking a way to become more social. Her father's response? "Why do you need to date? You're so busy with other things." Not only was her father enabling Shannon to avoid socializing with her own friends, he was creating a situation in which each depended on the other for all emotional support. Shannon's father was in some ways lonely since her mother's death, and he had confused his own need for companionship with his daughter's dependence.

In contrast, Bill, age twenty-eight, received the kind of empowering that enabled him to make a change for the better. He still lived at home with his mother, a travel agent, when he began taking classes to become a paralegal. At first, he was sluggish, taking only a class or two per semester and working one day a week in a convenience store. But his mother pressed him to arrange a better schedule that allowed him to progress through school at a faster pace and take on extra hours at work, which meant extra income for Bill, a portion of which his mother required him to pay toward household expenses. When his mother and her boyfriend traveled, they stopped including Bill, explaining to him that he was on his own, an adult, and could arrange his own trips when he could afford them. His mother knew what she was doing. By making it less and less convenient to live with her, she was showing Bill that he could have more independence, more freedom, if he lived on his own. Soon, Bill was able to find a roommate from the college. Eventually, he got a job as a paralegal and a place of his own. His mother had empowered him to become independent, and both were grateful for her courage and persistence.

Parents themselves are often confused by the idea of enabling their children to avoid anxiety-producing situations. Recently, I received a call from the mother of a twenty-seven-year-old man inquiring about my sociability program. The first step, I told her, would be a consultation with her and her husband to discuss dependency issues relating to her son, who was still living at home and had little social contact outside of work. "I don't understand," she said. "My son is an adult. He's twenty-seven years old. Shouldn't you treat him independently? Why do you need to meet with us?"

This question is typical, yet profound in its implications: In thirteen years of offering this therapy program, I have found that six out of ten calls come from parents concerned about their overly dependent—and not very social—children. Although there may be signs of "trouble" in childhood—few friends, a tendency

to avoid peer situations, being a "loner"—the severity of the social anxiety problem may not be obvious to parents until it is almost too late. "He'll grow out of it." "She's just going through a
shy phase." These statements—excuses, really—can often make a
bad situation worse by allowing it to continue. Parents of pre-
teens, adolescents, and adults who exhibit the symptoms of social
anxiety we discussed in earlier chapters will find this chapter to be
a practical guide toward helping their children to become independent, productive people.

How do I determine whether a person is overly dependent on his
or her parents? For one thing, if a person is independent enough—
however anxious—to place a call to me on his own, then I feel
comfortable meeting with him alone. (Similarly, if you have obtained this book on your own, you may well be capable of attaining
a new level of social independence on your own, without directly
involving your family in your self-help program.) But if it takes a
parent to seek out help for an adolescent or adult child, then I feel
that there are some dependency issues that must be clarified before
treatment can begin. (In fact, even when an otherwise independent
person relies on parents to pay for therapy, I am inclined to bring
them in so that I can assess the degree of dependence that is
present.) When a parent makes that phone call to me or obtains
this book for a child, it could be the beginning of empowerment, of
giving that child the tools for independent living. Or it could merely
be a continuation of the enabling that has perpetuated the problem.
The key lies in the follow-through. Later in this chapter, I'll offer a
set of guidelines that will help parents to become empowerers and
abandon their role as enablers of social avoidance.

When evaluating a new client for degree of independence, I
consider four factors:

1. *Emotional issues:* Does the person have good resources within
   himself or herself for coping independently with emotional
   issues that come up, or does he or she turn to parents not only
   for advice, but for cues as to how to react to the event in
   question?

2. *Financial issues:* Does the adult child earn an adequate living on his or her own, or does he or she rely heavily on parental input for things such as job contacts, supplemental funds, or housing?
3. *Practical issues/interactive situations:* Can the person manage day-to-day living, finances, nutrition, exercise, and housekeeping?
4. *Career/education issues:* Does the person have a rewarding job or career that is commensurate with his or her abilities and offers the potential for further success? Is the person willing to learn new things to increase his or her productivity or compensation?

These are basic skills of living, many of which are addressed in the social ability questionnaire. Just as there are levels of social functioning, so too there are levels of independent functioning. *All three of the following levels describe an adult with some degree of dependency problems.* A healthy adult is someone who is independent financially, is able to manage practical and interactive issues, and who stays in touch with family but does not rely almost solely on family for emotional support.

Level 1—Low functioning

Emotional issues: Lives at home with parent(s) or away from home in a fully structured or supervised environment.

Financial issues: Contributes virtually nothing financially to the running of the household.

Practical issues: Chooses clothes to wear that day, but does not manage own wardrobe (i.e., laundry, shopping, etc.). Relies on family members to buy food and prepare meals. Does few household chores, if any. May try a few tasks when asked, but seldom follows through until the job is finished.

Career/education issues: Is not able to keep a job, and therefore does not earn an independent living. Extremely resistant to learning new skills or changing responsibilities.

Level 2: Moderately functioning

Emotional issues: Lives either at home or nearby and calls home every day. Relies on parents to discuss all details of daily life, from what happened at work or school that day to what to wear the next day. Will call home for advice rather than trying to figure something out for him- or herself.

Financial issues: May rely on parents for supplemental income—parents may supply car, apartment, etc. May be employed by parents at an inflated salary for a job with very few responsibilities. May be irresponsible about paying bills.

Practical issues: Is able to make daily decisions about clothing, but may rely on parents when shopping for clothing and other items. Neglects household responsibilities such as laundry, cleaning and meal planning.

Career/education issues: Has a job, but is unable to cope with much on-the-job stress; job is therefore only minimally challenging, or a major source of anxiety—discussed in detail with Mom and Dad.

Level 3: Functioning

Emotional issues: Lives away from home. Calls home a few times a week, relies on family for emotional support and most socializing. Few friends.

Practical issues: Handles all aspects of daily household management independently.

Financial issues: Is financially independent, pays bills on time.

Career/education issues: Has achieved some moderate success at work. Is willing to seek new information, even to take an occasional class to improve skills.

As you consider these levels of daily functioning, keep in mind that you, as a parent, may perceive a much higher degree of independence than is actually present. It may take some further investigation to determine exactly where your adult child fits in the spectrum. A single factor—a good job, nice clothes—is not enough to determine overall functioning level. What you want to consider is the extent to which your adult child relies on you to manage the activities of daily living such as household duties, financial planning and responsibilities, and basic coping and decision making. Be objective, parents! A hard look at reality may be uncomfortable, but you owe it to yourself and your child to be honest. Don't participate in denial.

This reminds me of one woman who called me to discuss her daughter Julie, who, although she was maintaining a respectable B average at a college an hour away from home, called almost every night in tears over some new "crisis." Her mother's response? "Julie really needs a break from school," she told me. "I encourage her to come home some weekends, since it's so close. That way, she can concentrate on studying and won't have to worry about anything else." The occasional weekend soon became *every* weekend. Finally, her mother did ask Julie whether she wouldn't rather stay on campus to have fun with her friends. But Julie just said no and quickly changed the subject.

Julie's grades that semester were excellent, but she seemed distracted and unhappy. Her mother, still concerned about how well her daughter was coping, came to see me. After hearing her out, I told her what I thought. By reacting strongly to every new "crisis," and encouraging Julie to hide out at home every weekend instead of attempting to manage her newly independent life on her own, this well-intentioned mother was *not* being supportive. "But I'm only trying to help her through a difficult time!" the mother told me. What she needed to understand was that, in smoothing things over, in letting her daughter revert to little-girlhood, this woman was encouraging dependence—and rewarding her daughter's dependent behavior.

Separation issues often surface during young adulthood, so it was not unusual for this girl to have conflicting emotions about coping. But these issues, if not dealt with when they first arise, continue to crop up in later years. One couple contacted me about their daughter Alison, who at age thirty-one worked at her father's small printing company. The family was close, and Alison enjoyed tagging along on outings with her parents and their friends, including a few trips with tour groups. But the couple worried that their daughter had no friends her own age and, after a few brief, unsuccessful relationships in her early twenties, had not dated at all. When I tried to point out that she was overly dependent on her parents for emotional support, her father cut me off defensively. "But she lives alone," he said, "and she pays all her own expenses."

"True," I countered, "but she relies on you and your wife to initiate any social activities and vacations, and she isn't really doing the kinds of things that people her own age like to do." They saw my point; after all, that was why they had asked me to treat her, wasn't it? Alison, I explained to them, didn't socialize with her peer group because she didn't feel she needed to. She had everything covered—her work life and her social life were all wrapped up in her parents' lives.

Alison turned out to be a tough sell when it came time to ask her to work on her social anxiety issues. But this didn't surprise me. As I said, with all her needs being met, why change? She would scarcely admit to anxiety, saying only that she didn't usually get on well with people her own age. Of course she was in denial. How could it be worth forgoing a known situation—a situation that was comfortable and familiar, that she had in fact known for her entire life—for all the unknowns and anxieties of making friends and meeting men? In Chapter 2, we discussed the reasons why it *is* worth the trouble. People are social animals. They want friends. In time, Alison came to accept these truths.

I wasn't surprised to meet with resistance on Alison's part because

I had seen it so many times before—even in people who come to me on their own for help. I typically encounter one of two basic attitudes in people with sociability problems: They are either *cooperative* or *resistant*. This is true for both children and adults. Parents of younger children, however, are generally even more resistant because they fear the stigma of therapy. "How come my child is in therapy? Have I failed as a parent?" (Children, too, may feel a stigma associated with being in therapy.) Parents also can become quite preoccupied with appearances, worrying about what kind of people are in the therapy groups, and what *their* parents are like. In fact, I think fear of failure is where some of the resistance over involving parents in therapy sessions comes in. Parents may be afraid of blame. But looking at these issues is not a question of blame. Rather, it is a way of letting the individual evaluate the past and present, acknowledge it, take responsibility for it, and *move on*.

Whether a client is cooperative or resistant, denial of the problem may be evident. In a cooperative person, someone who has come in either at someone else's suggestion or on his own, but who truly wants his life to change, denial may be more subtle: Not "I don't have a problem socializing" but "Of course I'd like to go to the singles group at the Y, but I've got too much work to do to prepare for my meeting next week." Tricky, huh? In fact, the person who said this to me very much *wanted* to meet other singles but was afraid to express the desire and was even more afraid of the unknown situation and the anxiety it might cause. Still, in cooperative clients, denial isn't as big a stumbling block, and the focus is more directly on the anxiety and the avoidance it causes.

Where there is resistance, denial is far more pronounced, and treatment usually begins not at the person's own request but as the result of family intervention. In fact, it's fair to say that the more denial there is, the more dependence there is likely to be. Conversations with resistant people usually sound something like this one I had with a twenty-eight-year-old man who worked part-time in a video store:

"I don't know why my sister wanted me to come here. There's nothing wrong with me."

"Well," I said, "your sister tells me that you don't get out much at all, except when she and her husband ask you to a movie or something. Is that true?"

"I do go to work," he argued. "I just don't feel like seeing people when I'm home. What's wrong with that?"

"She says you don't have any friends. Do you have anybody you like to do things with?"

"I do things with her. I don't need friends."

I don't need friends. I have heard this excuse literally thousands of times. The assertion is denial, plain and simple. If you don't need something that you don't have, why seek it? But we all need friends. If "need" makes you uncomfortable, it is enough to say that we all *want* friends. And it is possible for all of us to have friends, if we would only admit that we want them and then do what we can to make ourselves available for friendship.

This portion of the chapter is directed at those of you whose son or daughter or other relative is in denial about his or her social life. No matter what your relationship is to this person, you need to tell yourself—daily, if necessary—that it is okay to want this person to become independent. Right now, the person is a burden to you. It is not selfish of you to want to lessen the burden of being the sole emotional support of someone else. It is selfish of the other person to ask you to be that support. But you have every right to try to foster, nurture, even at times force a healthy independence. There is an old saying that you may want to keep in mind as you proceed: "It is better to teach someone to fish than to fish for him." It is better, much better, to give someone the courage, strength, and skills to become socially independent than to be that person's entire social world. You'll feel better. And the person you care about will ultimately feel better too.

The No. 1 piece of advice that I give parents who want to help their adolescent or adult child is this: *Use your influence to help your child face up to his or her anxiety.* It need not be done all at once. I'm not suggesting you walk your child to the mouth of the volcano and leave him there, but you need to be the one who never falters. Your child, who suffers anxiety in social situations, will inevitably backslide from time to time. His improvement will be steady, but it will not be constant. So you have to be there to provide firm support and active, vocal encouragement throughout his journey to socialization. What I am asking you to do is nurture your child's independence. Do not rescue him from what he fears. Do not confuse *nurturing*—saying to him, "I know you are afraid, but do the best you can because I believe you can succeed"—with *rescuing*, saying, "I know you are afraid, so I'll call and cancel your plans and maybe you can attend that club meeting another time when you're more ready." Do not confuse teaching him to fish with fishing for him.

And incidentally, if *temper tantrums* are a part of your relationship now—those angry outbursts or the silent treatment—it is natural to fear the reaction you might get as you try to get the socially anxious family member to confront his fear. One mother I met with had a twenty-five-year-old son who was a rock drummer living at home with her. Onstage he was a captivating performer, and women paid attention to him, but on his own, he felt extremely anxious and seldom dated or socialized. When his mother asked him to get a "day job" so that he could bring some steady income to the household, he flew into a rage, and his angry outbursts became personal attacks on his mother's ability to manage. These verbal attacks continued. They made the mother feel terrible—and terrified. Soon she became avoidant as well, in an attempt to keep the household free of conflict. But inside she was angry and hurt and wished to find a way to make her son more independent.

Temper tantrums at any age are controlling behavior. But don't let that kind of acting out undermine your commitment to nurturing your child's independence. Don't allow your anxiety as a parent— fears of what will happen if you take action now—keep you from thinking about her future and what will happen to her once you are gone and she has no choice but to live independently. One of my clients left the program with her father's blessing after just a few months of participation. How did she persuade him to let her stop coming? Although I had warned him that Jenny would be extremely resistant to change, her father could not withstand her verbal assaults against him. As basic issues were raised, Jenny began acting out her anger and defiance. Her father simply couldn't cope. "If this is the result," he told me, "I'd rather assist her in living her own quiet, isolated life. I can't take it." Fear of retaliation—emotional or physical—does occasionally keep parents from intervening. But careful planning can make intervention more bearable. If you as a parent are especially resistant to suggesting change in your socially anxious child, follow the guidelines later in this chapter to firm up your own commitment (see p. 69), and then arm yourself with the stress management techniques outlined in Chapter 6.

"HE'LL GROW OUT OF IT"

I have seen this confusion take its toll in socially anxious children of all ages. Six-year-old Jimmy, for instance, was singled out by his elementary school physical ed teacher for his skill at tumbling. His proud mother signed him up for Saturday gymnastics classes at the local recreation center. When he went to the first class, he felt anxious and clung nervously to his mother, who stayed for the full one-hour session. When the next week's class rolled around, Jimmy cried and said he didn't want to go. His mother's response? "Okay, if you don't want to go, you don't have to." End of story, but the beginning of a lifetime of rescuing or enabling interaction between mother and son.

I don't advocate forcing a child to attend enrichment programs that don't interest him. It would *not* have been better for Jimmy's mother to tell him, "You're going to gymnastics and I don't want to hear anything more about it." That would have scared him even more, and made him feel further out of control. Instead, it would have been good for Jimmy—and his mother—to discuss *why* he didn't want to go. Can a conversation about feelings be of any benefit when the anxious person is all of six years old? You bet. Let's imagine:

"Why don't you want to go to gymnastics class today, Jimmy?"
"I just don't feel like it."
"You don't like tumbling anymore?"

"I like tumbling but I don't like balance beam. They make you do balance beam there."

"Why don't you like the balance beam?"

"I think I'll fall off because I don't know how to do it."

"If the teacher showed you how to do it, would that be okay?"

"Yeah, but I wish Mr. Graham would show me."

"But he's your P.E. teacher at school. Miss Lacy is your teacher at the rec center."

"I don't like her."

"Why not?"

"She's new."

Fair enough. By having a conversation with Jimmy, his mother finds out that he is worried about two things: that he doesn't know how to use the balance beam (this may mean he's afraid of getting hurt, but more likely that he's afraid of being humiliated in front of the new teacher, and all the new kids in the class) and that his teacher is "new" and unfamiliar to him. What can Jimmy's mother do with this information? Without a lot of extra effort, she can try to smooth the way for Jimmy by arriving a few minutes early to let him get to know Miss Lacy. If Jimmy is still hesitant, she can tell him they are going to stop in to see her for just a minute, and that if he doesn't want to stay, he can decide then. Miss Lacy may even have a minute to talk to him about the balance beam. Chances are, once Jimmy feels comfortable with the new situation, he will feel much less anxiety. And his mother has done more than just get him to attend gymnastic classes. She has shown him that it is okay to talk about your fears, and that there are steps to take to help confront them.

If only all parents and children were able to talk things out along the way. It is very rare that the parents of an anxious young child will contact me for help. Invariably, they assume "shyness" is a phase the child will grow out of. Sometimes children do abandon their reserved persona for another, better-adjusted one. But if a young child spends most of his time alone, seldom speaks in class, and expresses no interest in typical childhood pursuits such as interacting with other kids in an age-appropriate manner, playing with toys, engaging in sports, and even watching television and talking about fantasy characters, there could be a problem. One important key along the way is communication. "Do you feel okay?" "How do you feel about the kids at school?" "Do you want to invite someone over to play tomorrow afternoon?" When your child answers, the way she addresses these questions is as important as the words she chooses. Does she seem sad or listless? Defensive? Apologetic? Fearful? If so, then there may be a problem. If you are concerned that your child's social anxiety is making it hard for her to cope, talk to her teacher or a school counselor. The same thing holds true for children as for adults: *Social anxiety is a problem when it prevents you from doing things that you would like to do.*

In determining the social ability level of your preteen, consider the following behavioral symptoms of social anxiety. Note that while some of these symptoms relate exclusively to this age group, others may carry over into later developmental stages. Also keep in mind that these symptoms may be indicative of other problems. For our purposes here, it is the overall pattern of social anxiety that will become evident.

Preteen Warning Signs

> Lack of peer relationships outside the family
> Difficulty engaging in age-appropriate conversations
> Social skills difficulty
> Inability to make and keep friends
> Obvious anxiety, fear of social situations
> Afraid of groups
> Angry outbursts
> Restlessness
> Inability to concentrate
> Temper tantrums—sustained argumentative or "acting-out" behavior
> Inability to complete projects
> Clumsiness—not good at sports
> Poor muscle coordination

Poor academic skills
Depressed mood, seems withdrawn
Stress-related physical symptoms
Insecurity
Limited tolerance of frustration
Fear of new situations
Learning disabilities

THE STORM OF ADOLESCENCE

Once a child enters adolescence, it may become increasingly difficult to raise these issues. Because adolescence is a time of rebellion—of self-definition, of distinguishing oneself from parents and peers—there may be less communication than ever. It is also a time of great emotional and physical change—and therefore a time of intense confusion within. If the adolescent child's self-image gets lost in the shuffle, there may be years of hell to pay. Doug is thirty now, and his life is a lot different than any of his high school basketball teammates might have expected. A star player, Doug was offered several college scholarships, but he lost the one he accepted because his grades were poor. After flunking out of college, he went home to live with his parents. More than ten years later, he still lives there. Occasionally he drives a cab, but he spends most days and nights hanging out with a crowd of unemployed high school dropouts who watch TV and smoke marijuana all day (studies show that drug use is common among "shy" boys). Doug conforms easily to peer pressure, so desperate is he for friendship. But the valuable aspects of intimate friendship are entirely missing from his life at this point. And Doug still spends a great deal of time alone. If Doug is home, he's in his room, alone.

Despite his abhorrent behavior, Doug's parents have never really stood up to him, and their own anxiety makes them too afraid to use the "tough love" approach I would recommend in such a case. The few times they have tried to talk to Doug, he has simply gotten up and left the room, closing the door behind him. When they suggest he get a job, he becomes hostile because he resents the fact that they won't take him into the family business. But they in turn are angry that the few times they have let him work, he has been rude to customers and has come and gone as he pleased.

They came to me, seeking some workable remedy, but Doug refused to get help. "How can you embarrass me by taking me to a therapist? There's no problem. I like my life just the way it is." No steady job. No expenses. No pressure. No wonder. But obviously, something is very wrong. And not just with Doug. His parents, by allowing his irresponsible behavior to continue, by paying his way and letting him abuse their kindness and concern for him, are enabling his conduct to continue.

And it all started when Doug was still a teenager, when he just dropped out of college and his parents ignored the early symptoms of social maladjustment.

Adolescent Warning Signs

Lack of peer relationships outside the family
Anxiety in social situations
Difficulty with social skills such as keeping a conversation going
Depression, withdrawal
Confusion
Sexual identity problems
Interpersonal problems—trouble interacting with people
Sleep problems, including excessive sleeping
Stress-related physical symptoms
Feelings of persecution
Family conflicts
Antisocial attitudes
Overdependence on TV, computer, or video games
Using subjective symptoms as a way of avoiding responsibilities
Procrastination
Fear of groups

Lack of planning or organization
Difficulty making decisions
Difficulty with self-expression
Feelings of loneliness
Physical complaints
Difficulty making and keeping friends; stormy relationships with
  peers
Fear of new situations
Rationalization about lack of social life
Learning disabilities

THE SOCIALLY ANXIOUS ADULT

In the previous chapters, we have already looked at the symptoms of social anxiety typical of "shy" adults. In this chapter, we are addressing the issues faced by parents of socially anxious children of all ages and are outlining a progression from childhood through adolescence to adulthood. Because it is the parent who is making the initial layperson's diagnosis—not the actual individual—the symptoms outlined here are shown from the point of view of the involved observer. These symptoms are the ones that would be most obvious to family members. Aside from examining the level of independent functioning of the socially anxious adult, watch for the following behavioral symptoms:

Adult Warning Signs

Lack of peer relationships outside the family
Feelings of guilt or shame
Difficulty with social skills such as keeping a conversation going
Difficulty with intimacy in relationships
Sense of being different, alienated from others
Drug or alcohol dependency
Feelings of loneliness
Depression
Suicidal thoughts

Quick temper
Difficulty making or keeping friends
Devastated reaction to rejection
Fear of humiliation
A sense of reality as black or white
Distorted body image
Anxiety attacks, especially in social situations
Difficulty making decisions
Anxiety reactions in restaurants, banks, movies
Persistent difficulty with job, career
Sexual-identity problems
Physical complaints/hypochondria
Self-destructive behavior
Stress-related physical symptoms
Fear of groups

In reviewing these generalized behavior surveys, you will become more aware of when to intervene. *And remember, the earlier the better.*

Once you have decided to help your child to overcome his or her social anxiety and move toward truly independent living, you will need a plan of action. Your role is a vital part of enabling your child to do more than just survive—but to *thrive* as an independent, fully social person.

TOUGH LOVE

You may have heard the phrase "tough love" applied to treating drug- or alcohol-dependent adolescents. Like drugs and alcohol, avoidance of interactions is an addiction, and those addicted will do anything to hide out from the things they fear. Tough love does not mean throwing your adolescent or adult child out on the streets. Tough love means limits, boundaries, rules, and consequences for breaking them. Tough love is positive pressure. It is turning your dependent relationship around. Right now, your child depends on you for support—emotional, financial, or practical. Your goal is to foster independence. How can you do this? By turning that dependence around. Your child depends on you—let him depend on you for guidance through this difficult transition. Tough love may be your best investment in a productive, fulfilling future for your son or daughter, provided it is done at the right time.

An interesting case comes to mind that illustrates the complex issues surrounding tough love. Billy was a bright fifteen-year-old whose social anxiety led him to decide that he was not going to school anymore. He had no friends, and relied solely on his parents for a sense of acceptance and approval. Outside the home, he was withdrawn and monosyllabic. His parents begged him to go into therapy to discuss his anxiety and avoidance, but he refused, first quietly, and then with violent tantrums.

On my advice, his parents tried the tough love rules-and-consequences approach. They resolved to make Billy less comfortable at home, taking away TV privileges, then his computer, then his baseball card collection. But there was no progress. So long as he was home from school, away from his peer group, Billy seemed content.

Upon returning home one afternoon, Billy's parents were perplexed to discover that Billy, who had been fairly negligent of household chores in the past, had not only vacuumed and dusted as they had asked, but had also cleaned the kitchen, right down to polishing the silverware! Wasn't this improvement?

Not exactly, I explained. I interpreted Billy's behavior this way: "Please, Mom and Dad, I'll do whatever you want. I'll be the perfect son. Just don't make me face my fears." Time for step two. I advised his parents that the physical comforts they had deprived Billy of were of less value to him than their approval. Their displays of affection were signaling to Billy that his avoiding reality was okay with them. In fact, it was not, and their withholding is what told him so. When Billy behaved unreasonably, or let his fears get the best of him, his parents were firm and direct, not affectionate and forgiving. Soon there was progress. And eventually Billy began therapy and resumed ninth grade.

That Billy appeared content, despite the fact that he had no relationships with anyone except his parents, is a warning sign.

Socially anxious people of any age are likely to deny their problem, to assert, "I'm perfectly happy. I don't need friends." As a parent, it is your job to step back and look objectively at the situation. If your child—of whatever age—sees no one of his own peer group except at school or on the job, then there is a problem. What you're seeing is *avoidance:* Of course the person appears content when there is no possibility of humiliation, rejection, or scrutiny, the three things he most wishes to avoid. He or she doesn't want friends? Don't buy it.

It's up to you to take action. The older your socially anxious child gets, the more difficult it will be to change his behavior. If you are waiting for the "phase" to end, you will wait forever. If you are waiting for a day when your resistant child of whatever age will become more reasonable and agree to get help with anxiety on his own, you may wait forever. Keep your expectations reasonable, and know that your own commitment to nurture your child toward independence is what will correct the situation. You want the best for your child, and the best includes experiencing the pleasures of friendship and romantic love. Nurture independence, don't enable unhealthy dependence. Here is a plan of action.

GUIDELINES FOR FACILITATING CHANGE

NOTE: The use of the word "child" in the following guidelines refers to children of all ages, preteen through adult.

1. *Develop positive mental attitude* (PMA). You must believe that change is possible. With PMA, there is an excellent chance that there will be progress and growth. Without PMA, the status quo will remain. A uniformly positive message is crucial, so be sure the whole family is behind you to the fullest extent possible. Social anxiety is curable or controllable, but a negative or confused attitude during rehabilitation can result in a chronic social disability. Your child depends on you. Transform that dependence—turn your *rescuing* into *nurturing.*

2. *Acknowledge that a social anxiety problem exists.* Identify the degree to which it affects both the individual and the family using the surveys, indexes, and profiles in this book.
3. *Realize that your child will not simply "grow out of it."* The only way out of it—at any age—is to learn a way out of it. A step-by-step program, reinforced by your PMA, is the only way. Your child needs your help.
4. *Think of the future.* Ask yourself: "What will be the outcome of the present situation if no change is made? And if change is made?"
5. *Establish short- and long-term goals.* It is important to be realistic. During a session with the parents of a twenty-year-old young man who had dropped out of college, I asked them, "What do you think is a reasonable goal to try to accomplish with your son this month?" The father replied, "I'd like him to feel good about himself." Again, the best intentions, but that's a lifetime of work in just a month. I asked the father instead to redefine the goal into something attainable and concrete: "I'd like him to identify something he accomplished around the house that was helpful to the family." Same idea, right? But it's not a once-and-for-all statement of self-esteem. Start small, and work steady!
6. *Understand that your child probably has an avoidant and dependent personality.* She avoids social interaction because she fears humiliation and rejection. He depends excessively on family members because he has difficulty with self-reliance and is unsure how to go about establishing a peer support network.
7. *Focus on the present, not on the past.* If you realize now that you have enabled your child's social anxiety by rescuing him or helping him to avoid the situations he fears, accept that as past behavior and move on. Don't be negatively controlled by guilt. The past does not equal the future. I am reminded of Jay, a twenty-year-old who moved back home when he dropped out of college. Jay was angry and resentful that his parents had sent him to boarding school for ninth and tenth

grade; his bad experiences there, he believed, were their fault, and he never let them forget it. They in turn felt they were to blame. But again, the past does not equal the future. Make a stand. If you deny your role in your child's dependent behavior, there is a good chance that his social anxiety will be permanent. Instead, turn your role around: Your child depends on you, so let him depend on you now to teach him independence.

8. *Develop a strategy or game plan.* Realize that your first objective is to help your child change her attitude. If the attitude changes, behavior will eventually change too. Take responsibility for creating appropriate communications with your child. If you have been an enabler or rescuer in the past, it may take some hard work to get your child to see you in a new light. But do everything you can to make your child take your new stance seriously. If at this point she acknowledges the problem and admits she wants help, then much of your battle is won. But as I explained, denial is common, so expect it. In order to improve the situation, you must confront resistance.

9. *Understand your role as enabler.* The socially anxious person has an addiction—an addiction to avoidance of things that make him anxious. It is a habit that is hard to break, but with your help—and by your example—he will be able to confront his fears and begin working to overcome them.

10. *Become an empowerer.* This means that you take the role of helping your child to confront and even master the difficult situation instead of enabling him to avoid it.

11. *Make a list of the inappropriate ways your child is dependent on you.* These will be most obvious when considering adult children: financial, emotional, and practical needs could be met by a healthy adult, but instead an unhealthy adult relies on you to meet them. In younger children, inappropriate dependence may mean an elementary-age student relying on Mom to choose his friends and invite them to do things with him, or an eighteen-year-old who refuses to learn to drive

because his dad takes him wherever he wants to go. This list is the beginning of your power: Use it to negotiate in a productive manner when you are faced with a lack of reason.

12. *Present a united front.* Both parents should be perceived as being on the same team. Consistency is essential. When you disagree, do so behind closed doors. The socially anxious individual has learned to play family members off one another, manipulating them both consciously and unconsciously. Manipulation is easy when parents disagree on how the situation should be handled—your child knows this, and will use this knowledge to create chaos and avoid taking responsibility for his or her behavior.

13. *Understand that your child relies on defense mechanisms.* Usually, when confronted with honest, direct communication, he or she becomes uncomfortable or anxious. This may result in a temper tantrum—acting out aggression, making threats, or withdrawing even more than normal. These tantrums will not go away overnight. Often, things get worse before they get better. Your child has relied on his avoidance and dependence as a way of life for as long as he can remember. When you ask him to change, he will resist. Expect that, and be firm. You are in control.

14. *Fight temper tantrums:*

(a) *Define your own tolerance level* so your child knows the limits of what's acceptable. *Establish consequences* your child must face if he persists in his bad behavior. Mean what you say. Never, never threaten any consequence you do not follow through on. Without actual consequences, the negative behavior will remain the same. Enabling is great if you can afford it. I know one wealthy man who supports his daughter and "incorrigible" son-in-law with $100,000 a year just because enabling them to be irresponsible financially makes *his* life easier—he no longer need worry about their financial status. Not the best way to encourage independence, but that is his choice. On the other hand, I know an elderly woman who can ill afford to send $10,000 or so a year to her son; but she does it anyway, because she fears what his reaction will be next time he's in dire straits. Again, make your limits clear.

(b) *Learn to manage your own stress.* This is extremely important. You may have learned a thing or two from your avoidant child and may therefore back away from stressful situations (believing that it's easier, short term, to just go ahead and fish for him than to teach him to fish). This new program will be stressful. But it will eventually end in success. Don't give in just because you are tired. If you do burn out, refer to the stress management techniques in Chapter 6. To renew your commitment to helping your child, think again about the long-term consequences of doing nothing.

15. *Learn what "tough love" means.* Confront problems actively and honestly, and insist that your child do the same. Again, mean what you say. Behavior equals consequences. Does that mean throwing your adult child out on the streets? Absolutely not. There are many, many steps to take before resorting to such a drastic measure. Growth occurs by confronting fear and anxiety.

16. *Place positive pressure on the socially anxious child—using gradual steps.* To break the negative balance, establish limits, responsibilities, and consequences.

17. *Become your child's teacher.* You are there to teach your child what he does not know. "But I don't know what to say when I invite Bob over to watch football," your adult child says. "Let's practice: How about 'Hey, do you want to come over and watch the game Monday night?' " It may be as simple as putting words in his mouth. The role of teacher can be very productive if handled right, so find out just what information or skills are lacking, and start teaching.

18. *If you need to seek professional support, identify your options.* Some counseling or psychotherapy may be in order; Chapter 10 will address when this is necessary and give tips on how to shop for a therapist.

Remember, your child looks to you for guidance. Your influence—your consistent, positive support—may save your child from a life of persistent failure, loneliness, and anxiety. As you proceed through this book, pay special attention to any references to parents or other relatives. You will always be a part of your child's system, whatever his or her age; our common goal, however, is to ensure that he or she does not just survive but thrives in a social support network of his or her own creation. Although I am speaking directly to readers who are suffering from social anxiety problems, everything I am saying can become part of your success strategy with your preteen, adolescent, or adult child. Understand it, then do all you can to make it an integral part of your family dynamic. With a positive mental attitude, you can make a difference!

CHAPTER FOUR

The Deciding Factors: Avoidance, Dependence, and Low Self-Esteem

Working with independent adults who have made a conscious decision to fight their social anxiety is the most rewarding aspect of what I do. It is also much easier than working with someone who is resistant to change because of deeply ingrained fears. Naturally, there is some degree of resistance in anyone for whom social anxiety is a problem. In a mid- to high-functioning person, the results of my social therapy program are often dramatic, and the person integrates a positive attitude and healthy behaviors into his or her life in a progressive manner. Commitment to change is essential, and what makes commitment possible is PMA—positive mental attitude—a vital component of anyone's eventual success. Without an optimistic outlook, change is extremely difficult. Consider the following scenarios, which delineate three different levels of social anxiety:

Ellen: Ellen, forty-two, is a graphic designer for a small advertising company. Her art training has given her a good sense of color, which she uses both in choosing her clothes and in decorating the condominium she bought last year. She enjoys going to museums, and has pursued painting as a hobby for many years. Ellen often goes on these outings alone, but she does occasionally invite a friend to join her. Usually, though, it is the friend who calls to invite Ellen, not the other way around. Ellen, like many socially anxious people, avoids telephone contact. Her answering machine is her guard dog—it's always on, screening her calls. When she returns a call, she usually does so when she knows the person won't be home, so she too can leave a message and avoid a real conversation. As far as friendship goes, Ellen has told me that it's the follow-up that bothers her: She truly dreads getting to know anyone well enough that they would have any expectations of her. The stress of giving is too much; Ellen is afraid to let other people down. Basically, it is a problem with intimacy; she feels that if they got to know the "real" Ellen, they would judge her negatively or even reject her. So the quality of her friendships is not always satisfying. She enjoys going places in a fairly structured environment, where expectations are clear (such as a lunch date or museum excursion), but she is quite uncomfortable sharing her feelings. Outwardly successful, Ellen knows inside that she falls short of self-actualization because she herself can feel the emptiness in her friendships. Yet her social anxiety keeps her from really trying to fill the void.

Joe: At twenty-six, Joe lives in a New York suburb with his parents. He is a computer technician who earns a good mid-range salary. Occasionally, Joe dates a woman from his church, but he spends most of his free time tinkering with his own computer at home or maintaining the BMW that is his pride and joy. He also belongs to a health club and is very proud of his physique. Joe claims he lives at home for "financial reasons," but anyone can see that he could afford to move out if he really wanted to. His parents have made it easy for him not to, setting up an "apartment" in the basement (though he still comes up for meals, which they pay for). In public, Joe exaggerates his career success, and talks vaguely about women he "knows" as though they are past girlfriends (they're not). To him, his suit, briefcase, and cellular phone represent success. But beneath the shell is a lonely, dependent person who has so far managed to avoid confronting his insecurities and pursuing intimate friendships and other relationships. Joe is moderately dependent and avoids confronting his fears by making excuses.

Wayne: Wayne lives in a trailer his parents bought for him four years ago, on some land in upstate New York that has been in the family for years. It's a beautiful spot, but Wayne is no nature lover; in fact he could not care less. He spends all his time indoors, flicking the channels to see what else his satellite dish will tune in. Unemployed since the year after high school, Wayne, now thirty, relies entirely on his parents to fund his existence. He feels justified in this, as he tells them in long, angry phone conversations, because, he says, "they made me like this! It's their fault I can't do anything and I don't know anyone." But because of his severe social anxiety Wayne makes absolutely zero effort to venture out and meet people. The guilt he causes his parents to feel creates a situation in which they further enable his avoidance and dependence. When he needs groceries, his father actually makes the two-hour drive to deliver them! Wayne literally will not leave the house, and his parents are enabling his behavior to continue by supporting him in his dependence.

As you can see, there are many variables that make up the balance of avoidance, dependence, and resulting low self-esteem, and there are different degrees of incapacity due to social anxiety. This chapter will help you to determine what the balance is for you.

LOW SELF-ESTEEM

Characteristic of most people with social anxiety is low self-esteem. I showed you the sequence in Chapter 1. What is the connection between low self-esteem and social anxiety? A person who has experienced years of failure and frustration will suffer from a lack of self-confidence unless he or she learns appropriate strategies that can break the cycle of negative thinking and allow real behavioral change to take place. In some cases, early peer rejection has caused the socially anxious person to develop a poor self-image. In other cases, negative reinforcement (harsh criticism at home, poor performance in school or on the playing field) has turned self-doubt into self-reproach. Eventually, that element of "self"—the inner voice—becomes far more judgmental than any outside person or group could be. The inner voice then chastises the person into silence and, finally, retreat.

The following statements indicate low self-esteem and may have a familiar ring:

- "I don't say things that interest people."
- "No one can find anything to say to me."
- "I'm not good at doing things other people like to do."
- "People think I'm unattractive."
- "I'm not good enough."
- "I know I'll fail."
- "I am uncomfortable with change—I tend to hang on to what's familiar, even when I'm not very happy with it."
- "People are always judging my efforts at work or school."
- "I have trouble expressing emotions, such as disappointment or anger."
- "I generally have a pessimistic attitude."
- "I am inhibited from recognizing new opportunities in my career and social life."
- "I hesitate to take advantage of new opportunities in my career or social life."
- "I have trouble making decisions."

If you have low self-esteem, you believe you can see yourself through other people's eyes, and you judge yourself by what you imagine other people's standards to be. As your own personal sequence of self-esteem has progressed, you failed to develop an inner feeling of confidence and satisfaction (this is the definition of self-esteem). Without a sense of personal value, disappointment becomes a disaster, so attuned are you to other people's reactions. Perhaps worse, if you suffer from low self-esteem, you may begin to believe your acquaintances hold the same low opinion of you that you hold of yourself. Often, you may force the issue, secretly expecting the rejection that will confirm your fears.

A case in point: When Raymond first came to me for help with his social life, he insisted he simply had not met the right people.

More than anything, Raymond said, he wanted to "find a woman." By no means afraid to seek out companionship, Raymond would recount situation after situation in which everything seemed to be going along well for one evening or even two, only to erupt in a telephone argument or terse note explaining why the relationship could not continue. As we talked, Raymond revealed that he had in fact never had a successful romantic relationship, and his desperation was quite apparent. I asked him to pay close attention to the kinds of things he said to his dates. Was he making them uncomfortable? Did his desperation show?

The following session, he reported another blowup. His new "girlfriend" had gotten angry when Raymond asked her to cancel her plans to attend a concert with friends. How had the whole thing started? "I called Denise up and said, 'I'd like to take you out to dinner Tuesday, unless you don't want to go out with me.' " When Denise said she'd made other plans, he assumed (wrongly, it seemed) that she was rejecting not just the date, but Raymond himself. After several such instances, Raymond began to see how his neediness came through in the way he expressed his wishes, forcing the very thing he feared most: rejection. Raymond had a lot of work to do before he could get beyond his fear of rejection to achieve the quality of intimacy he truly desired.

Low self-esteem can also prevent you from living up to your career potential. Carla, a client of mine, left the work force to raise a family after three years as an administrative assistant. With her children approaching college age, she decided to shift her focus away from the home and back to a career. Having helped her husband with his computer firm, she decided to take an advanced computer course to improve her skills. The course was extremely difficult, so tough, in fact, that twelve of the twenty-four students dropped out after the first test. But Carla got an A. Even so, she belittled her accomplishment, trying in vain to persuade me that it was an easy class and that she probably could never be qualified to find work in that field. In fact, Carla is quite gifted, but without the requisite self-esteem she will have great difficulty selling herself in this competitive job market.

"I Think I'm Ugly"
"I'm ugly." I've heard this phrase so many times from people in my program. Low self-esteem can often manifest itself in your perception of how others see you. I've treated sufferers from social anxiety who, objectively speaking, were attractive, but whose poor physical self-image led them to fear rejection. One young man would not even talk to women because he was so sure he was repulsive to them; when I asked him why, he cited few specifics, except for the thick glasses he had worn since childhood. In reality, he was reasonably good-looking, and, once he was able to work through his self-esteem and social anxiety issues, was rather enjoyable to be around. Another woman, fearing her legs were "too chubby," refused to wear skirts or dresses, even to formal occasions, and would avoid talking to men. Social anxiety can lead to distorted perceptions, and the fear of outright rejection based on looks diminishes as self-help techniques work to boost confidence. In isolation, you tend to obsess on your negative thoughts. Learning to control your anxiety will allow you to get out there and gain some positive experience. In the end, physical attractiveness is only one part of interactive chemistry. People enjoy interacting with those who take a genuine interest in them, and who are energetic and positive.

Changing Your Opinion
Think back to the low-self-esteem statements you identified with, bearing in mind that, no matter how you came by your low opinion of yourself, you *can* change it. As Eleanor Roosevelt once said, "No one can make you feel inferior without your permission." You own your self-image, and you can feel about yourself whatever you choose to feel. Throughout this book, there are exercises to help you change how you feel about yourself. And in the next chapter, we'll look at some ways to set social goals. For now, try repeating what Mrs. Roosevelt said: "No one can make you feel inferior without your permission." Give yourself credit for seeking help with your social problems. You care about yourself, and that counts for a lot.

Social anxiety and low self-esteem go hand in hand. In fact, many people simplify so-called "shyness" as a self-esteem problem. The reality is, however, that poor self-esteem is a by-product of social anxiety. It is the social anxiety that comes first, not the other way around! Social failures cause anxiety, which causes avoidance, which causes low self-esteem. As a person's confidence dwindles, the fears become greater, until eventually the individual simply stops trying. With fewer and fewer opportunities for social interaction, there are also fewer opportunities to receive positive feedback. This combination of factors perpetuates low self-esteem, which cannot be replaced with a healthy self-image until the avoidant behavior ceases.

If you experience feelings of inadequacy and low self-esteem, your poor self-image may keep you from exploring your social self and getting to know others. When fear causes inhibition, your chances of interactive success are severely diminished. Eventually, it will seem easier to avoid the anxiety of socializing than to go ahead and risk failure. The more you avoid these situations, the more you depend on family members for all your emotional support. In my treatment of individuals with social anxiety, these are the two personality profiles that inevitably surface. There is a direct connection between the two: If you avoid doing something that needs to be done, you probably depend on someone else to do it for you. For example, if you habitually avoid going to the bank, or making a phone call, how do these things get accomplished? Ask yourself: "When I avoid these things, who picks up the pieces?" You can't have avoidance without an element of dependence. Now ask yourself: "If I did it myself, what would the outcome be?" And then: "If no one did it, what would the outcome be?" I am reminded here of a client in his early twenties who had gotten about twenty-five speeding tickets over the course of a year or so. Somehow, his parents managed to cover up for him to the point of acquiring a new driver's license for him whenever his was revoked. While it is true that this did get him out of trouble, it also perpetuated dependence on the rescuing relationship.

Experience can be the best teacher. In my own life, when I am faced with something stressful, I sometimes recall an experience I had during my last year in graduate school. I was working with kids—street-smart kids—who had criminal records ranging from drug dealing to robbery and murder. Believe me, I had a lot of anxiety! As the only white staff member at a youth center in the heart of the Bronx, I had more than a little anxiety about going in to work every day. At times, I even wanted to quit. But I stuck with it and eventually found the common ground that would get me through my tenure there: basketball. Being on the court together—on *their* turf—gave us a better understanding of each other, and in time, I became less nervous. I use my memories of the anxiety I felt to remind myself that I can get through just about anything if I adopt the right attitude.

In this chapter, you will come to understand the personality components of avoidant and dependent behavior, identify the symptoms that apply to you, and begin to assess the extent to which avoidance and dependence are controlling your social life.

AVOIDANCE

When your social fears control you, you may go to great lengths to avoid interacting with others. Think about how other people manage to get out of many of the normal social obligations or other interactions in their lives—they may flatly refuse to go, or, if they do attend, they may do whatever they can to avoid mingling with people who make them uncomfortable (help out in the kitchen, sit and read a magazine, play with the kids). To avoid dealing with his fear of addressing a group, remember how Alan—an otherwise well-adjusted young man—almost abandoned his dream of graduating from college because he was afraid to take the public speaking class that was required of him.

In the short run, these solutions work. You are capable of identifying what makes you socially anxious and steering clear of it. But in the long run, if you simply avoid anxiety instead of learning to confront it, you limit yourself in ways that will ultimately cause loneliness in your personal life, a lack of productivity at work, and ultimately depression.

The *Diagnostic and Statistical Manual of Mental Disorders,*[*] which is the reference manual used by mental health professionals to diagnose psychological problems, defines the avoidant personality disorder by saying that this personality type has the *"essential feature of hypersensitivity to potential rejection, humiliation, or shame. . . ."* Avoidant people are always afraid of "messing up," "saying or doing the wrong thing," "getting caught," "not being good enough," and so on. They do anything to save face—even, and this is the extreme, not showing their faces at all.

The *Manual* goes on to describe *"an unwillingness to enter into relationships unless given unusually strong guarantees of uncritical acceptance. . . ."* Most avoidant people do whatever they can to keep relationships superficial or nonexistent, unless they are sure that the person will accept them without judging them; often, they turn to relatives for emotional support, perceiving them as "safe." Even if superficial friendships do exist, it is unlikely that an avoidant person will take the perceived risk of sharing intimate thoughts or feelings, for fear that the acquaintance would find "the truth" horrifying or even merely unattractive or unacceptable.

"Social withdrawal in spite of desire for affection and acceptance . . ." Avoidant people may look and act like "loners," but they're not. Many of the people I have worked with in my social therapy program start out saying that they are perfectly fine *without* friends, even though they have sought out treatment for depression or anxiety. The truth is, most people truly want companionship, even if they can't verbalize the desire. Avoidant people are no exception; the only thing that makes them different is that the fear of rejection we all feel to one degree or another has become so great in their minds that they have trouble controlling it. With effort, though, avoidant people can learn to overcome their fear of rejection and seek out the friendship and even romance that they secretly want.

"Low self-esteem." As I've explained, most people who fear rejection act as though they have some terrible secret that would

[*]Third edition, revised (Washington, D.C.: American Psychiatric Association, 1987).

mean instant loneliness if it were discovered. Usually, we are much harder on ourselves than others would ever be. For people whose low self-esteem is a stopper, it *seems* as though the whole world sees them the way they do, and that only magnifies their poor self-image.

"Individuals with this disorder are exquisitely sensitive to rejection, humiliation, or shame. Most people are somewhat concerned about how others assess them, but these individuals are devastated by the slightest hint of disapproval." So sensitive to disapproval, in fact, that they will avoid it at all costs—*even if it means forgoing job opportunities, social events, or intimate relationships that they would truly like to pursue.*

To determine ways in which avoidance is limiting you, examine the list below, which explores the ways in which avoidance affects different areas of your life. As you consider these examples of avoidant behavior, think about why you behave as you do. Does your fear of rejection or humiliation inhibit your interactions? What is the worst thing that could happen? What would make it easier for you to interact?

1. I have difficulty accepting challenges.
2. I'm afraid that if I try something and then can't do it, people will think I'm a failure.
3. I cut situations short—even when I'm enjoying myself— because I fear others are bored with me or because I'm uncomfortable.
4. I tend to put things off—deadlines, phone calls, social engagements.
5. I often cancel plans I've already made.
6. I make excuses to avoid things I think I'll do poorly.
7. I make excuses to avoid things that might be fun if I just let myself go and enjoy them.
8. I fear taking on added responsibility at work.
9. I avoid interacting with authority figures such as supervisors at work.
10. If I make a mistake at work, I try to cover it up to avoid confrontation.
11. I prefer to stay home.

12. I seldom invite people to visit.
13. When people drop in unexpectedly, it makes me uncomfortable and sometimes even angry.
14. I have trouble starting and ending a conversation because I'm afraid I'll say something foolish or stupid.
15. I have trouble asking questions, because I'm afraid people will think they are inappropriate or feel I'm prying.
16. I have trouble making eye contact.
17. After the first few sentences of a conversation, I don't know what else to say; I'm afraid to take a chance because I'm sure I'll say something inappropriate.
18. I try to avoid social obligations such as parties.
19. I seldom accept social invitations.
20. I avoid phone calls, both at home and at the office.
21. I am resistant to changes in my work or school environment.
22. I feel uncomfortable when I talk about myself.
23. I have difficulty eating in restaurants.
24. I seldom date. If I do have a date, I often get anxious and think about canceling at the last minute; sometimes I do cancel.

As you think about these symptoms, you will see that a pattern is emerging. *Even though you want to interact, your fears keep you from it.* You are letting your anxiety control how you spend your time. In your mind, the social event has taken on such mammoth proportions that it is entirely unmanageable. Many people get somewhat nervous before a social engagement—especially a first date or formal gathering, where expectations may be a little more charged than usual. But to be so fearful that you choose to stay home alone rather than attend is avoidant behavior. Don't let avoidance be the order of the day.

DEPENDENCE

If fear and anxiety inhibit the degree to which you interact, you may tend to rely on others to do things for you. Even if you appear to outsiders to be a highly functioning, successful person in school or career, if you scratch below the surface, you may discover some dependence hidden beneath a few clever rationalizations. In some instances, these things may not seem very significant, and you yourself may justify them quite convincingly: "The other sales reps are better at coming up with new marketing plans, so I don't need to participate in brainstorming sessions. I'll just sit quietly and take it all in." "My sister has such good taste—she knows more about what looks good on me than I do. I'll get her to come shopping with me." Of course, even if it meant a little extra effort on your part (and possibly making a few mistakes along the way), you *could* take more responsibility for your career, appearance, or whatever other aspect of day-to-day life you are now surrendering to other people's control.

One client of mine, a college student, insisted that he had no problem with dependence, until one day he casually mentioned that his mother, a college professor, had picked up all the books he needed to write a paper. "It was no big deal," he said. "She was going by the library anyway." But her "little favor" had big implications: Mothers who do research for their college-age sons are enablers, pure and simple. Eventually, this client learned to insist on doing his own work, and to deny his mother's well-intentioned "favors." (By the way, once you get over your dependence, you may actually find, as this client did, that it feels good to be self-sufficient; your resourcefulness will then build your self-esteem and give you confidence.)

When your reliance becomes more pervasive, and you start expecting family members or one or two friends to provide significant emotional support and guidance as well, the issue of dependence becomes more complicated. Because you are afraid to live independently, without the same security you enjoyed in childhood, you may have chosen to live with your parents well into adulthood, even though you earn enough to support yourself financially. Or you may live alone but continue to rely on your parents' input about the major decisions you make, and to accept some supplementary income for living expenses or recreational costs.

Donald, for example, would seem independent on first meeting.

But in fact, he is emotionally dependent on his parents. Donald also uses his parents as an excuse to avoid taking a risk he would really like to take. In his words: "I want to open my own accounting firm in Colorado; I've always dreamed of living there. But my parents need me here. They would be very upset if I moved away." Donald himself might have mixed feelings if he ever did indeed move. But depending on his parents to hold him back is a pretty powerful way to avoid making a decision to venture into the uncharted territory of a new town and business.

The *Diagnostic and Statistical Manual of Mental Disorders* says that someone with a *dependent personality disorder "passively allows others to assume responsibility for major areas of his or her life. . . ."* As I have explained, healthy adults should function independently, without looking to others to absolve them of responsibility for the practical aspects of living. It's okay to seek support and advice, but be sure that it is an active, conscious choice. Don't let others develop or maintain a habit of making your decisions for you. Break your own habit of dependence, and then keep to it!

". . . Because of a lack of self-confidence and an inability to function independently . . ." It may be easier to let others do things for you— whether large or small—but if you consider it honestly, you will eventually see that giving over your responsibilities has undercut your self-confidence. Because you don't do something, it may feel as though you *can't* do it. If you think of yourself as a can't-do, it is difficult to regard yourself as someone others would respect and appreciate. Dependence takes a huge toll on self-esteem, and self-esteem is an essential component of a healthy social being. *"Individuals with this problem invariably lack self-confidence. They tend to belittle their abilities and assets. They may refer to themselves as stupid."*

"The individual subordinates his or her own needs to those of others on whom he or she is dependent in order to avoid any possibility of having to be self-reliant. . . ." Rather than risk inconveniencing anyone with your desires, you simply "go with the flow," relying on family members to make all your plans for a time and place convenient for them.

"Such individuals leave major decisions to others." To do otherwise

might entail taking responsibility for one's own desires, something that is virtually impossible for a dependent person. Having no say at all appears to be easier than taking a stand and risking independence.

This index will help you determine the ways in which you are overly dependent on others. Again, as you look at each statement, decide whether it is true for you. It is not important to keep score. Rather, take a few minutes to consider how each statement has affected your life, and try to identify the ways in which dependence has inhibited your interaction or kept you from self-actualizing.

1. I rely on others for at least some financial support.
2. I have one or two friends or relatives that I call too often when I have a problem.
3. I rely heavily on my parents' advice and opinions.
4. I often allow others to make even minor decisions for me.
5. When it comes to major purchases or decisions, I defer to the judgment of others.
6. Usually, someone else makes my appointments for me, and keeps track of my medical needs.
7. I have a hard time shopping for myself and prefer to have someone else along to help me choose; sometimes, others do my shopping for me.
8. Someone else handles my finances.
9. I seldom answer the phone because other people in my office or household are willing to do it for me.
10. I usually get another member of my household or office to make calls on my behalf.
11. I screen calls with an answering machine so that I am not caught off-guard.
12. I depend on my colleagues to do work assigned to me if the task makes me uncomfortable.
13. I depend on work for most of my social interaction.
14. When I socialize or participate in recreational activities, it's usually with family members or one of only a few close friends.

15. I seldom initiate social events, leaving it up to others to decide what to do and when.
16. I seldom drive myself places.
17. I become anxious when I have to go someplace new, and rely heavily on others to help me find the way.
18. I rely on others to handle my household management.
19. When I'm alone, I often have a feeling of indecision when faced with a dilemma.
20. Because I don't like how it feels to have a lot of time on my hands, weekends and vacations make me uncomfortable.

WHEN SOCIAL ANXIETY BECOMES SOCIAL PHOBIA

When your social anxiety becomes so great that you have to avoid the specific situation that causes it, you are dealing with a social phobia. In movies and on television, in both serious and comical contexts, we have heard of many phobias: fear of heights, fear of trains, fear of bridges, fear of crowds. And this, according to the *Journal of Psychiatry,* is the decade of social phobia. What is social phobia? As we discussed earlier, social phobia is essentially performance anxiety. Here is how the *DSMIII-R* defines it:

"The essential feature is a persistent irrational fear and compelling desire to avoid situations in which the individual may be exposed to scrutiny by others." In other words, the avoidance typical of social anxiety sufferers becomes so extreme that it overshadows any desire to participate in the situation. The fear of being scrutinized by others includes not only the evaluation of the performance but also a fear that anxiety symptoms will become obvious. Obsessive thought patterns ("They can tell I'm nervous," "They can see I'm sweating") are common, along with the actual physical symptoms. Both mental and physical symptoms become as stressful as the situation itself.

"There is also fear that the individual will behave in a manner that will be humiliating or embarrassing." Again, the individual is preoccupied with fear of failure or performance anxiety.

"Marked anticipatory anxiety occurs if the individual is confronted

with the necessity of entering into such a situation." Even the thought of being evaluated causes the social phobic reaction, so ingrained is the anxiety response.

Where social phobia exists, there is a pronounced inhibition of interaction on all levels. The individual is so preoccupied by fear of symptoms and by finding a way of avoiding the situation that he cannot successfully interact. Some specific social phobias are included here:

- Fear of public speaking
- Fear of participating in a group presentation
- Fear of eating in a restaurant
- Fear of raising a hand to talk in class
- Fear of writing a check in front of someone
- Fear of using a public bathroom
- Fear of dating
- Fear of participating in an activity with other people
- Fear of attending public events

Think of social phobia as extreme performance anxiety about a specific act, such as those listed above. Where there is any chance of being evaluated by others in the situation he fears, the social phobic will experience extreme anxiety and will do all he can to avoid the situation.

AN EXTREME CASE: AGORAPHOBIA

Many people confuse social anxiety and social phobia with agoraphobia. Agoraphobia literally means "fear of the marketplace" in ancient Greek. Psychologists use the term today to refer to the fear of open spaces. Whereas social phobia refers to the fear of interacting with others, agoraphobia is a more generalized fear of being away from the controlled environment of home. The *DSMIII-R* calls agoraphobia the *"fear of being in places or situations from which escape might be difficult or embarrassing or in which help might not be available in the event of panic."* This fear manifests itself in situations such as the following:

- Being outside the home
- Being in a crowd
- Standing in line
- Traveling across a bridge
- Traveling inside a car or bus

Agoraphobia and social phobia overlap in many ways. Carrie, thirty, was homebound for ten years with agoraphobia. In that time, she became totally dependent on her mother, who supported her, shopped for her, and attempted to meet her emotional needs. Carrie's mother began bringing her for individual sessions with me, and I was struck by the severity of her fear. Seated in front of me and suffering excruciating pain from a tooth and gum infection, she nonetheless refused to see a dentist because she wanted to avoid the humiliation and embarrassment her condition would cause. With many agoraphobics I have treated, social phobia—the fear of humiliation or embarrassment—was at the root of the problem. In many of these cases, we are able to trace the agoraphobia's inception back to a humiliating or embarrassing incident. This leads me to conclude that agoraphobia is in some cases actually an extreme case of social phobia.

HOW DOES SOCIAL FEAR CONTROL YOU?

By now, you are beginning to see the ways in which social anxiety has prevented you from having a fulfilling personal life and career. *In fact, social anxiety builds on itself.* The more afraid you are, the more threatening even the idea of socializing becomes. Thus fear becomes phobia. To overcome your panic and make friends, you have to break the avoidance cycle and learn to depend on yourself.

Certainly, individual social needs differ from person to person, but the focus here is on finding a healthy and happy balance between private time and a rewarding social life. Each individual has the potential to develop a fulfilling social network and a better sense of self-worth. To reach these goals, it is essential to identify the severity of the problem (Chapter 1), understand its nature (Chapters 2, 3, and 4) and then take steps to correct your isolation by managing anxiety and refining your social skills. These indexes provide an important element of your map for change, and will be a useful reassessment tool in the months and years to come. Initially, you can use them to pinpoint areas for improvement; later, you will be able to take pride in areas that you are working on or that you have already improved or even mastered. In the next chapter, we will work on setting some specific, *reachable* interactive goals before we go on to discuss techniques of stress management and application of social skills.

CHAPTER FIVE

Goal-Setting: How to Build a Map for Social Success

When was the last time you left your house to go to the store? Yesterday? Last week? Some time ago? How did you get there? Walk? Drive? Whatever the case, you were able to negotiate going to the store via a very important process that you probably take for granted. Each street, every step, every turn, was part of a map you had programmed in your brain. Without this map or program, you would not have gotten there.

What frequently keeps a person from making a change is the lack of a map or direction. The first four chapters of this book have provided you with substantial information regarding your map for social change, a map you will soon develop, and will continue to use throughout this self-help program. You have created a number of self-profiles that are the basis for changes that you are going to make; consider these the key for the map you will make. Now, let's take a practical view of these profiles before we move on to the how-to component of this self-help program. Then, with an understanding of what these case studies reveal, we will focus on your social goals, looking at where your life is now, and where you want it to be.

Before we begin, *activate your PMA* (positive mental attitude). Remind yourself that you *can* achieve interactive success. Now, in a positive, can-do frame of mind, list three reasons why you want to change your social life:

1. _____
   _____

2. _____
   _____

3. _____
   _____

Motivation is the crucial concept in bringing about change. Motivation is the fuel you will use, the energy you will spend to *actualize* the changes you want to make. How motivated to change do you feel right now? Let's measure your degree of motivation.

5 —*Extremely motivated.* You recognize your potential for happiness and have a sense of urgency about remedying the problems that inhibit your quality of life. You are totally independent and take responsibility for problem solving. You persevere, keeping in mind the old saying, "If at first you don't succeed, try, try again." You haven't given up, and you understand that the route to success has not only ups but downs.

4 —*Substantially motivated.* You understand the importance of resolving problems. You are fairly consistent, and are able to commit to many of the projects you wish to complete. You want to create change, but you sometimes question whether change is worth the effort—especially when you meet with failure.

3 —*Fairly motivated.* You know *something* is wrong, but you aren't ready to admit it's the poor quality of your interactions. At times you want to change, but you go back and forth about it, saying it's "not worth it," or "things are fine the way they are," even though deep down you know that it would be worth it and things are not fine. You hesitate to take responsibility for your own happiness, refusing to see your role in the reality of the situation. You may give up on the task at hand, especially

when the anxiety of confronting your fears increases to the point that you are uncomfortable.

2 —*No real motivation.* You are considering change, but this is mainly at the urging of others on whom you are dependent—in order to avoid conflict with them, you tend to agree, however halfheartedly, to try harder to be independent and social. You have succumbed to the problem—you let your anxiety and fear control you. As you see it, there is very little hope. Occasionally, though, you do have positive feelings, but they are quickly overwhelmed by feelings of anxiety when you are confronted with stress.

1 —*Nonfunctional.* Motivation is an abstract concept for you— social anxiety is something that others experience. You maintain that you are content, that you don't want or need to change. "Problem? What problem? I prefer to be alone. I don't need friends." You probably would not even look at your social situation were it not for the consistent pressure of others, and even then, you usually remain in an extreme state of denial. You are immersed in an unhealthy balance of living, avoiding what you fear and depending on a few relatives or close friends for all your emotional and social support. Because you avoid interacting, it is difficult to point to interactive problems (they simply don't come up because you don't interact), though they are present. Total camouflage exists.

What is your level of motivation? Do you feel you have been objective in your assessment? Obviously the higher the level the more potential for success exists. If your level is on the lower side, ask yourself the following questions:

1. Do I want to change? Why or why not?

_____

_____

_____

2. Do I think change will happen by itself—without my involvement?

_____

_____

_____

3. Do I think that life goes on forever—whether I have a satisfying life or not—so that what is happening now really does not matter?

_____

_____

_____

4. Am I blaming someone else for my problem? Am I caught up in the process of blame to the point that I cannot address my own role in my social anxiety?

_____

_____

_____

5. Is my current life situation what I really want? Am I challenged and fulfilled in my work? Am I content and satisfied with my personal relationships? Or am I rationalizing because of my various fears and anxieties?

_____

_____

_____

Take a moment to think about these questions, and the answers you've written. You are probably familiar with the word *fantasy*. Think of it as unrestrained imagination. We're going to use this imagination to help you set your goals. Everyone has the ability to do this kind of exercise. Let me prove it to you. How many windows are there in the bedroom of your house or apartment? That's right . . . how did you get the answer? You pictured your home in your mind. So use this ability now to begin picturing yourself as a person who interacts successfully. Before we begin, I want to stress that *you must actually do these exercises* to benefit from them. Reading through them is not enough. Take responsibility for your self-help by committing to do each and every exercise in this chapter and throughout this book. If you skip any exercise, you are not empowering yourself to change. Work step by step, however, and you are giving yourself a gift for the future. Now to the exercises.

Sit back, take a deep breath, and allow yourself to relax. Close your eyes. Use the television screen in your mind to visualize what interactive success means to you. You are walking into a social situation. You were invited because the other people enjoy your company and look forward to spending time with you. Imagine that there are other people there. What are they doing as you enter the room? They are glad to see you. What do you say? What do they say to you? Stay with this picture for a few moments. As you move around the room, picture your body relaxed and at ease with the situation. You are in control. How does it feel? Open your eyes.

Now sit back comfortably once again. Take a deep breath. Close your eyes, and picture yourself in a work environment. See it very clearly. Use your natural senses to develop the image. You were asked to make a presentation to your associates. You've been preparing for months. All your materials are in order and everyone is eager to hear what you have to say. What are your associates doing as you enter the conference room? They seem interested in your ideas. What do you say? What do they say to you? Your bosses are there. How do they respond? As you flip through your materials, you can feel that your body is relaxed and moving easily. You are in control. How does it feel? Open your eyes.

When you first work with imagery, you may feel self-conscious or embarrassed. The more you work with imagery the easier it becomes. Think of it as behavior rehearsal. We will continue to use imagery throughout this process, especially in the exercises in Chapters 6 (stress management) and 7 (self-awareness). Imagery will help you to visualize yourself as someone who interacts successfully—the ultimate goal of this self-help program. Remember, this is your time, and it will serve you best to be as open and honest as possible.

Planning Each Goal
In the blanks below, write whatever comes to mind. *Do not skip any questions.* Every step is essential.

My overall goal for social or interactive change is:

_____

_____

My timetable for meeting this goal is:

_____

_____

I have chosen this timetable because:

_____

_____

This is a reasonable timetable because:

_____

_____

Meeting my goal according to this timetable is important because:

_____

_____

In this next part of the exercise, you will examine several areas of your life. Later, in Chapter 6, you will refer back to these areas when you draw your "Pie of Time"—the actual percentages of time and energy devoted to each, and then your ideal allocation. For now, identify your goals concerning each of the following:

Area of Concern	Goal	What I Will Do
Personal		
Career/School		
Family		
Social		
Other		

It is essential that you allow yourself to come up with objectives in each of these categories. If you have trouble coming up with a goal for a particular category, think about the issues we've been exploring and how they affect your life (avoidance, dependence, low self-esteem, denial). One client, Andrea, skipped the family category completely, though I knew there were issues there to be addressed. After breaking it down by issues, however, she was able to state her ultimate goal with regard to her father: "I would like to make decisions about my career without feeling as though my father disapproves." Later on in this chapter, you will begin to break down your strategy step by step. The steps Andrea identified to reach her goal included working to identify her own personal career objectives and standing up to her father by declaring these objectives to him. Eventually, she was able to confront her father and tell him: "My career goals are important to me, Dad, and while I appreciate your input and concern, I need to make these decisions on my own, and I hope that you will support me in what I choose." So think again about these areas of your life and what you would like to achieve with each.

This next exercise moves you closer to creating the map for step-by-step change that will help you to reach your goals. Here you will identify things that may get in the way of reaching your goal, such as past situations that have set patterns, and you will also single out solutions that may include enlisting the support of someone you know. Think of this exercise as research and development—you are researching your own history with regard to the goal (similar situations, difficulties you might encounter), and developing a mode of operations that could include independent action as well as coordination with someone close to you.

My aim is to:

_____

_____

A similar situation in the past is:

_____

_____

Difficulties I might encounter include:

_____

_____

Possible solutions to these difficulties include:

_____

_____

Whom can I count on to help me to come up with an independent solution?

_____

_____

How?

_____

_____

Identifying Avoidance—and Avoiding It

In previous chapters, you have identified the situations that make you anxious or fearful. When setting social goals, it is a good idea to zero in on the problems that *most* interfere with your life. With an eye toward setting a plan of action, list the top three situations or places that you avoid:

1. _____

_____

2. _____

_____

3. _____

_____

What effect does avoiding each of these situations have on your life? Consider:

- *The psychological manipulation you go through to avoid it.* If, for example, you avoid parties, you may tell yourself you're too tired, that you don't like the host's group of friends, that they don't really want you to come, and so on. At work, you might hesitate to accept challenges, fearing the anxiety and pressure to perform well. But you tell yourself it's because you are too busy, or that you're not the best person for the job (even when you are).
- *How your anxiety increases the more you avoid the situation.* Remember the first time you avoided the situation? You probably seized on a semilegitimate excuse. But when it comes to interacting, it's "use it or lose it." The more you avoid things, the less self-confident you will be. If you are in school, you may carry a fairly easy course load rather than challenge yourself with a more adventurous curriculum.
- *How much you lose—gratification, a sense of well-being, satisfaction, or success.*
- *How much avoiding it decreases your self-esteem and increases your feelings of failure.*

Write down some of the ways your anxiety has interfered with your life.

CAREER/SCHOOL: _____

_____

_____

SOCIAL LIFE: _____

_____

_____

Does avoidance make your life easier? How? Given all the things you miss because you avoid them, is the short-term solution really the best one?

Cause and Effect

Think about how you learned to avoid. You weren't born with this problem. *You weren't born anxious.* You may have been set up for it by environmental programming—but you weren't born that way. Below, I've adapted the chart I used in Chapter 1 to explain the development of social anxiety. As an exercise, think back to when you were a child. Now fill in this chart, recalling a specific event and the ways in which it contributed to your anxiety.

AS A CHILD, I MADE A MISTAKE, WHICH WAS:

_____

_____

WHICH CAUSED FEELINGS OF CONFUSION BECAUSE:

_____

_____

WHICH CAUSED FEELINGS OF REJECTION BECAUSE:

_____

_____

FEAR BEGAN TO BUILD IN THIS WAY:

_____

_____

WHICH LED TO AVOIDANCE OF THE THREATENING SITUATION. I AVOIDED THE SITUATION IN THIS WAY:

_____

_____

THIS LOWERED MY SELF-CONFIDENCE BECAUSE:

_____

_____

THIS IN TURN DECREASED THE CHANCES OF SUCCESS BECAUSE:

_____

_____

THIS CREATED MORE POTENTIAL FOR CONFUSION AND REJECTION, CAUSING ME TO FEEL:

_____

_____

ULTIMATELY, THIS INCREASED MY ANXIETY AND LACK OF FULFILLMENT, WHICH MADE ME FEEL:

_____

_____

There were probably situations throughout your childhood and adolescence that made you uncomfortable, situations that you now understand made you feel embarrassed or rejected. When you experienced these situations, you began to realize that if you avoided similar ones in the future, you would not experience the pain of failure.

Countless clients have described to me their memories of teachers calling on them in the classroom, usually in elementary school, and how a humiliating episode resulted in patterns of avoidance. Others recall being embarrassed in front of their peers in free-play situations, or feeling humiliated by a parent in front of others.

When avoidance becomes pervasive, it is known as *phobia*. Phobias develop in different ways. A phobic reaction is one in which a person feels his environment has let him down. An essential component is a perceived loss of control. One of the first clients I ever worked with was Anne, a married woman of twenty-five who had developed a phobia of trains. When she traced the development of her problem, she vividly remembered her first trauma. During a train trip, her hemorrhoid condition began to bleed, the blood seeping through her pants. Mortified, she ran from the train, experiencing a desperate sense of losing control. This was the start of her phobia.

Another person remembers being mortified as a nine-year-old gifted child. After completing a challenging homework assignment, the girl joined her classmates in school. Because she was known to be a gifted student, the other kids teased her about being a "smartypants" and a "know-it-all." When the teacher had corrected all the papers, she made an announcement that was intended as praise. "Katie, you can go outside to play. Everyone else will have to stay in to do this assignment again. Katie was the only one to do it correctly." By itself, the event might not have been traumatic; but taken together with other, similar responses, a pattern developed that included headaches and a tendency to avoid making friends. Outside of the structured classroom situation, in spontaneous free-play situations with her peers, she had trouble interacting, which only increased her anxiety. Katie tended to be a loner, because she became so afraid of being identified as "different." By the time the child had become an adult, she chose to avoid many situations—in school, at work, or socially—that might cause her to feel singled out.

Eventually, both Anne and Katie learned to confront their fears; although they continued to feel anxious, they began to manage that anxiety. You too are learning to approach—slowly but surely—the threatening situations that you tend to avoid. As you identify these situations, and project ahead to a time when you have mastered them, you will use them as part of your map for change.

If you identified with the dependency issues in the last chapter, think about whether you depend on other people in a negative manner to do things that you really could or should do for yourself. Obviously, depending on others can be a healthy part of friendship and intimacy. But unhealthy dependence robs you of self-esteem and allows you to avoid those situations that make you anxious, thereby intensifying your overall problem. In this chapter, we are further examining the negative aspects of dependence, the ways in which it holds you back, keeps you from living the life that you want. The key determinant is whether you would be healthier if you handled these aspects of your life on your own.

List three ways that you depend negatively on other people:

1. _____
   _____

2. _____
   _____

3. _____
   _____

What effect does this dependence have specifically and generally on your life? Consider:

- *The psychological manipulation involved in dependence.* Do you make excuses to justify your dependence? "It's not that much trouble for my colleague to return some of my phone calls for me." "My lab partner really likes to make the oral reports—I'll stick to the written stuff."

• *The way your anxiety increases the more you continue to be inappropriately dependent.* The less familiar you are with certain tasks and situations, the more you fear them, and the more likely you are to avoid them.

• *The loss your dependence causes: loss of gratification, success, lack of intimacy.* Are you held back in your job or career because you are unable to take on responsibility yourself?

• *The way dependence robs you of self-esteem and self-confidence.* Do you secretly feel like a failure because you are unable or unwilling to attend to the responsibilities in your life?

Write down your feelings about the effects of negative dependence:

_____

_____

_____

_____

_____

_____

While you weren't "born shy," you were born dependent. As an infant, you relied on your parents for all your personal care. But as you grew older, the natural progression was toward independence, toward the separateness of adulthood. If you are experiencing problems with dependence now, it is in part because the people you depend on are *enabling* you to depend on them. You ask for their help, consciously or unconsciously, and they give it to you. They may tell themselves it's easier to do something for you than to risk your negative, even agitated, response at being denied. They play into your own *denial* of the problem by rationalizing their objections. Just as you maintain that it's not that big a deal for your lab partner to handle the oral report, your lab partner, knowing you get anxious when you have to address large groups, may tell herself the same thing.

Think about how you might have learned dependence. Did your parents exhibit a willingness to rescue you from new or stressful situations? Do you remember your response? If your parents taught you to avoid stress and anxiety because they would "take care of it," you began to believe it was easier to rely on them than to risk failure on your own.

At twenty-two, Jim was an A student at college. Despite a learning disability, he has succeeded in school and entered graduate studies in library science. A few years earlier, at the time he had started my program, he had no social life. Except for his academics, Jim depended totally on his parents. He did not drive. He did not take the bus or train alone. He had extreme difficulty making phone calls. He did not even know how to do his own laundry. As we delved through layers and layers of dependence, it became clear that Jim felt an extraordinary degree of social anxiety. Having relied on his parents to such a great extent, he had no social self-confidence and had learned to avoid most social situations.

Let's now consider the physical sensations that make you feel uncomfortable, the *negative stress responses*. These are actual feelings that have allowed anxiety to control you. In Chapter 1, you identified the specific symptoms that anxiety causes you to experience. Now that you understand avoidance, it should be clear to you that *the more you avoid, the less you experience your symptoms of anxiety*. If your goal is to stop experiencing symptoms, then you are succeeding. If your goal is to be able to interact successfully on both the social and career fronts, you have a long way to go. Goal-setting can help. How? By providing a map for change.

All too often, an individual who comes to me for help with anxiety is preoccupied with the symptoms themselves. Do you think about your sweaty palms, wonder whether everyone can see that you're blushing? You exaggerate the symptoms in your mind, just as your body is exaggerating the emotional response to stress. You have learned to *somatize* your response to stress—in other words, your emotions are repressed and are now manifesting themselves in your body.

How does somatization occur? A thirty-three-year-old woman sought my help for her panic attacks, which consisted of common symptoms such as rapid heartbeat, sweating, nausea, fear of passing out (the thought was a lot stronger than the likelihood that the event would occur), and an overall fear of losing control. In counseling, she became aware that her communication with her husband was not good. She was not assertive or even expressive. Instead, she kept most of her feelings in. These unexpressed feelings led to a backup of energy internally. The result? Her body would say what her voice could not. As she learned a healthy way to express herself, the symptoms diminished.

Anxiety is a natural part of life, and anxiety symptoms apply to everybody. Reflecting back on your physical symptoms and thought patterns can give you a valuable history to draw from. To gain further insight into your own anxiety symptoms, use imagery to recall the following:

1. When was the first time you experienced the symptoms that now control you?

   _____

   _____

2. Where were you, and with whom?

   _____

   _____

3. What happened after you experienced the symptoms?

   _____

   _____

4. What was going on in your life at this time? Were you experiencing change (in home life, work, or school)? What major issues were you addressing?

   _____

   _____

If there was no organic or physical cause for these symptoms, they were the result of stress. To control your symptoms, you must learn to manage stress. In the next chapter, we will explore stress management in depth. For the time being, understand that a very important component of your map is to be able to control the symptoms so that you do not live in fear of them. Once you gain control, you will find it much easier to confront the situations you fear.

THE TEMPER TANTRUM

One way I explain the exaggerated physical response to stress is to call it a *temper tantrum*. We've all seen children become enraged and throw screaming, sobbing fits at inappropriate times, usually much to the embarrassment of their helpless mothers and fathers. But anxiety reactions in adults can include temper tantrums, too. You may recognize this in a boss who rages when something goes wrong, or in contrast, the boss who gives employees the silent treatment for days after a project goes awry. Both reactions are temper tantrums, or what is sometimes called acting-out behavior: The child inside is upset. What is the "child" inside of you? It is a part of your personality, a specific ego state. The child within is where your emotions are located. Part of diffusing the tantrum is nurturing that child, addressing its fears and concerns, and becoming allied against the offending stress—not by running from it, but by confronting it.

How can you nurture yourself? The same way you would nurture someone else. Growth and self-actualization involve confronting fear and anxiety, and nurturing yourself—supporting yourself as you address your stressors—is the only way to get there. Here are some guidelines for nurturing:

1. *Acknowledge the fear objectively*—without judging whether it is rational or not.
   Say to yourself: "I know I'm afraid to:
   . . . ask for a raise."
   . . . meet this authority figure."
   . . . give this speech."
   . . . go on a date."

2. *Look realistically at the problem.* Is this something you *could* do if you had the courage?
3. *Take responsibility for the problem.* No matter where it all started, it's yours now, and it's up to you to perpetuate it or discard it through anxiety control.
4. *Understand the emotional conflict* that gives rise to the exaggerated feelings and the resulting physical symptoms.
5. *Learn how to control these feelings and symptoms* by confronting the problem.
6. *Learn relaxation* or internal self-regulation.
7. *Learn to use healthy communication* and self-expression.
8. *Apply* these attitudes and skills.

As part of goal-setting, list the three symptoms that you would most like to gain control of. If you like, refer back to Chapter 1 to help refresh your memory.

1. _____

_____

2. _____

_____

3. _____

_____

Gaining insight or awareness is an important part of the getting-well process. Chapter 7 offers several exercises in self-awareness, designed to put you in touch with your strong points and help to clarify your goals further. People vary in their ability to become aware, and, once they have gained insight, in their ability to use this information effectively. And—this warning comes from my years of practice as a psychotherapist—*beware the "I-Don't-Know" disease!*

When people seek help, part of the goal is to change the negative balance that exists in their lives. Much of this unhealthy balance has arisen because of a lack of awareness, and a tendency not to take responsibility for various aspects of their lives. Self-awareness can be a difficult thing to attain, and the learned reflex—the answer to any even vaguely threatening question—is "I don't know." But "I don't know" is not a brick wall. It is a door to be opened. Find out what's behind it. If you're having trouble, keep knocking until you get an answer.

The sociability profile has provided you with a more concrete understanding of your social strengths and deficits. Using this profile, along with the symptom profile and the avoidance and dependence profiles, get ready to clarify your objectives.

As you set your goals, remember to break them down into short term, intermediate, and long term. Don't start out with "Goal: to become completely comfortable in every social situation." That is not possible—yet. Breaking it down into a step-by-step process is crucial to your success. Often, the failure to achieve stems from having unrealistic expectations. Don't do that to yourself! Don't let impatience get in your way. Start small and work steadily. Think of your own social success program as a staircase. Start at the bottom and, using this book as your handrail, work your way to the top, one step at a time. Keep your eyes on the top of the stairs, but don't try to get ahead of yourself. That goal is not going anywhere, so take your time.

Alan, whose public speaking anxiety I mentioned earlier, was good at identifying his objectives, and that is what helped him to achieve a rewarding social life. How did he set his goals? He had two basic objectives: the short-term goal of controlling his fear enough to take the required public speaking class, and the long-term goal of moving out of his parents' house, an important step in becoming an independent adult. With the help of his therapist, Alan created a sequence of steps. It went like this:

Short-Term Goal: To feel comfortable with public speaking.

Step 1: Talk about your fears.
Step 2: Learn to relax.

Step 3: Rehearse.
Step 4: Stop manipulating to avoid the situation.
Step 5: Do it. Put yourself in the situation.
Step 6: Keep doing it!

The sequence for the longer-term goal of moving out of the house was as follows:

Long-Term Goal: To live independently.

Step 1: Talk about your fears and conflicts.
Step 2: Develop strong motivations. Believe it's the right thing to do.
Step 3: Establish a budget and work to save enough money for a deposit.
Step 4: Stop procrastinating; look for a place.
Step 5: Do it!
Step 6: Keep doing it!

Now it's your turn. Use the following guidelines to chart your goals and create a map for change:

My *Long-Term Goal(s)* (again, consider Career/School, Family, Friends, Relationships, and Other):

_____

_____

_____

_____

_____

_____

_____

_____

In order to achieve them, I must accomplish the following *Short-Term Goal(s)* (again, consider Career/School, Family, Friends, Relationships, and Other). But this time, cite specifics: Find an apartment; change jobs; have at least one social engagement per weekend; meet new people, and so on:

_____

_____

_____

_____

_____

_____

_____

_____

_____

_____

_____

For each goal, write down steps, as Alan did, and establish a planning date. Then note the following:

What will I do?

_____

_____

_____

_____

When? Where?

_____

_____

_____

_____

What do I have to learn?

_____

_____

_____

_____

What difficulties may I encounter?

_____

_____

_____

_____

How will I handle them?

_____

_____

_____

_____

Follow-up
Later, use these questions to guide you through the assessment stage
of your progress:

What things went well?

_____

_____

_____

_____

What things need further work?

_____

_____

_____

Am I ready to work toward the next goal?

_____

_____

_____

_____

If you feel you would like to set goals specifically related to your dependency issues, use the following as a guideline to work toward changing your relationships with those on whom you depend:

In My Relationship With	Goal	What I Will Do Differently
Mother		
Father		
Sibling		
Sibling		
Sibling		
Others		

As you plan for change, work out a step-by-step map that tells you what you need to do. Without such a map, you may veer off the track in your quest for independence. George, a client of mine, was unable to stick to his goals because he lacked such a plan of action.

An attractive young man, he was all set to become independent at age twenty-seven and was fortunate enough to have his family's support in this goal. His aunt gave him a house she had purchased on foreclosure, with the understanding that he was responsible for all expenses related to it. These expenses totaled about $12,000, not an unreasonable sum for a working person with George's qualifications. Unfortunately, George was unwilling to take the extra step toward finding permanent employment. He usually dressed in sloppy jeans and T-shirts and refused to cut his long ponytail, despite the negative responses he had received on the few job interviews he was willing to go on. Although he sometimes worked as a carpenter, he was essentially unemployed. George refuses to recognize his lack of motivation, and tends to blame his family for all his problems. With only a small savings account, and no job prospects, George would be in dire financial straits if not for his well-meaning (but enabling) family. Eager to escape the trap George's dependence has locked them in, his family members have tried to confront him about the practical issue of how he plans to support himself and meet his end of the bargain with the house. But when they do try to discuss his map for change, George blows up, accusing them of lacking confidence in him. The truth is, George is having trouble staying on track. Having no map for change can mean a lot of trouble.

Moving Forward

Throughout this first section, you have completed a number of profiles to help you determine your degree of sociability, the extent of your social fears, the ways in which avoidance and dependence have affected you, and to establish your goals. Your step-by-step outline of what you must do both in the short and long term to achieve your interactive goals is your *map for change*. Refer to it, as I will, throughout the rest of the book. If necessary, update your goals as you learn more of the skills it will take to meet them. But save your original maps; they will be valuable tools for reviewing your progress and giving yourself credit for your true commitment to changing the way you interact. Remember, this book is constructed as a step-by-step process. You must complete each step before moving forward. If you haven't given this chapter all you should have, please complete the exercises again.

The next chapter is designed to provide you with the stress management techniques that will allow you to make your goals become reality. Again, it will be helpful for you to refer back to previous chapters from time to time to reflect on your specific symptoms. As you do so, you can explore the ways in which your newfound skills can help control or alleviate your anxiety responses. And, as always, keep that positive mental attitude. You *can* have a healthy, fulfilling, productive life!

CHAPTER SIX

Managing Stress and Controlling Anxiety

By conservative estimates, at least 70 percent of all visits to physicians are stress-related. What exactly is stress? It is not something abstract. It is not something up in the sky. According to the late psychologist Hans Selye, who was perhaps the world's leading authority on the subject, stress is best thought of as "adaptation"— immediate or long term. Think of stress as the result of emotional, psychological, physiological, situational, and environmental stressors. When these stressors appear, they require you to adapt—physically and emotionally. Most indexes designed to assess your likelihood of serious physical illness list major life changes such as marriage or divorce, new residences or jobs, birth or death of a child or other relative, and fluctuations in financial status as the most profound stressors. The more major changes, good or bad, the more likely you are to suffer a stress-related physical illness such as hypertension, diabetes, asthma, ulcers, or even cancer. It follows, then, that the more adaptable you are, the better equipped you will be when stressors do arise.

Adaptation takes on special meaning for the individual who is struggling with social anxiety. For a person who has any degree of social anxiety, interaction represents change or newness. Avoidance and dependence may have limited the socially anxious person's interactive experiences. Poor self-esteem may cause him to doubt his instincts, second-guess his words and perceptions, and finally, in many cases, to allow his body to begin the fight-or-flight response that typifies anxiety. This sequence—where initial experiences lead to increased anxiety and then low self-esteem and even avoidance—develops in different degrees depending on an individual's background and experience. Again, for the socially anxious person, the key is adaptation. A new or unfamiliar situation usually takes longer to adapt to, and mind and body may overreact. Where stress is adaptation, anxiety is overadaptation—an overreaction of mind and body. The result? Symptoms can include irregular breathing, rapid heartbeat, cold, clammy hands, tense muscles, and recurring negative thought patterns. Without frequent, successful interactive contacts, these symptoms perpetuate themselves, and any situation can become a new and threatening entity to which the mind-body has to adapt.

Stress is adaptation. Picture yourself on a busy street. As you step off the curb to cross, a car appears as though out of nowhere, narrowly missing you. You didn't see it coming, and you're startled. There is no time to think, only to react: Your pulse quickens, your muscles tense up, you start to perspire—your body is focused on adapting to that moment. The anxiety response to interaction is no different, though there are varying degrees of severity. For example, a person who has muscle tension as a result of anxiety may develop a tension headache. Another person whose anxiety manifests itself in recurrent thought patterns related to unresolved emotional issues can develop insomnia. Symptoms vary from person to person, but the cause is the same: anxiety.

To explain the way in which your personality adapts to change, I am going to draw on some concepts from a form of psychotherapy known as "transactional analysis": the Parent, Adult, and Child within you. The Parent is the part of you that is both critical and nurturing. The Parent develops and teaches values, and plays a major role in both finding fault and promoting growth. The Adult is objective—think of it as an energy source that processes information like a computer; you use the Adult for logic and precision. The Child is full of feeling and emotion. Like the Parent, it has two roles: the free child, fun-loving and spontaneous, and the adapted child, conforming, compromising, and manipulative.

Understanding these three components of our personalities helps us, in calmer moments, to review anxiety-filled situations objectively (using our Adult component) for the purposes of problem solving and stress control. It is the objective Adult who will recognize the motivations of the Parent and the Child within you. No doubt you have already used the Adult to answer some of the indexes in previous chapters. In the stress management arena, the Adult is responsible for the following:

1. Identifying the stressor or problem
2. Identifying the cause
3. Identifying choices
4. Setting priorities
5. Making decisions
6. Following through

The Adult is the keeper of your problem-solving method, and an essential part of a healthy personality. Why? *The more control you have, the less stress and anxiety you have.* Wouldn't it be nice if our Adult were always in control? How easy problem-solving looks on paper! But at the very least, we can train our Adult to step in and follow these steps when anxiety starts to build. Think of your Adult as a trusted friend whom you can count on to see through the emotions or logistics of the problem to the bare facts beneath. Let your Adult be the foundation of future change.

Caroline used her Adult problem-solving method to resolve a conflict she was having at the office. As executive secretary to her company's vice president, Caroline had a lot of responsibility and generally liked her job. But when Mitch, a mid-level executive, was transferred from another branch, things got complicated and Caroline's anxiety rose. While Mitch's job description included preparing his own reports and proposals on computer, he routinely requested that Caroline handle them, even though she was assigned exclusively to the vice president. Soon, Caroline found herself falling slightly behind in her own duties. Worse than that, she left work every day feeling angry and resentful and powerless. What complicated matters was that Mitch seemed to have a close friendship with the vice president; Caroline even wondered whether they were dating. How could she approach her supervisor about this problem when she might well side with Mitch? This only added to Caroline's feelings of helplessness.

Here's how Caroline solved the problem, using the Adult problem-solving method outlined here:

1. Identify stressor:		Mitch gets me to do his work for him.
2. Identify cause:		I can't seem to say no.
3. Identify choices:	a.	Keep doing the work.
	b.	Tell the vice president it's a problem.
	c.	Go over vice president's head to discuss with president.
	d.	Get feedback from other colleagues.
	e.	Flatly refuse to do the work.
	f.	Do it, but make it clear that it's extra.
	g.	Tell Mitch I'd be glad to, but I have to check with my boss.
	h.	Tell Mitch I'll do it as soon as I'm finished with my other work.
4. Set priorities:	a.	Keep my job!
	b.	Get my own work done first; do it as well as I can.
	c.	Maintain good relationship with the vice president.
5. Make decisions:		After weighing the choices, I decide to keep it between Mitch and me and I will tell him I'm glad to help out once my own work is done. Going to my supervisor could have backfired (she could say she wants me to help him!). And refusing to help could get back to her through Mitch. If I'm lucky, Mitch will probably get the point and do it himself,

rather than having to wait for me to be ready for him.

6. Follow through: The last time Mitch asked for help, I did just as I planned, and he went ahead and did the work himself. No hard feelings. Actually, he was pretty nice about it, so if I ever do have time, I really won't mind pitching in—though I think I will let my boss know what a good team player I am.

Caroline succeeded in allowing her Adult to step in and nurture her Child to provide a solution that proved workable and productive. To do so successfully, you have to perceive the emotions and the reality clearly, as Caroline did, before you decide on a solution.

As you can see, recognizing the stressor and determining choices does not mean removing stress from your life by running away. In fact, it is impossible to remove stress from your life. You can, however, control stress by mastering techniques for relaxation and incorporating stress management strategies into your life. By gaining control of the anxiety symptoms, a socially anxious person will be able to step forward and adapt to "new" interactive situations in much more comfort than before. And then, with practice, the situations will seem less threatening, and less difficult.

Relaxation and internal self-regulation have many payoffs for those who learn to incorporate them into their lives:

- Lessening of stress-related symptoms
- Increased feeling of well-being and self-esteem
- More mental and physical energy
- Increased feeling of self-control
- Increased productivity and even creativity

And remember, anxiety is incompatible with relaxation.

Anxiety can produce some extremely debilitating symptoms. Renata was a thirty-three-year-old homemaker or "domestic engineer," as she called it, when she came to me with all the classic signs of anxiety and panic disorder: heart palpitations, dizziness, increased muscle tension, fear of passing out, fear of losing control. Sometimes, she did lose control, and, at her worst moment, refused to leave the house for three weeks, cutting off all social contact and becoming totally dependent on her husband. Her physical symptoms were so severe that she made appointments with ten different specialists who put her through almost every test imaginable. She was convinced that her problem was physical and was terrified of what the tests would show. But every test came back negative.

Far from feeling relieved, Renata became panicked, and even suicidal. Eventually she was referred to a psychiatrist, but when that doctor suggested medication, she balked: Was he suggesting it was all in her head? In search of an alternative, she came to me.

In our first few sessions, we focused on two things: the reality that Renata's tests had come back negative, demonstrating no physical cause for the condition, and the possibility that her stress was the cause of her symptoms. As therapy progressed, Renata developed an understanding of stress, and she began to take responsibility for getting well. Soon, she abandoned her search for a physical cause of her problems, and gave herself over to the two vital therapeutic components that saved her. First, she was able to address her own emotional conflicts and social fears. And second, she was able to learn stress management through relaxation training. The quieting response she learned enabled her to self-regulate her nervous system internally so that it no longer overresponded to stress. Soon, the self-awareness exercises translated into better self-expression, which vastly improved her communication skills and problem-solving abilities.

Relaxation works. This chapter will show you how to make it work for you. There are three components of relaxation-based stress management:

Learning the Difference Between a Stress Response and Relaxation

To get in touch with yourself when under stress and when relaxed, finish the following sentences:

When I feel stress, I feel or experience _____

When I feel relaxed, I feel or experience _____

Do not use the words "stress" or "relaxed" in formulating your answers. Rather, identify the specific mind-body responses that you recognize as your symptoms of stress and your signs of relaxation. For example, if you know your hands become cold and clammy when you are under stress, include those symptoms as part of your definition. If you also know that your hands become warm and dry when you are relaxed, then include that information in your description. Even breathing, moderate pulse rate, loose, limp muscles—all of these signs of relaxation create a concrete mental picture for you to try to achieve. You have worked through other chapters to identify symptoms of distress, and in this chapter you must identify symptoms of relaxation. Relaxation must not be an abstract concept to you. You have to have a mental picture and a verbal definition of both your stress and relaxation.

Look again at your responses above. Discipline yourself to identify your most basic internal sensations, both in an anxiety state and when you are relaxed. You may not know quite what to call what you are feeling. But if a word or phrase conveys to you what you mean, then use it. For example, one of my clients was at a loss to describe the rapid pulse in her forearms until I asked not "What is the symptom?" but "What does it feel like?" "It feels like I have electric current running through my arms," she said, giving both of us a vivid picture of what she meant.

Take a minute to describe in more detail your feelings or symptoms of relaxation and anxiety. Then, use these descriptions as the tags for sensations you do and do not want to experience.

Relaxation

_____

_____

_____

Anxiety

_____

_____

_____

Learning Relaxation Skills

Renata learned to cure herself of her crippling anxiety by incorporating relaxation techniques into her daily life. They became her natural medicine. Relaxation and internal self-regulation were the key to regaining control of her life. Remember, control starts from within. If you can control your responses to stress, you will be in a far better position to confront your fears and move forward toward self-actualization.

Applying Relaxation Skills

Relaxation techniques can be applied creatively and flexibly once they are learned. Jennifer, thirty-six, used to experience emotional and physical anxiety symptoms any time she was in a singles-oriented situation, such as a cocktail party or social group. Because she had a strong desire to overcome her fear, she worked hard to conquer the problem, and in time she became very good at applying relaxation techniques. The relaxation response became so automatic that she merely needed to give herself the suggestion, "My hands are warm," and the anxiety response would diminish. Learn these relaxation techniques and practice them daily. Even relatively small physiological changes can result in substantial control of anxiety and symptoms. New advances in technology have made it possible to see and hear your stress response through the use of sophisticated noninvasive instrumentation, a practice that actually helped Jennifer learn to adjust her anxiety level. Even without the use of instruments, there are ways to evaluate and readjust your psychophysiological reaction to stress. This chapter explains them.

Biofeedback-assisted relaxation, internal self-regulation, progressive relaxation, meditation, "the relaxation response" . . . There are many stress management techniques. How do you know which one is best for you? Try as many as you are able to, and work out the combination that suits you. There are many relaxation exercises introduced here that you can teach yourself, techniques I have relied on to help my clients become more productive and control their anxiety. The biofeedback-based relaxation technique that follows on p. 131 will be especially valuable as a process to train both your mind and your body to relax; practice it every day for three weeks, supplementing your program with the other techniques detailed in this chapter. Remember, any effective combination of the following stress management techniques is appropriate—so long as you feel the techniques enable you to control your anxiety.

How do you achieve relaxation? These guidelines will help put you in the right frame of mind to begin practicing relaxation techniques:

1. *Give yourself permission to relax.* You must nurture yourself. Even if it has been difficult for you to relax in the past, now is a new beginning. It may not be easy at first, but in time, and with practice, relaxation is possible for everyone.

2. *Create the right environment.* This means no distractions: no TV, no telephone, no music, no food. This is a time for you to be at peace with yourself. Wear comfortable clothing and allow yourself to focus only on the present. Allow yourself to let go, to relax emotionally as well as physically. Be careful not to think of letting go as losing control. The opposite— holding on—is what causes heightened anxiety. To really control anxiety, you have to let go of it, become familiar with it, and then find a new way to lessen its intensity. The process of letting go and achieving relaxation can sometimes feel uncomfortable. But it is this uncomfortable feeling that has to be worked through to achieve success.

3. *Learn diaphragmatic breathing.* Diaphragmatic breathing is the basis of all relaxation and internal self-regulation. Often, breathing exercises of this type are in and of themselves a good means of stress management. Start breathing deeply to slow your body and mind down in preparation for relaxation. Con-

scious breathing is an essential part of this exercise. Inhale through nose, draw slowly into stomach (diaphragmatic region) and exhale through your mouth. This process should be done slowly and rhythmically.

4. *Learn muscle relaxation.* This is fairly easy to learn. The first step is to become aware of the difference between tense muscles and relaxed muscles. Then, learn to make your muscles feel limp and heavy.

5. *Cultivate warm, dry hands.* As you relax, your blood vessels dilate and the peripheral blood flow (at the skin's surface) increases, resulting in warm hands. Anxiety is related to the fight-or-flight response. When confronted with stress, the body naturally sends blood away from extremities toward the torso in preparation for escape. While normal body temperature is 98.6 degrees, hand temperature is slightly cooler, and varies considerably depending on the degree of stress or relaxation. Don't confuse the two—extremities are always cooler. Remember the mood rings of the 1970s? True, they were a gimmick, but they relied on stress-related surface temperature changes to create the desired effect. Bio-dots and stress cards available today work the same way, and can be a useful tool in learning to bring yourself down from an anxiety state. Still, you may not need a machine or other equipment to tell you how cold your hands are. If your hands feel cold to you, they are responding to stress. If your hands are warm and dry, you've achieved relaxation.

A PERSPECTIVE ON MEDICATION

Most of my therapy is based on the concept of individuals taking responsibility for themselves and the quality of their interactions. My goal is for people to be as qualitatively independent as possible. In my practice, we try to do our work without medication to the fullest extent possible. If clients come in who are already on medication, it is often an eventual goal to get them off drugs when appropriate, especially if they are relying too heavily on medication to mask their uncontrolled anxiety. Of course, there are situations and conditions that warrant medication. But I believe medication is appropriate for anxiety sufferers only when it gives the short-term relief necessary to focus on appropriate emotional and psychological issues. In recent times I have seen a definite pattern in which adults and teenagers are relying on alcohol to relieve anxiety. *Remember, alcohol is the most commonly used drug in our society.* I would like to caution anxiety sufferers that dulling the physiological sensations with prescription or other drugs or even alcohol enables avoidance by taking the edge off. Action—confronting that which you fear—is what will ultimately relieve anxiety. Controlling your symptoms naturally is the most productive way to nurture yourself toward action.

METHODS OF RELAXATION

Any of the following methods could be the answer to controlling your stress response. Everyone is able to learn relaxation scientifically. It is not always easy, and it does take discipline, but the results will change your life! People learn at different speeds. It is possible to affect your own hand temperature after the first few practice sessions, or it could take thirty sessions. For example, often your hand temperature will first decrease before relaxation sets in and then increase. Everyone is different. The important thing is to remain committed to learning. Where relaxation is concerned, the control lies in letting go. Consider all the self-help methods described below and follow the specific instructions for each. After each exercise, be sure to evaluate how you feel and determine which symptoms of both anxiety and relaxation are present.

Biofeedback
Biofeedback is a scientifically based stress management technique that allows you to gather information about your stress and then use that information to develop control over how you react to stress. You can learn some biofeedback techniques on your own, by concentrating fully on your response to stress; several biofeedback tech-

niques are described in this chapter. As we discussed in Chapter 1, an anxiety attack is a psychophysiological, or mind-body, response that is one example of distress. You can actually view your stress response on a biofeedback machine, and see the cause and effect. The learning process involved in controlling anxiety with biofeedback is the same as in learning any other physical skill—namely, trial and error. For example, a person learning to throw darts makes an initial throw, sees the result, then tries to adjust for inaccuracy, to correct his or her aim on the next throw. "Information" about the accuracy of the first attempt at controlling nervous tension "feeds back" into the learner's autonomic nervous system, and he or she can practice relaxing. Without this feedback—without knowing where the darts landed last time—you could not learn to hit bull's-eyes.

How does machine-assisted biofeedback work? Sophisticated instruments measure muscle tension, skin resistance, skin temperature, and brain waves and provide scientific data about your stress responses.

EMG (*electromyograph*): Measures muscle tension and relaxation in terms of microvolts at various locations on the body.

GSR (*galvanic skin response*): Monitors emotions as information is provided about your arousal system and "mental" energy. Measures skin resistance or perspiration.

Temp (*thermograph*): Measures temperature on the surface of the skin, which is the result of your peripheral blood flow. Changes in the dilation or constriction of blood vessels lead to changes in blood flow.

EEG (*electroencephalograph*): Measures brain waves (beta, theta, alpha, and delta).

Under the guidance of a trained biofeedback professional, Renata learned to relax by checking the biofeedback results in front of her to determine her level of relaxation. As she practiced, alternately thinking calm, then thinking about an anxiety-producing situation, the machines took her readings. One sensitive receptor, held on her finger by a cloth ring with a Velcro closure, fed the skin temperature reading into a digital display facing her. A second finger strap conveyed the degree of skin resistance—moisture or clamminess—to a display on a second machine. The third machine informed her by means of a sound-equipped dial, whose clicking sounds conveyed the degree of muscle tension in the face, fed from three receptors on the forehead that were held in place by a loose headband. In time, supplemented by relaxation tapes for home use, Renata learned to relax. A biofeedback program is an excellent way to learn internal self-regulation and stress management. As Renata's internal self-regulation skills increased, she used biofeedback as a maintenance program, checking back periodically to track her success. (If you wish to make machine-assisted biofeedback a component of your self-help program, and need information on how to locate a qualified professional, write to the Association of Applied Psychophysiology and Biofeedback, 10200 West 44 Ave., Wheat Ridge, Colo., 80033.)

Is biofeedback only possible in a clinical setting? No. In fact, you probably already use a kind of biofeedback throughout your day. Every time you gather information that changes the way you proceed, you are letting your observations "feed back" into your brain to inform your course of action. Even something as simple as stepping on a scale, determining you are overweight, and adjusting your diet is a type of biofeedback process.

While machine-based biofeedback training is effective, there are other ways to learn biofeedback-based relaxation. Think about how simple biofeedback is. You now know that warm, dry hands are a symptom of relaxation. You can check your body against that ideal, and then give yourself the suggestion, "My hands are dry and warm," to elicit that physical response. Look at your face in the mirror. Tense and relax the muscles. Furrow your brow. Then release. This give you the information you need to alter your state of mind.

In using the biofeedback-based response that follows, you are familiarizing yourself with your own mind-body responses. After you have learned to distinguish relaxation from tension, you will be able to get in touch with your relaxed self by referring back to this exercise.

A Relaxation Exercise

This biofeedback-based relaxation exercise is designed to help you learn, step by step, how to relax. *Practice this exercise for 21 days in a row.* Set time aside for it when you are alert, not tired. The goal is relaxation, not sleep, so do not begin this exercise after a heavy meal or right before bedtime. Remember, you are trying to learn a new skill, and the learning process deserves your full attention and energy. If you do fall asleep, it may be a signal that you are burnt out (emotionally and physically exhausted) or depressed.

Before you begin, make a list of the physical sensations you are aware of. Use whatever words come to mind. Use this list as a basis of comparison for what you are experiencing now to what you feel when the exercise is over.

Before:

_____

_____

_____

Wearing loose clothing, assume a comfortable position in a chair. Hold your head, neck, and back in a straight line. Try not to slouch or arch your back. Your feet should be resting flat on the floor, and your hands should rest on your thighs; there should be no tension, so do not let them hang at your sides. If you wish to use armrests, you may do so, as long as your shoulders are not hunched as a result. You should not feel any pull or strain on your shoulder muscles. The goal is comfort and ease. The more comfortable your body is, the less it will distract you.

Give yourself permission to be passive. Concentrate only on this exercise, and on how your body is feeling. Activate your positive mental attitude (if you like, you can imagine a switch in your mind that turns your positive mental attitude on full throttle).

If you find yourself losing concentration or experiencing any intruding thoughts, let them flow through you until they pass. Allow yourself to breathe them in, then out.

Now focus on your breathing. Take your time, breathing slowly in and out. Inhale through your nose, slowly drawing the oxygen down into your abdomen. Hold it for a few seconds. Now slowly exhale . . . 5 . . . 4 . . . 3 . . . 2 . . . 1 for a total of up to ten seconds (with one to two seconds between counts). Again inhale, hold it, and exhale . . . 5 . . . 4 . . . 3 . . . 2 . . . 1. Remember, don't push or force the air in and out of your body. Continue to breathe slowly and deliberately, until the pace feels natural. Concentrate on the process. Inhale the oxygen, exhale the carbon dioxide. Inhale the energy, exhale the excess tension. Feel yourself settle further into your chair, and continue breathing in a normal and relaxed way.

Next, focus on your muscles. Start with your right hand: Make a fist. Hold it . . . feel the tension. Memorize it. Then slowly let the fingers open up, releasing tension. Feel the tension disappear as relaxation overtakes it. Repeat the exercise until you have memorized the difference between a tense muscle and a relaxed one.

Make mental contact with your right arm. "Feel" it with your mind. Feel the muscles in your shoulder, then focus on your biceps, elbow, forceps, wrist, moving into your hand and the very tips of your fingers. Imagine the muscles releasing their tension, becoming soft and loose. Think the words "soft and loose" to yourself. Then, begin to experience your right arm as "heavy and limp." Say three times to yourself, "My right arm is heavy and limp."

Once again, if you experience any distracting thoughts, let them go. Focus on your breathing.

Switch sides now, making a fist with your left hand. Hold it, feel the tension, and then release. Replace the tension with relaxation as your fingers open up.

Next, make mental contact with your left arm. Again, "feel" it with your mind: shoulder, biceps, elbow, forceps, wrist, hand, fingertips. Feel the muscles relaxing. Feel them becoming soft and loose.

As you feel yourself settle further into your chair, resume concentrating on your breathing: Slowly inhale through your nose, drawing the oxygen into your abdomen. Hold it for a moment, then slowly exhale, counting backward from 5 to 1 as before, with one to two seconds between each number.

Renew your mental contact with your right arm. This time, say to yourself, "My right arm is warm . . . I feel the warmth flowing through my right arm." Spend about thirty seconds repeating these phrases. Then expand your focus to include the sensations of heaviness and limpness. Your body should feel totally passive, with all your thoughts focused on that one arm.

If you like, use imagery to picture yourself lying on your back at the beach in the warm sun. You feel the sun's rays warming the palms and fingers of your right hand. You are completely still and have no wish to move. As you experiment with imagery, you may find that your mind starts to drift to other thoughts. To regain focus, simply concentrate on your breathing and in a relaxed, nonpressured way, return your attention to the task at hand.

After a minute or so, move your awareness to your left arm. What does it feel like? Say to yourself, "My left arm is warm . . . I feel the warmth flowing through my left arm." Again, repeat these phrases for about thirty seconds. Then, for another thirty seconds, say, "I feel the blood flowing through my left arm." Note any sensations you feel in your left arm. Is there a tingling sensation? During the relaxation process, tingling is a good sign.

At this point, go back to that sunny beach in your mind. Imagine yourself placing your hand in warm, still water, or basking on the sun-baked sand.

Let go of all intruding thoughts. Focus on your breathing: slowly, naturally, passively.

Now, move your awareness to your face. Allow the muscles of your forehead to soften. Picture your forehead smoothing out as your furrowed brow and other wrinkles dissipate. Feel the tension melt away. Let your jaw slacken and drop slightly. Let go of the tension in your jaw. Move up to your temples, then to your eyes, releasing the tension as you go. Find a comfortable position for your eyes and let them rest. Feel them become still and calm.

Focus on the tension in your stomach. Hold the muscles of your stomach in, and then let them go. Let everything sink, and feel your weight being pulled into your chair. Allow all the muscles of your torso to let go completely.

Let your whole body go further and further, as you seem to sink deeper and deeper in your chair.

As you continue to breathe deliberately and deeply, bring your focus back to the abdominal area. Fill the area with air, and then count backward from 5 as you slowly exhale. Feel the tension flow from the body every time you exhale: Energy in, tension out. Energy in, tension out.

Continue this process, focusing on your abdomen moving in and out with each deep breath, for several minutes. Let go a little more with each exhalation.

Allow your body to take on the breathing process, and breathe naturally. Close your eyes now, and for a few minutes concentrate on your body's natural rhythm. Your eyes will open only when you want them to once you are ready to end the relaxation.

Now that you are finished, write down some words to describe your relaxed state. Just jot down whatever comes to mind, staying with the feeling of relaxation as you write:

After:

_____

_____

_____

This exercise is intended to build relaxation into your life as a daily ritual. Again, you must practice for twenty-one days straight in order to maximize the productivity of your relaxation training and to truly incorporate the stress management process into your life. Each time you achieve a state of deep relaxation, make a note of it, commit the feeling to memory so that you can go back to it as a mental goal next time you are trying to "come down" from excess stress. After twenty-one days, you will probably have memorized the process. Continue to practice, but this time close your eyes. Just as tennis players rely on "muscle memory" to execute the same basic moves again and again, so must you develop a "relaxation memory"—a blueprint to refer to every time you want to relax.

By now, it has been several minutes since you finished the exercise. How do you feel: relaxed, or under stress? What sensations do you associate with each? What physical sensations are you experiencing: heaviness, limpness, warmth, tingling, regular breathing? Write these feelings down.

_____

_____

_____

_____

_____

This list of sensations will become your "relaxation memory"—refer to it often to remind yourself that regular breathing, warm, dry hands, and soft, loose muscles are your ideal relaxed state.

OTHER RELAXATION TECHNIQUES

There are many other stress management techniques that can help you to "bring yourself down" quickly when you are highly stressed. You can use them *before* a situation where anticipation raises tensions that do not automatically subside after a few minutes. You also can use them *during* an interaction or when a surprise threatens to escalate your stress out of control. Or use them *after* an encounter has raised your stress level, if it is not subsiding naturally.

Mental Imagery

You experimented with mental imagery in the previous chapter on goal-setting. The use of mental imagery also can be an effective tool for anxiety control. Think of it as a new application of skills you already have: memory and imagination. When I asked you earlier to recall how many windows there are in your bedroom, you used imagery to retrieve the information. Mentally, you went into the room, looked from wall to wall, and counted. That process is mental imagery.

From a relaxation perspective, your nervous system cannot distinguish between reality and imagery. Material passed from the body to the senses, whether real or imagined, is processed the same way. Therefore, imagery can play an important role in inducing internal self-regulation and relaxation. If there is a particular image—such as the warm, sandy beach of the previous exercise, a cool forest clearing covered with a blanket of pine needles, or even a clear blue sky—that represents relaxation to you, it would be valuable for you to be able to tune in to it whenever stress threatens to interfere with your life. Be sure to conjure up the reactions of all five senses: Imagine the look, sound, smell, taste, and feel of your surroundings. Mental getaways are a valuable part of the relaxation exercise we just went through. And it is important to be aware that your nervous system—which is what overreacts in a stressful situation—cannot distinguish between reality and imagination.

Here's how to use mental imagery to create a mental getaway:

(a) Choose a favorite place, a pleasant, relaxing setting that you have enjoyed in the past or one you would enjoy visiting in the future.

(b) Close your eyes and think about the scene. Use your senses of *hearing, smell, sight, taste,* and *touch* to develop the scene. Put yourself there. If your mind wanders a bit, that's okay. You'll drift back to the scene after a short while.

Behavior Rehearsal

So far, we have used imagery to place ourselves in ideal relaxed settings. But mental imagery is also a valuable component in behavior rehearsal—picturing yourself succeeding at a stressful task. For example, a basketball player can imagine shooting the ball into the basket as a way of improving his or her performance. A golfer envisions putting the ball right into the hole as a means of practice. Both are relying on imagery to improve their games.

When should you use imagery? In gearing up for public speaking class, Alan used imagery quite effectively—putting himself in front of a group, giving his speech successfully—just after doing the relaxation exercise we just went through, because the mind and body are more receptive to imagery in a relaxed state. I myself use imagery in preparing to give a speech—I find it useful to picture myself giving the speech, and to imagine the reaction of the audience. Again, practice makes perfect, and mental imagery offers an opportunity for a mental dress rehearsal of the situation you wish to confront.

To add behavior rehearsal into your daily relaxation ritual, try the following:

When you get close to the end of the relaxation exercise, when you know you are relaxed—right when you close your eyes—picture yourself in a group situation that so far has not been a success for you. Choose a scenario in which you would like to have success that does seem possible in the long term, such as a date, a work or school assignment, and so on. Walk into the room. Envision yourself as relaxed as you are now. You are in control. Your muscles are soft and loose, your face is relaxed, maybe even smiling. Your hands are warm and dry. Your breathing is even. If you get nervous as the scenario continues, pause to refocus your breathing and put your muscles at ease, pulling them back into a relaxed state. Experiment with behavior rehearsal as often as you like—this is a new skill, and there is no substitute for practice.

OTHER STRESS MANAGEMENT TECHNIQUES

Once learned, stress management techniques such as mental imagery become valuable aids to those who rely on them. Think of them as tools you keep in your pocket. When you need a tune-up—of confidence, or calm—simply pull them out. They belong to you, and you can use them whenever you like. Here are a few more to add to your repertoire. Combined with the daily relaxation exercise, these relaxation tools will make the difference in the quality of your interactions.

Thought Stopping

Thought stopping is a stress management technique designed to interrupt obsessive thought patterns. If you find yourself continually going over and over a stressful situation in your mind, without arriving at a solution, and without determining any course of action, your thoughts may become obsessive. Think of it as "analysis paralysis": You are analyzing something to the point of being unable to do anything *but* analyze it. Here's what you do to end this circuitous thinking:

(a) Shout the word "STOP!" to yourself.
(b) Visualize a red stop sign.
(c) If the thought continues to recur, place a rubber band around your wrist. When the thought pops into your head, snap the rubber band.

Internal Coaching

Internal coaching will help you to manage stress by accentuating your positive mental attitude. Internal coaching works best with short, clear messages that specifically target the behavior or attitude you would like to adopt. Here are some positive messages that you may find helpful to tell yourself:

- "I am under control."
- "I can get through this. I've done it before. I can do it again."
- "I am okay. I will be okay."

NOTE: *When you give internal coaching suggestions to yourself, be sure to leave out the words "no" and "not."* A sentence or phrase such as "I will not fail" causes feelings of defensiveness and negativity. Take the negatives out so that your brain can process the suggestion in a positive way.

MANAGING THE ANXIETY OR PANIC ATTACK

The most severe and debilitating type of distress that a socially anxious person suffers is the panic attack or anxiety attack. These attacks manifest themselves in two ways: as a wave of free-floating anxiety, or in response to specific situations. Naturally, there are different intensities, just as there are different degrees of social ability, dependence, and avoidance. If you suffer panic attacks of any kind, you are not alone. In fact, an estimated 3 million people experience panic attacks about once a week.

In Chapter 2, we discussed anxiety symptoms in detail. What is the difference between an anxiety reaction and an anxiety attack? Perhaps it can best be explained by degree. The victim of an anxiety attack feels an overall loss of control, of being unable to cope with the situation that caused the symptoms. Thoughts such as "I'm afraid I'm going crazy" or "I'm afraid I'm going to pass out" or "I'm afraid I'm losing control" may occupy the victim's mind. For those who suffer repeated anxiety attacks, fear of the anxiety symptoms, such as dizziness and sweating, may become as prominent as the fear of the event that causes the symptoms.

If you experience a panic attack, follow the steps below to bring it under control. Please note that these steps are not designed to "cure" the panic attack, but they will help you handle it better when it occurs. If you like, jot down these six steps and keep them handy (in your purse or wallet). That way, you'll have a plan of action the next time a panic attack occurs.

1. *Accept the reality.* Acknowledge that a panic attack is upon you. Admitting you are panicked does not mean agreeing to continue having panic attacks forever. All it means is that, for the moment, you have to accept the reality and learn to flow with it. Panic attacks do end, and with stress management, you will learn to control your anxiety.

2. *Roll with the punch.* Just as professional boxers are trained to roll with the punch instead of turning into it, so must you learn to go with the flow of the panic attack. Don't deny your feelings. Roll with them, and do what you can to make yourself as comfortable as possible until your relaxation techniques bring down your extreme stress level.

3. *Try to float with it.* Learn to get in touch with your relaxation response, and use deep breathing and mental imagery to float through the panic experience. Go with the force, not against it, to create a sense of ease. Think of a surfer riding a wave.

4. *Tell someone you trust.* If you are with someone who is close to you, you may feel better if you let that person know you are experiencing an anxiety attack. This can relieve a lot of internal pressure on you (you won't feel the need to cover up).

5. *Use relaxation techniques to bring down your stress level.* But this can only be applied once you have mastered the techniques. After you give yourself permission to roll with the attack, you can apply relaxation techniques to bring it down. An increase of even three degrees in hand temperature is enough to abort an anxiety attack.

6. *Remember FEAR means FALSE EVIDENCE APPEARS REAL.*

BLUSHING AND SWEATING

Many people have come to me because of a severe problem with blushing or sweating. Invariably, they feel they are completely alone with this problem. But blushing and sweating are very common symptoms of anxiety, and while they are not in and of themselves debilitating, the humiliation and avoidance they cause can be quite problematic. A businessman in the job market came to me because he found his severe sweating problem was interfering with his success in the interview process. He made sure to dress in a way that would compensate for the problem, but then spent the whole interview distracted by his increasing perspiration. He feared the interviewer could see sweat marks seeping right through his T-shirt and dress shirt and coloring his wool suit coat. This preoccupation, caused by a legitimate symptom, was in part keeping him from getting work; he simply could not present himself well when he was worried about his anxiety symptom.

A woman in my group program had a similar problem with blushing; in her case, she feared attending social events because she was afraid she would become anxious and start to blush. Like the businessman, her preoccupation with her symptom was causing avoidance. But the symptom was not always as obvious as she thought. Once, in group, she was talking about blushing and admitted that, in fact, she believed she was blushing right then. I told her I didn't see anything. Just then, another person in the group chimed in: "I think I see it. Yes, I definitely see a change in color." Until that moment, the woman was not blushing. But then the psychophysiological response, the adaptation, occurred. Once someone drew attention to her, she actually did begin to blush! Both of these clients were helped by stress management training. They were also comforted to know that thousands of people share their problems. Another client said her dream was to wear a silk blouse—something she believed her anxiety-related sweating made impossible. But anxiety *can* be controlled through the techniques in this chapter.

TOWARD A HEALTHY BALANCE

Achieving the ideal balance of responsibilities and desires is an essential part of a healthy lifestyle. The healthier you are, the more fulfilled and productive you will be. Time is not elastic; it does not stretch. It is finite. Life is finite. Learning how to manage the time you spend awake to get the most out of life is an essential part of managing stress. Just as there are only so many hours in a day, there are only so many years ahead of you. If your life is not what you want it to be, you should take a look at the time that has passed and ask yourself how long you are willing to wait. How long are you going to allow yourself to avoid making the changes that are within your reach?

Use the pie graphs below to work out your current "pie of time" and your ideal "pie of time." Assess how you currently spend your time on your personal interests, career, family, social life, and any other important factors. Then divide the pie into the appropriate portions. You will recall evaluating your goals concerning these areas of your life in Chapter 5.

To help you draw your "pie of time," take a look at Renata's "before" and "after" diagrams, which show where she felt she was when she first came to see me, and what her goals were in seeking change.

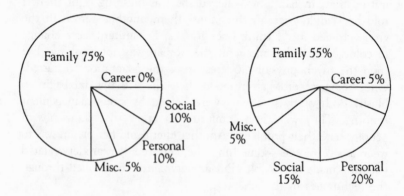

The percentage that Renata wanted to change was not overwhelming—20 percent. But it made a big difference to her.

Now, draw your "ideal" pie.

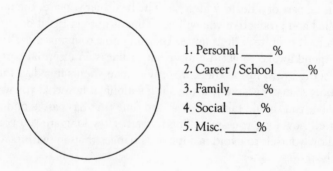

1. Personal _____%
2. Career / School _____%
3. Family _____%
4. Social _____%
5. Misc. _____%

What might you actually do to change the size of the various activity slices to make them more "perfect" for you? To facilitate this change, consider the following issues:

1. Which is the most satisfying or rewarding part of the pie?

    _____

    _____

    _____

    _____

2. Which is the most necessary part of the pie?

    _____

    _____

    _____

    _____

3. Which part causes you the most distress?

    _____

    _____

    _____

    _____

4. Which slices would you like to increase?

    _____

    _____

    _____

    _____

5. Which slices would you like to decrease?

    _____

_____

_____

_____

6. In which slice are you most productive with your time?

_____

_____

_____

_____

7. In which slice are you least productive?

_____

_____

_____

_____

Now that you've drawn your ideal pie, take a moment to outline the three areas to which you need to apply specific stress management techniques.

1. _____

_____

2. _____

_____

3. _____

_____

In which areas would you like to improve your interactive ability?

_____

_____

FOR A LONGER, HAPPIER LIFE

If stress is a major cause of serious physical illness, does it follow that reducing stress could actually prolong life? The World Health Organization says yes. WHO statistics estimate that an individual who is 45 years of age will live another 33.1 years if he or she integrates six to seven of the following healthy habits; if he or she incorporates only three or fewer, he or she will live just 21.6 more years. When you are talking about 11.5 years' difference, this isn't something to quibble about or make light of. Try your best to adopt these seven healthful habits:

Get eight hours of sleep per night
Eat a healthy breakfast
No snacking between meals
Keep your weight within healthy limits
No smoking
Moderate use of alcohol
Moderate, regular exercise (at least twenty minutes three times per week)

And one special note about recreation: Distracting yourself from the stresses of the daily routine is a vital component of stress management. When I meet a client for the first time, one of the questions I usually ask is, "What do you do for fun?" The number of people who have no answer for this is startling.

If you have trouble interacting, you may find it difficult to pursue interests outside of work, school, or television. Take a minute now to ask yourself the same question: "What do I do for fun?" In my own life, exercise and sports play a major role in stress management. You could say that exercise is my therapy. A good game of basketball can take away a lot of excess tension, and it provides a chance to get together with other people in a fairly low-key manner. The competition is good-natured, but the conversation is very light, and I feel free to concentrate on the game, to really let go and lose myself as I play. Of course, working up a good sweat means getting rid of excess adrenaline, which can build up and cause stress and anxiety symptoms.

These days, there are many different ways to enjoy yourself, and the interactive requirements vary considerably, so it wouldn't be too hard to find a group or event that allows you to function at your own sociability level. As you move forward through this self-help program, remind yourself that interactive health contributes to your overall health and longevity. Talking with others—sharing yourself and your experiences—not only makes you more productive at work and fulfilled in your personal life, it actually lowers your risk of disease. So stay committed to this program, and start to envision yourself as part of an interactive network. And keep in mind that having fun—alone or with other people—is one of your goals.

The bottom line with stress management is that all you can control is yourself. You cannot control others around you, which is especially important to understand. People do not always behave predictably or follow the course you would like them to. Situations are not always fair. But used appropriately, stress management can help you to control your reaction to these situations. Once you incorporate stress management into your life, you will find that it not only has the potential to improve the quality of your social interaction but it is also very much related to your overall health, feelings of well-being, and longevity.

CHAPTER SEVEN

Techniques for Self-Awareness

Chapter 6 introduced you to several strategies for managing stress. Your imagination can also be useful in presenting learning opportunities that imitate interactive situations in a safe, controlled environment. Just as children learn to socialize through play, so can adults improve interaction through role play, imagery, and other imaginative practices. Considering hypothetical, or "just suppose," situations will allow you to explore and experience new feelings, dimensions, and ideas—to enhance your self-awareness and better understand who you are, how you feel, and what you want in life. Feelings are important. The more you take responsibility for your feelings and emotions, the better off you are. As I said in Chapter 5: Beware the "I-Don't-Know" disease! When someone asks you—or better yet, you ask yourself—how you feel, you should make every effort to answer honestly and completely. Looking at yourself from different angles increases self-awareness. Think of self-awareness techniques as a means of reinforcing the known as well as finding out about the unknown. The more awareness you have, the more you are able to take control. Like the exercises in the previous chapters, these exercises require your full, active participation. Don't just skim through them. Really consider each one. Let your imagination work with you!

MENTAL IMAGERY EXERCISES

Imagination will help you to envision yourself from different angles and in different situations as well as help you focus your thoughts and articulate them clearly. You've already used mental imagery to picture the windows in your bedroom. Think about another room in your house—say, your kitchen. How many cabinets are there? Mental imagery allows your mind to take you into that room and look around. Experiment with the various mental imagery exercises listed here.

1. *The Mental Wastebasket.* Picture a wastebasket in your bedroom, kitchen, or perhaps at the office. You can throw anything into it that you wish to discard: an object, a person, a place, feeling, or situation.

   What would you like to throw away?
   Why? _____

   _____

   _____

   Toss it in there. How do you feel?

   _____

   What is the result of throwing it away?

   _____

   Do you wish to replace it with something else?

   _____

   What will you do with the space that it vacated?

   _____

   This exercise should give you an understanding of what things in your life may be causing anxiety or depression. By clarifying what remains, you also gain an understanding of what is left in your life once you discard these negative items. What is left is what is most important to you. In reality, you may not be able to "discard" the unpleasant or negative things you've thrown in your mental wastebasket. But you can begin to think about ways your relationship to those items, issues, or people might change for the better to improve your self-esteem and reduce your anxiety.

To get a sense of how this exercise can help, consider the case of Kelly, a twenty-six-year-old client of mine who was struggling to reconcile her relationship with her overprotective mother. Though she was angry, Kelly could not voice her feelings, and instead withdrew whenever a conversation turned into a fight, which was often. When Kelly and I worked on the wastebasket exercise, she made a breakthrough. "I want to throw my mother in the wastebasket," she said. How would this change the relationship? "If I throw her away, then I will free myself from her control," Kelly answered. I told her to picture herself throwing her mother into the wastebasket; she released a lot of energy and anger as she envisioned it.

When she had finished, I asked her how she felt. "Empty . . . but relieved," she answered. This was a strong beginning, and we further explored the full implications of her desperate act. In time, Kelly clarified her real wish: to discard the "sick" relationship with her mother and replace it with a "healthy" one in which both women respected each other as independent adults. In time, Kelly became motivated to spend time with her friends, and eventually, she and her mother developed a healthier relationship.

Try it! The wastebasket exercise can be liberating. Let it empower you toward healthier interactive relationships.

2. *The Environmental Overhaul.* This exercise is similar to the Mental Wastebasket, with one major exception—if you wish, you can actually *make* some of the modifications you desire.

Look around where you live. Choose a room that you would like to improve.

What would make you more relaxed, comfortable, or happy in this room?

_____

_____

Imagine changing the furniture: What would you buy?

_____

What would you throw away?

_____

You can paint the room any color you want: What color will you choose?

_____

Which changes are feasible right now?

_____

Create an action plan to make some of these fantasies real (steps might include reorganization, cleaning, painting, shopping for furniture, getting rid of certain objects, and persuading family members to accept the change):

_____

_____

_____

_____

_____

_____

Changing your immediate environment can be an important step to building confidence and trust within yourself. It can also be very empowering, because it enhances your sense of organization and self-control and lets you know you have choices. You may not be able to change an entire room at once (or your entire self) but little things add up to a big difference.

If there are people close to you, you might enlist their help in executing your plan, if it seems appropriate. But be careful not to let them make your decisions for you—this is your choice, and it is important for you to keep it your own. At any rate, don't be impatient, or you could become overwhelmed. Instead, make one or two meaningful changes at a time.

3. *Developing concentration.* As you learned in Chapter 6, concentration is the key to overcoming interactive anxiety about other people and what they will think of you. If you are able to focus constructively on your physiological responses, you can learn to control them and diminish your anxiety reaction. In social situations, concentration is essential. For example, I sometimes find I have trouble remembering people's names— even people to whom I was introduced just five minutes earlier! When I am able to channel my energy toward the introduction by concentrating on what is being said, though. I remember more accurately and feel more comfortable.

   Where self-awareness is concerned, concentration is everything and involves all five senses: hearing, sight, touch, smell, and taste. The following exercises are designed to heighten your awareness of what is around you. You need not follow the order listed here. Instead, become familiar with the exercises and then practice them when an appropriate situation arises. You may designate a special time for each of them, or you can do them while you are traveling, waiting in lines, or in any other given situation. The most important thing is that you do them consciously and with full awareness of the specific sense that is your focus for that exercise.

NOTE: *Practice your most effective relaxation techniques before you begin these exercises (refer to Chapter 6 if necessary).* People are better able to concentrate when they are relaxed.

Listening

- Pay attention to the sounds coming from outside: from the street, from above in the air, from as far away as possible. Then focus on one sound only.
- Pay attention to the sounds coming from a nearby room—the kitchen, living room, etc. Identify each one, then focus on a single sound.
- Pay attention to the sounds coming from the room you are in: the windows, the electrical appliances. Then focus on one sound only.
- Listen to your breathing.
- Hear a short tune and attempt to re-create it.
- Listen to a sound, such as a ringing doorbell, a knock on the door, a telephone ringing, or a siren. How does it make you feel?

_____

_____

- Listen to a voice on the telephone. Really focus on it.
- Listen to the voices of family members, colleagues, or fellow students, paying close attention to their intonation, pacing, and accent. What mood are they conveying?

Looking

- Look around the room and differentiate colors or patterns, such as straight lines, circles, and squares.
- Look at the architecture of the room. Now close your eyes. Can you describe it? Could you draw it?
- Look at one object in the room: chair, desk, chest of drawers, whatever. Close your eyes and try to picture the shape, the material, and the colors.

- Notice any changes in your environment at home, at school, or in your workplace.
- Look at magazine photos and try to guess what emotions the subjects' expressions show.
- Observe the effect of light around you. How does it change shapes? Expressions? Moods?

Touching

- When shaking a person's hand, notice the temperature of the hand. Then notice the temperature of your own hand.
- Hold an object in your hands, such as a cup of coffee, a brick, a tennis ball, or anything else that is available. Then put it down. Close your eyes and remember the shape, size, and texture of the object.
- Feel different objects and then, with your eyes closed, touch them again. Be aware of how the sensations change.
- Explore different textures and surfaces with your eyes first open and then closed.

Smelling and Tasting

- Be aware of the smells around you; come up with words to describe them.
- Try to remember the taste of a special meal that you enjoyed in the past. Use words to describe the flavors—not just the names of the dishes.
- Search your memory for important smells or tastes.
- Think of places with a strong tie to smell.

These sensory exercises are an excellent way to boost your awareness and increase your ability to concentrate. What is learned in the fullest way—using all five senses—is unlikely to be forgotten. As you learn concentration, you will find that you are able to be more in tune with what is going on around you in a social situation, which in turn allows you to interact more fully.

WORDS AND SELF-IMAGE

Because most interactive situations involve talking to other people, you have to train yourself to understand not only words but their context—what people mean by what they say, and how what is said fits in with the conversation at hand or the event that is taking place. One of my clients, a secretary, recalled having a boss who would often rant and rave when a customer had disappointed him. If a ringing phone stopped him mid-sentence, he would glare at her and yell, "Answer the damn thing!" The young woman would feel terrible because she thought he was mad at her.

Misinterpreting a situation because you don't understand its context could cause great anxiety. But you can learn to pick up on the subtleties and variations of spoken words, which are altered by tone of voice, facial expression, and body language. Experience is certainly the best teacher; but the following exercise offers a chance to explore your own feelings about certain words and phrases.

What adjectives would you use to describe yourself?

_____

_____

_____

_____

_____

_____

Divide them into two categories—positive and negative—to gain insight into your self-image.

POSITIVE   NEGATIVE

_____   _____

_____   _____

_____   _____

_____   _____
_____   _____
_____   _____

Which category has more? _____

Which words would you like to change?

_____

_____

_____

The negative words you used to describe yourself are things you *can* change. While I don't recommend trying to change everything at once, I do suggest that you identify a few small items that you feel you can change for the better without undue stress. Make a list of the aspects you would like to change. Then ask yourself:

Why do I want this change?

_____

_____

_____

Who can my role model be for this change?

_____

_____

_____

Where will I start?

_____

_____

_____

Following Through
Sometimes you may find yourself unable to follow through on a plan of action. Follow-through is a crucial part of interactive success. You may start something but lose the rhythm of the task and somehow not get back to it. This is frustrating and interrupts your concentration. Anxiety sets in, and soon you will start looking for a way out. This exercise will help you explore your feelings about "what happens next."

Look at a magazine. Find a photograph in which some action could follow. What action do you think will come next?

_____

_____

_____

Would you do the same in this situation?

_____

_____

_____

What are some other possible outcomes?

_____

_____

_____

Now watch the first five minutes of a movie or television program. What do you think will be the outcome of the story?

_____

_____

_____

When the story ends, write down why your analysis at the beginning was correct or incorrect, and explore how you got the ideas that you did.

_____

_____

_____

_____

_____

Next, go back to the imagery mode. Imagine these situations to follow through on: asking for a raise, asking for more responsibility at work, asking for a date, and making social plans with a friend. Picture yourself following through in each of these situations. What happens? How do you react? How do people respond to you? Write down what you envision for each situation.

_____

_____

_____

_____

_____

_____

_____

_____

Object Objectives

We are surrounded by objects, many of which seem to shape our lives. Some of them are very familiar, and we utilize them fully.

Some may be hard to use. Some seem to have no practical value but are important in decorative or sentimental ways. As you become more aware of the objects in your life and what they mean to you, you will grow more selective in choosing them.

Which objects represent a positive emotion such as happiness or hope? Why?

_____

_____

_____

Which objects represent a negative emotion such as fear or failure? Why?

_____

_____

_____

Where do you keep them?

_____

_____

_____

Make a list of objects that you don't need.

_____

_____

_____

Make a list of objects that you want to acquire.

_____

_____

_____

How Do You Feel?

Your emotions and feelings are a central part of your capacity to interact successfully. Without an awareness of them, you will be unable to reach your full potential in your career and social life. Recognize that your emotions and feelings are valid. Understand the emotions and feelings of others, even when you disagree with them.

Think about the positive qualities of people you interact with. How do you feel about these people? How do they make you feel about yourself?

_____

_____

_____

_____

_____

_____

Anger

Over the years, I have treated hundreds of people whose anxiety and depression masked anger related to family issues, relationships, and their current situation. The frustration of limited interactive ability is certainly a cause for anger. Indeed, repressed anger is a major cause of distress, which in turn causes numerous debilitating problems, not the least of which are anxiety symptoms and depression.

Anger can be present on the surface, as I've seen with clients who are belligerent, resistant to treatment, or just plain defensive. Or it can lie closer to the core, taking shape as blame. (Some of my clients have been so angry with their parents that they blamed them for their social misfortunes. This allowed them—for a while—to avoid taking responsibility for their own unhappiness.) To get in touch with your anger, consider the following questions:

Are you aware of anger in your life?

_____

_____

_____

On a scale of 1 to 10, what is your average level of anger? _____
On a scale of 1 to 10, how angry do you get at your peak? _____
What are you most angry about?

_____

_____

_____

Toward whom do you feel the most anger?

_____

_____

What situation are you most angry about?

_____

_____

_____

Do you believe the anger is resolvable? Can you let it go?

_____

_____

_____

What is an objective and responsible way to handle your anger?

_____

_____

_____

In order to nurture or take care of yourself, how will you express the anger?

_____

_____

_____

YOUR SELF-IMAGE AND SELF-ESTEEM

As you have worked through the exercises in this chapter, you have begun to get a clearer picture of who you are and what you are about. Your awareness is increasing. Now, let's take a look at the "whole self."

The Imaginary Mirror

Imagine a mirror that reveals your true self. How will this self be seen by those who are important to you (your parents, siblings, friends, teachers, colleagues)?

_____

_____

_____

How big a difference is there between what others see and who you really are?

_____

_____

_____

What can you do to narrow this gap?

_____

_____

_____

Where will you start?

_____

_____

_____

What will you gain from this change?

_____

_____

_____

Who can be your real mirror? Who could you ask to give you feedback?

_____

_____

_____

The Real Mirror
There are two parts to this exercise:

1. Find a full-length mirror. Fully clothed, stand in front of it for at least a minute. Look at yourself. How do you feel? How do you look? What qualities do you like? What qualities don't you like?
2. When you are really comfortable (give yourself time), repeat the exercise again, unclothed. Again, assess how you look and feel. Which parts of your body do you like? Which parts would you like to change? Change is possible: weight, hair style, beard growth, makeup, and so on.

ROLE PLAYING

Most of us play several roles in our daily lives. We might play the role of an employee, a spouse, a lover, a teacher or student, a son or daughter, a sibling, and so forth. Each of these roles requires a different outlook and a different way of responding. Putting yourself in the shoes of different people within your various relationships will help you to reduce your inhibitions and explore the attitudes and feelings of others. And practice makes perfect—role playing is helpful as preparation for real situations.

The following role-playing exercises are structured to help you experience many situations in which you can explore other people's perspectives. Do not try to do all these exercises at once. Rather, concentrate fully on each—one at a time. Try out every role in every situation. Note that the main elements in building a character are physical presence, age, sex, clothing, general attitude, experience, temperament, and personal beliefs.

Replay each situation again and again until you feel confident. If you are comfortable doing so, you might ask someone close to you to participate by playing one of the roles opposite you. One important tip: Don't simply describe the scenario. Act it out as though it is a real-life situation. Don't plan in advance what you will say or how you will act. Just go with the flow of the conversation.

NOTE: In the Father/Child and Mother/Child scenarios, I am drawing on my clinical experience with sufferers from social anxiety, who often reveal a pattern of home life that includes the traditional roles of the father as distant and controlling, and the mother as more accessible and controllable.

1. *Father/Child—Experience the roles of both father and child:*

   - The father does not accept the child's staying out late. The child tries to persuade him.
   - The child wants to buy a car, and gives her father reasons why and a financial plan.
   - The child tells the father about a new love interest. The father does not approve. They argue.

2. *Mother/Child—Experience both of these roles:*

   - The mother is asking for help. The child doesn't have time.
   - The child is asking for money. Mom agrees/disagrees.

- The child tells the mother a secret. She is surprised and angry/she understands and gives advice.
- The child is angry at the mother. The mother doesn't accept the anger.

Repeat this exercise until you feel that your way of expressing yourself is clear to the other person. Make sure that you are not hiding your real feelings, but also make sure that you are not coming on stronger than you naturally would wish to.

3. *Teacher/Student—Experience the roles of both teacher and student:*

- The student disagrees with the teacher's grading and explains why.
- The student is punished by the teacher and says how he or she feels.
- The student doesn't understand the lesson and asks for help.

Now, use role playing to envision the following situations:

4. *The Job Interview*—Try playing both the interviewer and the applicant for the following positions:

- Management position. How do you introduce yourself? What first impression does each person make?
- Office worker. What is the organization looking for in an employee? Why is this person the best candidate for the job?

Come up with a list of jobs that would interest you. Act these interviews out as well.

5. *The workplace*—Try playing both the supervisor and the employee.

- You need to ask for more time on a project. You go to the supervisor to discuss it.

- You have to delegate work to someone else. The person doesn't want to do it. You negotiate a compromise.

6. *Dating*—For people with social anxiety problems, dating can be difficult (even relatively confident people can have trouble sometimes!). You may fear being rejected. You may think the other person is better than you are. In short, you may enter the situation with social fear and low self-esteem. Let's use role playing to improve your interactive skills in this area:

- Introduce yourself to a new person. What are the qualities you wish to convey to this person?
- You are talking on the phone. Tell the other person about yourself.
- Ask someone out. You've seen this person before, now you'd like to take it one step further. Give some hints to determine whether there is any interest. What will you say?
- Sometimes, we have different feelings, views, and needs from our friends. We have to be able to say so and yet still maintain the friendship. Act out a scene with a friend where you are angry or sad. Try to make sure your friend won't be hurt or angry but, rather, understanding and sympathetic.

After you've completed these role-playing exercises, write down your thoughts and feelings. If possible, discuss your experiences with other people (if you are role-playing with a partner, discuss it with him or her). Emphasize the characteristics of the people whose conflicts you acted out, and identify the major factors governing each situation. After further consideration, you may choose to re-play the situation with more emphasis on the characters, language, feelings, or some other aspect of the exchange.

Mastering the self-awareness techniques in this chapter has added to your understanding of your *interactive identity*—who you are and how you relate to other people. In the next chapter, you will combine stress management and self-awareness with social skills strategies and so prepare to increase your interactive ability and further enhance your social system.

CHAPTER EIGHT

"Hello. My Name Is . . .": Mastering Social Skills

Why is one person comfortable meeting new people and capable of interacting easily, while another finds the process painful and difficult and avoids it to varying degrees? Usually, the answer lies in how much social success the person has experienced in the past. If you are uncomfortable with the social process, it is likely that your social skills are in need of improvement. In Chapter 6, you learned some new ways to manage stress. Controlling your anxiety is essential to developing or refining good social skills. Simply put, if you are anxious, you are probably more focused on your own anxiety than on the person or people you are talking to. By improving your social skills, you will gain the following rewards:

- more effective interaction
- improved self-esteem and self-confidence
- a lessening social anxiety level
- improved image in the perception of others
- increased ability to negotiate
- more potential for closeness or intimacy in relationships
- a larger number of relationships

When we say social skills, we mean the techniques involved in approaching and speaking to others for the purpose of interaction—

how you stand, and how close, what kind of eye contact you make, what types of things you talk about. This is not a question of which fork to use or when and whether your elbows can be on the table. Good manners are important, but here we are not talking about matters of etiquette; if you would like to perfect your social manners, consult your library or bookstore for books on that subject. If "knowing the rules" gives you confidence, then so much the better. As the legendary Green Bay Packers coach Vince Lombardi used to say, you have to know your fundamentals to play a good game. Studying the finer points of good interaction will help you to perfect your ability. Consider this chapter as your basic playbook, and adapt the concepts and techniques to your specific interactive needs.

The most basic concept to learn is that of *interactive chemistry*— the positive exchange of energy in which you yourself feel comfortable and others are at ease with you. Interaction should not be hard work. A good balance of interactive chemistry requires managing your anxiety, feeling confident, and using appropriate social skills. When you have developed a repertoire of strategies that allows you to achieve this balance, you can enter the game of interacting with the confidence that you've got the fundamentals down cold. The rest is just refinement.

What does it take to develop good interactive skills? You must perfect the ability to process information—take it in, store it, and retrieve it—as you interact. A recent report in the *Journal of Cognitive Psychotherapy* shows that "socially anxious individuals engage in self-focused thinking which may impair their ability to process social information." The more attention you pay to yourself, the less attention you are paying to others, and the less approachable you will seem. In working out a stress management strategy that you can take with you to interactive situations, you are taking a major step toward interactive success. Once you realize you can count on your "Adult"—the objective, computerlike part of your personality—to identify stressors and take steps to desensitize you to them, you can begin to feel more confident socially.

Two of my clients, Phil and Evelyn, are typical examples of how patterns of behavior have particular social consequences. Although both had had social difficulties and experienced loneliness in the past, they managed to make significant progress. By learning to handle their social anxiety, they brought their fear under control to the point of being able to interact successfully. But without the necessary social skills, each found it difficult to make a smooth transition from failure to success.

Feeling mutually understood is what makes any kind of interaction successful. When that certain something "just clicks," both parties feel at ease and the relationship can progress further. Being able to read other people is an essential part of good chemistry. And no matter what your initial hopes or expectations may be, being able to adapt them based on the new information each interaction gives you will make you feel comfortable and in control. If, for example, you spend time with a member of the opposite sex, hoping the relationship will turn to romance, you should feel that the experience is valuable even if your hopes are not met. Adaptability to change in the initial stages of interaction will make for a healthier, more fulfilling interactive life all around.

Phil had not mastered the finer points of interactive chemistry. In fact, he had been socially anxious—and lonely—for most of his life. By his early twenties, though, he had worked through some of his anxiety and had just started to acquire the social skills that his peers possessed and took for granted. Phil had made several male friends but felt intimidated by women, although he longed for female companionship.

One of Phil's new friends invited him to a dinner party, where he met a woman he became interested in. They began talking, and Phil felt as though they had a lot in common. After a short conversation alone on the patio, Phil invited her out on a date. She accepted.

On the following Saturday evening, Phil picked Carol up and took her to a local restaurant, then to a movie. The evening started out well enough, but somehow conversation became a bit tedious and forced midway through dinner. Carol fidgeted and looked distracted. For his part, Phil could vaguely sense that the chemistry wasn't right but he resolved to try even harder and found himself saying just about anything to fill the awkward silences. When Carol moved away, he edged a little closer.

The movie was a little easier—sitting in the dark, without the pressure of conversation, Phil could maintain the illusion that the date was going fine. But afterward, as they approached Carol's house, Phil was faced with reality once again. Still determined to impose "success" on the evening, which he had hoped would be the beginning of a romantic relationship, he asked, "Can I see you again?" "I don't know," she answered, without much enthusiasm. "Call me."

At this point, Phil's instincts were telling him that Carol wasn't interested, but he pressed on, clinging to the image he had had in his mind since he first met her. "Can I have a goodnight kiss?" For Carol, that was the last straw. "I don't think so," she said, and bolted into the house.

When Phil called Carol the next day, he got her answering machine. And so it went all week long. Carol never returned his calls.

Phil had not done anything terribly offensive. But his inability to read the situation properly created some awkward moments for both him and his date and ultimately caused a more obvious and disappointing rejection than was necessary. Even without a hint of romance, the possibility for friendship was there until Phil forced the issue. It's true Phil was polite—devising the makings of an enjoyable evening, letting Carol know he liked her company, inquiring whether he could see her again, asking to kiss her—but he allowed his expectations to limit his success. If Phil had responded according to the chemistry that developed, he might have gained a friendship of a different kind; while a romance didn't develop, the chance to add to his social contacts by getting to know Carol and her friends might have led to some satisfying relationships of whatever kind.

Evelyn was married to Emile, a French doctor who had recently moved to the United States. Together, they enjoyed a very comfortable lifestyle. Emile seemed unaware of Evelyn's bull-in-a-china-shop personality, and in fact, appeared to admire what he called her "American spirit."

But Evelyn was restless and unhappy. Despite her new social status, she was no more accepted—had no more friends—than when she was single. To outsiders, Evelyn appeared extremely confident. She spoke out on any topic and had no fear of expressing her opinions. The problem was that she didn't know when to stop. She could not read the chemistry between her and others. Instead, she would ramble on without giving other people a chance to speak. She was entirely too focused on her own performance even to notice how others were responding to her. Because she wanted so much to be entertaining, she neglected to offer conversational openings for her guests. Interaction is a two-way street, and the best chemistry allows people on both sides to contribute to a conversation. After a social engagement, Evelyn would remember herself as having been vivacious and entertaining and had no idea why she couldn't seem to establish any friendships. She simply couldn't perceive chemistry correctly.

Evelyn's boorish behavior masked a lack of confidence. Because she was poor at interaction, she tried extra hard—too hard—to be the life of the party and focused entirely on herself. Despite her anxiety, she wanted to be thought of as an excellent conversationalist and believed that her bold speaking style would create that image. Again, however, the inability to read others' reactions caused social failure.

Conversation doesn't have to be difficult. In fact, conversation is natural when you are prepared to talk and when you seek out someone who is likely to be open to talking to you. This chapter outlines the basic building blocks of interaction and will help you to work on the specific skills related to it. As you begin to develop these skills, you will start to experience the interactive success you hope to achieve. Remember, these are *practical* skills, and there is a wide range of ability even with those who experience social anxiety. Whatever your comfort or ability level, start slowly. A safe and comfortable way to begin is to allow one small social success (perhaps a quick verbal exchange with a stranger in a store, for example) to lead to greater accomplishments later (a plan to meet with a new friend, for instance, or a weekend date).

SOCIAL SKILLS AT PLAY

In order to put social skills into perspective, let's look at the way that children learn to socialize. The so-called normal child acquires social skills through free play. Parents should encourage a child to play with other children of a similar age both at school and at home. At first, children may play next to each other independently, but eventually they will engage in cooperative play, and the child learns what it means to be a friend: the give-and-take process of healthy socialization. And while this is a learning process, it is, first and foremost, fun for the children. Fun is the primary motivator, and continues to be throughout life. The reason people get together to socialize is to have fun and enjoy life.

Many of the adults I've worked with recall their childhood years as socially difficult. Their experiences with other children were not generally fun. Without the positive reinforcement gained from enjoying the company of other children, the developmental process of socialization becomes thwarted, and the result can be a socially anxious adult who lacks the skills and confidence necessary to seek out and enjoy the company of his or her peers. If this recollection is familiar to you, you may want to make a conscious decision to bring some fun and playfulness into your interaction with others. Earl, for example, had to do exactly that. When I first met him, a few years ago, he was forty-two, and trying to get back into the dating scene after a ten-year hiatus. As with Evelyn, his was a case of trying too hard. Earl was extremely particular, ruling out most potential dates before he had even spent time with them. When he did go out, it was for an extremely noncommittal cup of coffee at a local diner. If the woman in question passed this initial "test," he would invite her out again. But those first dates usually went badly. The women seemed to feel they were being interviewed. The interactive chemistry was terrible! Eventually, Earl learned to have fun on first dates—to choose a light activity that would be enjoyable whether the time spent resulted in romance or not. He lowered his expectations and increased his rewards.

So, try to have fun when you socialize. Think of it as an adventure.

The results you get depend on the frame of mind you have going into it. In other words, if you tell yourself that making friends is hard work, you may actually make it more difficult. But if you tell yourself that interacting is fun, you will seem friendlier and will probably enjoy more success. Use internal coaching to reinforce this idea in your mind. Tell yourself: "I am going to this party to have fun, and I will enjoy myself."

Right now, do a mental imagery exercise that lets you picture yourself as a social success:

Sit back, take a deep breath, and make yourself comfortable. Use the TV screen in your mind to picture yourself at ease in a social situation. Develop this picture clearly and use your natural senses as you have done previously. Incorporate some playfulness in how you respond to others. You are enjoying yourself. What do you look like? Others are having fun with you. How do they respond to you? As the conversation proceeds, take a risk—changing the subject, expressing an opinion, or inviting someone to do something. How does it feel? How do others respond?

As you emerge from this imagined interaction, what thoughts and feelings do you have about playfulness as an interactive skill? Write them down:

MAKING FRIENDS VS. HAVING ACQUAINTANCES

Many people make the mistake of confusing acquaintances with friends. I recently began treating a seventeen-year-old boy whose mother was concerned because he spent all his free time in his room playing video games or watching television. "Dean doesn't have a friend in the world," she told me. But when I asked Dean himself about his social life, he said he did have friends. How many? "Oh, six or seven," he answered. When I questioned him further, however, it became clear that, like so many socially anxious people, he confused acquaintances—his biology lab partner, his gym squad, the kids he occasionally sat with at lunch—with friends. As we discussed in Chapter 2, we may have many acquaintances—people we know slightly, whom we know by name, say hello to, may work or go to school with. But an acquaintance is not someone we spend free time with on a frequent basis. The distinction is important, because it affects the quality of the interaction.

A friend, after all, is a great deal more than that: someone who makes a difference in your life. Friendship entails having things in common and sharing aspects of your life. Having things in common, or commonality, is important. People generally like those who are like them in some way. Friends may have common attitudes, beliefs, values, background, and personality. They can argue often and vigorously when differences arise, but they respect each other.

Sharing is an important element of friendship because it establishes the bond upon which friendship is based. Sharing includes being involved in activities in which both friends have an interest, as well as an implicit or expressed mutual admiration or enjoyment of each other. With true friendship, there is an intimacy that allows for trust. A friend, quite simply, is someone you can count on in good times and bad.

How many friends should you have? There is no one answer for everyone. It is true that generally people have a few friends and many more acquaintances, but the number really is not important. Rather, it is the *quality* of the friendship that matters. In assessing the quality of your relationships, consider the following guidelines for establishing true friendship:

- Be selective about those with whom you associate.
- Take a warm interest in others and be a good listener.
- Do things together—shared experiences strengthen friendship.
- Be frank, open, and sincere at all times.
- Show empathy and compassion when others are in trouble.
- When friends make mistakes or upset you, be ready to forgive.
- When friends are slandered or unfairly criticized, be loyal and defend them.

BUT WHAT DO I SAY?

If you are most concerned about what to say when you first meet someone, you may be directing your attention to the wrong place. Only 7 percent of the message that people receive from you comes from the actual words you say. Your tone of voice accounts for 38 percent of the impression you make, and your nonverbal communication or body language accounts for another full 55 percent! Later in this chapter, we explore how to get beyond those first few seconds of the first impression—when body language is almost everything—into an actual conversation. But for now, let's start with the basics. What does your body say about you?

BODY LANGUAGE

Body language tells other people about your feelings before you even open your mouth. It conveys to others how receptive you are to communicating with them. A friendly first impression leaves room for social success. But an unfriendly first impression may mean there is no second chance with that person or in that situation.

Of course, the impression you give is only half the picture. There are actually two components to developing body language as a social skill: First, you must learn to project a friendly, open image to others; second, you must develop the ability to read another person's nonverbal behavioral signals, a much more challenging skill. In Phil's case, he worked so hard to make sure that his body language was friendly and open that he neglected to read Carol's hesitancy—the way she drew back, the way her eyes wandered and her attention seemed to drift. Giving and receiving the appropriate signals makes socializing much less of a guessing game and helps minimize the chances of approaching someone who will reject you. What are the basic nonverbal messages we send and receive? This overview will help you to identify them. But remember—use this chapter as a fundamental outline of basic concepts. Don't be robotic. Adapt these concepts naturally to your own life.

Posture

The first impression you make is likely to be from several feet away. An observer will assess your approachability from a general analysis of how you stand, so the right posture is something to be considered.

A closed posture—sitting with arms and legs crossed, often with a hand covering the mouth or chin—gives the signal: "Stay away, I'm not interested in speaking with anyone." Similarly, standing with arms crossed conveys defensiveness or displeasure, a poor impression to give anyone you'd like to get to know.

An open posture—arms relaxed, not crossed, hands away from mouth—says: "I'm available for a conversation, and I'm friendly. Come on over and approach me."

When you are working toward friendly posture, keep in mind that the degree of muscle tension is another clue to whether someone is open to being approached. A relaxed posture indicates that a person is more receptive. A tightened posture indicates that the person feels threatened. Think about the muscle relaxation exercises in the previous chapter: Remember how much calmer you feel when you have given your muscles the "soft and loose" command? Similarly, deep, regular breathing creates an impression of approachability.

Here is an exercise that makes use of biofeedback (information gathered, stored, and applied) to give you knowledge about your body language. Stand or sit in front of a mirror. Strive for an absence of tension. Look at your face. Use internal coaching to let your facial muscles go slack. Say, "My forehead, cheeks, and mouth are relaxed." If you see a furrowed brow or tight cheeks or lips, continue giving yourself the relaxation message until your face looks different. Then, imprint the muscle memory of relaxation into your mind. When you interact with others, try to recall this relaxed state.

Smile

By the time an observer has taken in the information conveyed by how you stand, you are likely to have noticed his or her attention. The next step? Smile. A natural, spontaneous smile indicates friendliness or willingness to communicate. We smile to say hello, and we smile to indicate approval or interest. A frown, of course, indicates unhappiness or a bad mood, as well as a lack of receptivity or skepticism.

The great thing about smiling at someone is that the person usually smiles back. Smiling is an easy way to say hello, and most likely will make another person more receptive and friendly toward you. But try not to act—the smile should be genuine. Be real, and others will recognize your sincerity.

A precautionary note: Make sure you combine smiling (and the other "accessible" behaviors described in this chapter) with an approach or attempt at conversation—or at least a warm hello at the right moment. If you smile for too long without further action, you may scare the other person away.

Body Orientation

When someone does approach and speak to you, pay careful attention to the extent to which you face that person. Facing someone directly communicates an interest in him or her, while turning the body away indicates a desire to avoid interaction. Similarly, when you are talking to someone, watch to see whether his or her body is facing you, indicating an interest in interacting, or turning away in an attempt to avoid the conversation.

Forward Lean

Just as facing a person directly demonstrates interest, so does leaning forward slightly. Leaning forward shows that you are actively listening. It's a kind of nonverbal compliment that tends to keep the conversation going. But pay attention to appropriate social distance (see p. 179, Proxemics, for more on this subject). You don't want to come on too strong.

Leaning back, especially with hands over your mouth or behind your head, communicates boredom or lack of interest. When others pick up on this, they will cut the conversation short and move on. When you perceive that someone you are talking to is leaning back, you may do well to change the subject, perhaps by asking what he or she thinks. If this produces no change in response, it may be time for you to move on. Don't take it personally, especially in a party environment. Most people who attend large gatherings are accustomed to moving from conversation to conversation and may not want to spend more than several minutes with any one person.

Eye Contact

Shakespeare called the eyes the windows of the soul. In fact, your eye contact signals more to another person than any other nonverbal behavior. When you first see someone across the room, catching that person's eye, like smiling, is a clear way to indicate interest. If someone meets your glance, it is an indication that he or she too may be interested in talking. As you evaluate the situation, keep in mind that there are degrees of approachability. Some people may be interested in no more than a smile or a brief hello, while others would enjoy a brief exchange or even a conversation. The trick is to provide enough of an opener that you will receive further information on which to base your next move. One thing you can be almost sure of, though, is that a person who responds to your eye contact by looking away is not interested in pursuing further interaction. It is also possible that the other person might feel anxious as well.

Reading other people takes practice. Sometimes a socially anxious person will look away—if you tend to do this, try to stop. As I said, looking away is generally read as a signal that you are not interested. If you avoid eye contact, the person you are talking to may read it as boredom. And some people read avoiding eye contact as a sign of dishonesty.

Once you are engaged in conversation, direct eye contact reiterates your interest and says that you are really listening to the other person. To maintain friendly, interested eye contact, use the guidelines below. But first, don't stare. Staring intently can make other people uncomfortable. Instead, vary your focus to different parts of the face, so long as it returns to the eyes.

NOTE: As you go through this outline of social skills, remind yourself that your purpose is not to be mechanical. Instead, use this chapter as a baseline of information that you can check against your own interactive skills.

Nodding

You can nod your head to show that you are listening and understanding what is being said. Nodding is a sign of approval, and encourages the speaker to continue talking. How often should you do it? Try not to nod mechanically throughout the conversation. Instead, choose to nod when you especially agree with what is being said. By saving the nod for times when you feel the strongest emotions, when you can best relate to what your companion is saying, you are participating in the conversation even without using words.

Touching

Like nodding, touching shows interest. Upon meeting someone, the best way to show respect and sincere interest is to shake hands. A warm, firm handshake shows that you have an open, friendly social attitude. Don't be afraid to be the first to smile, offer your name, and extend your hand—people will appreciate your interest and willingness to connect.

With whom should you shake hands? These days, it's appropriate to shake hands man to man, woman to woman, or man to woman—in both social and business contexts while exchanging names with other people. (Of course, a man should use a slightly gentler grip when shaking a woman's hand.)

A number of clients who have come to me say that their previous therapists or their parents have advised them to take a dance class in order to gain interactive skills and desensitize themselves to social anxiety. That's a good idea. But it's not that simple. The ideal situation would be one in which you could progress through the various levels of intimacy at a natural pace in an actual interactive situation. Developing a keen sense of interactive chemistry will help you to understand what type of touching behavior is appropriate.

As for other, more personal forms of touch, these should be undertaken more cautiously, and with keen attention to the body language of the other person. When it seems appropriate, gestures such as taking someone's arm or offering your own as you enter or leave a room or cross the street, touching a companion's back as you introduce him or her to an acquaintance—all of these are fairly noncommittal, but are a display of caring and interest. When you try these things, take special note of the response you get. Remember that body language involves communication between two people. Not only do you need to give signals of friendliness and approval but also to take cues from the other person involved.

Proxemics

Proxemics is the study of how people use space. As a rule, people reveal how they feel toward each other by the distance they maintain between them. You can test this by observing people's behavior in public.

Where you place yourself in relation to others gives them direct information as to how you feel about them. Where they place themselves relative to you communicates a similar message to you. You can use this to understand the messages that others send to you, and to make sure that you in turn are sending appropriate messages to them. Different levels of physical closeness are appropriate for different levels of intimacy. Familiarize yourself with the four conversation zones listed below, and use the knowledge to interact more effectively:

1. *Intimate distance:* From actual touch to eighteen inches away. This distance is reserved for those people we are emotionally closest to. Sharing this zone is a sign of trust and an indication that one's defenses have been lowered. When this zone is invaded inappropriately, we feel uncomfortable and threatened.

It was the inability to recognize this distance that got Phil into trouble on his date with Carol. In dating, observing your companion's reaction as you move into this zone is crucial. If you move within eighteen inches of your partner and he or she doesn't retreat, it is an indication that the other person is comfortable. If the person moves away—even slightly—it is an indication that you have entered the intimate zone prematurely.

If other indications suggest that this companion does in fact enjoy your company, continue to proceed. Most people will truly appreciate your ability to read them—much less awkward than having to discuss these things in the early stages of a friendship or potential romance!

2. *Personal distance:* Eighteen inches to four feet. This is the zone occupied by people who feel comfortable together. Eighteen inches is the distance at which most couples stand when in public, and the distance at which close friends might stand if they were having an intimate conversation. The far end of this range, from two and a half to four feet, is the zone beyond arm's length. While this distance still indicates a reasonably close relationship, it is not nearly as intimate as the range of one and a half to three feet.

3. *Social distance:* Four to twelve feet. Generally the distance between people who work together and between the salesperson and customer in a store. The span of seven to twelve feet is usually reserved for more formal and impersonal situations.

4. *Public distance:* Twelve to twenty-five feet. The closer end of the span, twelve feet away, is what teachers usually use in the classroom. Anything further away suggests a lecture situation, in which conversation is almost impossible.

Courting and Friendship Reciprocals

Reciprocals are the signals people give each other to indicate an interest in companionship. When there is physical attraction, these signals include smiling, repeated glances (perhaps with an extra second or two of direct eye contact), and straightening or smoothing of clothes.

Meeting and Greeting

1. Use eye contact and smiling as your first contact with others. In doing so, you can scout out the friendly, approachable strangers in the room and feel immediately more at ease.
2. Be the first to say hello. Stay calm if you are left alone to mingle—large parties, forgetful hosts, and friendly guests make this situation inevitable.

3. Introduce yourself to others. Offer your hand and say: "Hello. My name is . . ."

    A tidbit of information gives the new acquaintance something to build a conversation on: "Hello. I'm [your first and last name]. [The host's name] and I work together at the university."

4. As you shake hands, repeat the person's name. "Nice to meet you, Jack." This will help imprint the name in your own mind.

5. Make an extra effort to remember names and use them in conversation: "Don't you agree, Jim?" This makes people feel special.

6. Go out of your way to meet new people. They may feel as out of place as you do: "Hi, I don't believe we've met yet, I'm . . ." or "I don't know a soul."

7. Ask neutral questions that are easy to answer to convey the message that you'd like to get to know this person better.

8. Be prepared to say something interesting about what you do—but in small doses. No one wants to hear you talk exclusively about yourself.

9. Communicate a sense of enthusiasm about the event at hand or life in general. Focus on the positive.

10. Look for passing comments that could open up a whole topic of conversation. "The New York subways were a real experience for this country boy" could lead to a discussion of childhood on the farm, adjusting to city life, public transportation. . . . Clothes, jewelry, and accessories also make excellent conversation pieces. It's up to you to take the conversational ball and run with it, but be sure to pass it back to your teammate from time to time.

TURNING REJECTION AROUND

What if your friendly, hopeful conversation starter is not met with signals of approval or interest? If the person you approach is fidgety, avoids eye contact, appears uneasy, and exhibits none of the signals of welcome, chances are he or she is not interested in interaction—at least not at that moment.

The first thing to do is slow down. Be patient, and give the person time to relax with you. If you present yourself as relaxed and open to whatever develops (whether a good conversation, a valuable working relationship, even friendship or romance), your companion may in time relax too. Use your verbal skills to create interesting conversation and a sense of ease to break the tension.

Don't pressure yourself to be able to define a relationship from the first meeting. Keep your expectations general, and remember the playfulness factor. Enjoy someone's company with no strings attached. Don't fabricate obligations where none exist. It may take several conversations for a relationship to develop. If you had hoped for romance but the feelings appear not to be reciprocated, switch your interest to friendship, which has its own rich rewards.

What if you are outright rejected? Rejection at any point—at first meeting, during a date, or well into a relationship—can be painful and difficult for most of us. But there are ways to prevent it from being an all-out failure. One thing I like to tell my clients is that *the Chinese word for failure can be interpreted to mean "opportunity."* And opportunities, after all, are there for the taking. It all depends on how you perceive things.

There is a technique you can borrow from salespeople to counter your feelings of rejection. High-earning salespeople know that you can't succeed without being turned down at least occasionally. Some even look forward to rejection, because they know that being turned down this time brings them that much closer to succeeding next time around. They may even learn something in the process. So keep this in mind as you experiment with your new, social self: Hearing a no now may actually bring you closer to the bigger and better yes that is soon to happen!

Apply this idea as you practice interacting: Being turned down at any point in the process helps you to learn a little more—about how to approach a stranger, have a conversation, make plans, go on a date, or move toward intimacy. If you learn something positive from the experience, you can bring that with you into your next social situation. Just as in sales, the payoff in either romance or friendship is worth far more than the possible downfall or minor setback of being turned down.

A note on self-esteem: Rejection can hurt, but it certainly does not have to be devastating. It's okay to feel disappointed when we do not get the reaction we want. But all too often, people overemphasize the importance or meaning of rejection—especially where fairly superficial interactions such as a first meeting or casual date are concerned. Here are some tips to keep rejection in perspective:

- Don't overthink it. Overanalysis will only increase your anxiety.
- Keep the feelings of disappointment specific to the rejection situation at hand. Don't say, "No one ever wants to talk to me." Say, "Too bad the chemistry wasn't right for both of us."
- Learn from the experience. Ask yourself what you might have done differently, if anything, but then move on. Don't beat yourself up about it. If those thoughts start, use your thought-stopping techniques (p. 138) to control them.
- Use your "Adult" to look objectively at what happened.

Remember, rejecting your offer of conversation or an evening out does not mean rejecting your whole "being." You must continue to believe that you have something to offer, and that there are open, available people who would like to get to know you.

ANXIETY AND THE SOCIAL PROCESS

Generally, in life, we only make progress when we are willing to take risks. If you don't take risks in your life, it's probably because you are held back by anxiety. Because you fear that interaction will result in rejection, embarrassment, and scrutiny, you feel anxiety about it. After all, you tell yourself, why risk experiencing failure? But as we have discussed, rejection is not devastating; it is merely disappointing, and, with your anxiety under control, disappointment is entirely bearable. In time, and with practice and eventual success, your fear of disappointment will diminish.

Some people, far from shying away from social contact, actually look forward to meeting new people. Meeting new people does not in itself cause anxiety. The beliefs you hold cause anxiety. If you believe rejection will be devastating to you, and that rejection is highly likely to happen, you will feel quite justified in making sure that you never meet any new people at all. *But avoidance does not alleviate anxiety. It simply makes the problem worse next time the situation arises.* You need to tap into your positive mental attitude. Tell yourself: "Meeting new people is healthy, and by doing it, I stand a good chance of having a positive experience."

To summarize, here are some tips for interactive success. Try to integrate them into your being—make them part of your overall attitude toward interacting.

1. Anticipate success.
2. Be willing to risk.
3. Think positive thoughts about yourself to boost your self-esteem.
4. Think positive thoughts about others as well.
5. Be yourself.

This last point leads into a discussion of mental focus. It is typical of a socially anxious person to focus on himself or herself, to forget to read the nonverbal signals of others. Before you attempt to meet someone, it's a good idea to focus your attention in the right direction, not on yourself, but on the other person. Use your new skills of self-awareness and relaxation to enhance your focusing abilities.

Think of your attention as a finite resource. Is it really best spent on thoughts about yourself? ("Do I look okay?" "Can he tell I'm sweating?" "Can she tell I'm blushing?" "I hope I don't say anything dumb," and so on.) With so much attention directed inward, there is very little left to spend on the other person. One of my clients has so much trouble focusing on others in conversation that she developed a habit of pinching herself to stay on track. Do all you can to stop your inward thinking, because paying attention to the other person will provide you with the basis of an interesting and success-ful conversation. If you have trouble averting the focus from your own anxiety, try using relaxation techniques to bring your symp-toms under control. Diaphragmatic breathing, for example, can bring immediate relief.

"Party Phobia"

Many people who join my program or call in during my radio or TV appearances say they have "party phobia": They become extremely anxious about attending social gatherings and either avoid them or clam up as soon as they arrive. Technically speaking, "party phobia" would mean that you are so fearful that you avoid parties altogether. But even people who actually attend parties do experience various levels of party anxiety. Some nervousness is normal: You're meeting new people, perhaps dressing up a little. I understand the pain of anxiety, but you can learn not to let your anxiety exclude you from the fun. People give and attend parties because they want to enjoy the company of a group of friends and to meet other people whom they can bring into their social system. Here are some tips that you might find useful as you attempt to negotiate the party scene:

1. *Decide whether to arrive early—within the first half-hour—or late—an hour or more after the party begins.* Either could be advantageous, depending upon your specific issues.

   • The *early arriver* can position herself before most guests have arrived, and therefore ease into the scene, interacting with people as they arrive. In this way, some superficial bonds are formed that allow for a higher comfort level as the event progresses.
   • The *late arriver* doesn't have to go through that process. He may not meet everyone in attendance but can instead ap-proach just two or three conversational groups, fitting into the environment and mood that already exist.

2. *Try to circulate.* Don't "ambush" anyone (don't stay too long with one person, even if you don't know anyone else there). It's okay to introduce yourself to people.

3. *Be positive.* No one likes negative approaches or attitudes, so avoid talking about depressing subjects such as illness or bad experiences.
4. *Along these lines, don't be negative about yourself.* Present an open, friendly image. And don't choose to stay home because you think the hosts don't care whether you attend or not: *If you were invited, they want you to be there.*
5. *Have fun.* That's why you're there. Keep a sense of humor. Don't let others know you're working at it.
6. *Apply relaxation techniques* when necessary.

CONVERSATION GUIDELINES

What is the secret to good conversation? Shared interest in the subject; easy, natural flow from topic to topic; humor, when appropriate; the right amount of give-and-take—all of these elements are present. Countless people who have spoken to me about their social anxiety have said that their biggest social difficulty is having a conversation, whether it's beginning one or keeping it going.

How to start a conversation? When talking with someone new, it's a good idea to move from general to specific, starting with basic subjects such as the weather, news, and some reference to the event or situation at hand. From comments made in the first few minutes, you might move on to talk about what the person does for a living, where he or she lives, and what hobbies he or she pursues. Stay attuned to the interactive chemistry that is developing. Eventually, it may be appropriate to touch upon more personal topics: likes and dislikes, family life, values, and personal beliefs. This section will offer guidelines for starting a conversation, and tips on how to keep it going, when to change the subject, and how to create the opportunity for a graceful exit as the conversation ends.

Three Ways to Start a Conversation
It's a lot easier than you think. Over the years, countless clients have said to me, "But I don't know what to say! What is the perfect opening line?" Well, here's some good news: There is no "perfect"

opener! In fact, few people remember the first things they ever said to each other. Appearing comfortable and at ease socially is far more important than being witty or astute when it comes time to make that first impression. Just get the conversation going, preferably by encouraging others to talk to you. Here are a few ideas to get you started. Imagine yourself in each of these situations, and think about other things you might say.

1. *Ask a question.* Scenario: You are in a parking lot and see someone with a late-model car. "Excuse me," you say, "I'm in the market for a new car, and I'm considering one like this. What do you think of it?"

2. *Voice an opinion.* Scenario: During intermission at a concert or play. "I think they are absolutely terrific! What did you think?" If you're feeling a little more adventurous, follow up with a veiled invitation. "I think it's wonderful that they bring such talent to our area, don't you? I'd really like to come more often."

3. *State a fact.* Scenario: At an art gallery, showing the work of someone about whom you've done a little research (it never hurts, and gives you an air of being in the know). "I understand the artist spent several years in Haiti, working with native artists." Or, if you know next to nothing about the artist, "I'm intrigued by his work, but I know so little about his background. Are you familiar with it?" (This clever turnaround sets your new companion up as the expert, and works even if you actually do know a little something about the subject!)

Three Opening Topics of Conversation
Use your information-gathering skills to devise topics that would interest you both. As your conversation proceeds, listen carefully to the answers to your questions; they will provide you with material for further conversation.

1. *The situation you're both in.* For example, if you meet someone in a continuing-education class, you know that you share an

interest in learning, as well as in the topic of the course itself. Questions such as "Have you taken other adult education classes?" or "How did you become interested in English history?" should get the ball rolling. If you meet someone at a party, you might start off by talking about how you know the people throwing the party. "Oh, you and Bob went to sailing camp together? Do you still sail?" And so on. Take your cues from them, and let them know you are interested by following up—both verbally with questions, and nonverbally with your body language.

2. *The other person.* First, observe what the person is doing, wearing, saying, or reading. Look for things you share in common, or find something that you'd like to know more about. (But watch their body language to be sure they are approachable. A person who is busy changing a tire or engrossed in a book may not want to be disturbed, even by friendly, approachable you.)

3. *Yourself.* Talking about yourself is a step leading toward conversational intimacy. But it is only effective if you provide an easy way for your intended companion to turn the conversation around to him or her. A compliment such as "I wish I had your sense of color" starts out with you, but focuses on the other person. It makes her feel immediately appreciated, and offers her a chance to take the conversation further if she likes. When someone mentions something you know about or like, indicate it by nodding or by a short sentence ("I've been interested in gardening for years!"). Be careful not to talk about yourself too much—especially at first. That can be a real turnoff.

The Information Exchange

Good conversationalists know how to balance speaking and listening. Check the scale once in a while. If you are talking too much, subtly offer the other person a chance (with a follow-up question such as, "What do you think?"). If you have been listening passively, try to interject a comment or two.

To make sure there is the right amount of give-and-take in your conversation, imagine that the two of you are sharing a micro-phone. To be polite, and create the most satisfying conversation possible, offer your point of view, and then pass the microphone to your partner.

Changing Topics

Changing topics gracefully is the hallmark of an excellent conver-sationalist. Changing topics keeps the conversation fresh and allows you to explore further ideas of mutual interest. And if you detect that your conversational partner is uncomfortable with a subject, or not interested in it, changing the topic will be tactful and greatly appreciated.

Good conversations usually move naturally from one subject to the next. Sometimes, the movement will be to a somewhat unre-lated area. The important thing is to go with the flow.

The best way to change the subject is to guide the conversation based on information you were given earlier. Suppose your conver-sation focuses on volleyball, and your partner mentions having en-joyed volleyball on the beach in Florida last month. As the discussion of volleyball winds down, you might elect to return to the topic of Florida—when and where your partner visited, what places you are familiar with or would like to see, and so on.

A second way to change subjects is to branch off from the "avail-able" topics by referring to the event at hand:

At a party:
"Have you tried the crab dip? It's really terrific."
"Can I freshen your drink?"
"I simply must have some more chicken wings. The sauce is amazing!"
At a book club meeting:
"I wanted to go and compliment the author. I see he's free now."

These are friendly gestures, and leave open two possibilities: the chance for a graceful exit on either part, or the possibility of continuing the conversation at the refreshment table or in line near the author.

It's important to be able to change subjects quickly if you sense that your companion is losing interest or is sensitive to something you've touched upon (body language will tell you if words do not). Providing easy outs is the considerate thing to do.

On Paying Compliments

Compliments, appropriately timed, allow you to develop a greater sense of rapport with your interactive partner. Most people want to feel special and appreciated. Effective compliments focus on the following areas: the person's behavior, appearance, possessions, or performance. Be sure you are sincere in expressing your approval. Smile. Be specific, saying exactly what you like; make it unique to that person. Use the person's name, and follow up with a question. "You're a great dancer, Bill. How did you learn to dance so well?"

When receiving compliments, don't try to downplay what is being expressed. This makes the person paying the compliment feel unappreciated. Instead, look the person in the eye and respond positively: Smile, and say thank you. You can even say how you feel about the compliment ("That's sweet of you to say," or, "I'm glad to know my dance classes paid off"). There is no need, however, to return the same compliment to the person who just gave you one.

Keeping It Going

Asking questions may be the best way of keeping a conversation going. Not only can you express interest in what is being said, but you also demonstrate a continued desire to get to know the other person. Asking questions to find areas of common interest is somewhat like fishing: You throw out a line more times than you get a bite. So keep asking open-ended questions until you find an area that seems of interest to that person. Then, express your own interest or curiosity.

There are two types of questions, and a combination of both will serve you best.

1. *Closed-ended:* "Yes." "No." "True." "False." These are dead-end answers—a one- or two-word reply that probably leads nowhere. A question such as "Where are you from?" can be closed-ended if the person answers with the place name only. Follow up with an open-ended question, and you may save the conversation. But asking too many closed-ended questions in a row will seem like interrogation. Balance the conversation out with a variety of questions and comments, and you will discover greater interest and depth.
2. *Open-ended:* Open-ended questions are like essay questions— they promote thoughtful answers of several sentences, not just one or two words. Such questions include: "How?" "Why?" "In what way?"

When you ask the questions, you have control in the conversation. Don't waste the opportunity by asking general questions such as "What's new?" or "Tell me about yourself." Be specific. Of course, asking open-ended questions takes practice. Use the guidelines throughout this chapter to develop topics of interest between you.

Personal Questions
As you move further into the realm of conversational intimacy, you may be tempted to ask a more personal question. Such questions entail risk that you will offend the other person. Ask them with extreme caution—especially on subjects such as financial matters, past relationships, and religion. If you feel you are developing a close rapport, you could broach a subject carefully by softening it with a qualifier such as:

"Excuse me for asking, but . . ."
"I don't mean to get personal, but . . ."

Don't take it as a personal rejection should your interactive partner choose not to answer the question. Again, keep the conversation going. And if someone asks you a personal question that you don't wish to answer, be prepared with an easy way to demur: "I'd rather not talk about that. But I was wondering . . ." Then use the techniques described in this chapter to change the subject gracefully.

Being asked an overly personal question may embarrass you. Let your comfort level be your guide. If you do not wish to answer, that's okay. The person probably meant no offense and was asking only out of genuine interest. Try to continue on in the conversation to see what else is there. If you find your anxiety level rising, use relaxation techniques to bring it under control.

Active Listening

As a skill, active listening draws on many of the abilities you've developed so far, from your relaxation techniques to body language to conversation skills. Here are four ways to be a good listener:

1. Instead of thinking ahead or worrying about what you'll say next, focus on what the other person is saying right now.
2. Use positive body language to encourage the other person (maintain eye contact, smile, nod).
3. Occasionally restate the point the other person is making in another way (don't merely parrot their words), so that he or she knows you understand and are paying attention. Ask for and offer examples to support what is being said.
4. Look for hints of something that the person seems truly interested or involved in. Seize the moment with a follow-up question such as "Why do you say that?" or, "What happened then?"
5. Use self-awareness and relaxation techniques both to improve your ability to focus and to develop your listening ability.

Humor

Humor is a great social lubricator—it can make interacting go more smoothly. If you are good at telling jokes, try a few. Telling jokes is risky, however; do not tell ethnic, racist, or off-color jokes. And as always, pay careful attention to interactive chemistry. One high school student who attended my program reported that, although he tried to become part of a popular social group at his new school, playing on the football team and joining several clubs, he was not invited to socialize with the other kids off the field. He had become known for telling joke after joke, in vain hopes of being accepted. When we examined things more carefully, it became clear that his style of telling jokes—sometimes irrelevant, sometimes just plain corny—was not appealing to the peer group he was associating with. Quite simply, the chemistry was off.

If you wish to inject humor and levity into an interaction, it's better to tell funny stories. If the funny stories are about yourself, great: People enjoy mildly self-deprecating humor. You can also find amusing true stories in the newspaper.

Displaying Warmth and Empathy

Warmth means showing that you care about another person. *Empathy* is the capacity to share another person's experience, to "put yourself in his shoes," as the saying goes. Some ways to express warmth and empathy:

1. Use verbal and nonverbal signals to encourage the person to continue.
2. If the situation arises, describe experiences you've had that are similar to those of the other person, and explain that you can understand how he or she feels.
3. Use the person's name during the conversation (a person's own name is the sweetest sound in the world to him or her).
4. Become genuinely interested in other people, and show it.
5. Make the other person feel important.

Displaying warmth and empathy is a way of truly demonstrating to another that you value him or her, and is often the source of a person's immediate positive feeling toward you. In the words of psychologist William James, "The deepest principle in human nature is the craving to be appreciated." Conveying warmth and empathy, combined with being a good conversationalist, will help you to show appreciation for another person.

SELF-DISCLOSURE

In order to begin to reveal to your new acquaintance who you really are, it is helpful to discuss topics that are important to you. Be willing, as the conversation progresses, to share your beliefs, values, attitudes, and goals. These reveal a deeper level of what you are about. Self-disclosure includes facts, thoughts, ideas, aspirations, and deepest feelings.

The trick is timing. You don't want to reveal the really intimate, personal aspects of your life until you have known a person for some time, but you can build trust by gradually revealing your interests, hopes, and background. Sufficient mutual trust must be established so that both parties are comfortable. Then, more intimate details can be shared.

Three Levels of Self-Disclosure

There is a pattern of increased trust and intimacy. Becoming familiar with it may help you to develop a sense of timing when it comes to self-disclosure.

1. *Cliché greetings:* Responses to questions like "How are you?" and "How's the family?" Your basic answer should be brief and as positive as possible. This tells the person that your attitude is open, friendly, and available for conversation.
2. *Background of experiences:* Your job, where you're from, what you do for fun, activities you're involved in. At this stage, people actually began to know each other.
3. *Opinions and preferences:* Your attitudes, values, and concerns.

Some Conversational "Don'ts"

1. Talking about illnesses in detail.
2. Stating your opinions in a way that puts down anyone who disagrees.
3. Gossiping or speaking badly of others.
4. Spending too much time talking about yourself.

5. Revealing all your personal problems.
6. Using terminology or jargon unfamiliar to others.
7. Dominating the conversation.

HOW TO CLOSE THE CONVERSATION

Timing is crucial in closing a conversation. If you let your anxiety dictate your actions, you may end it too soon and lose out on the opportunity to move from the first conversational level to the second. If a conversation goes on too long, with one or the other doing all the talking, both you and your partner may feel drained or bored. Closing the conversation is similar to changing the subject. You can use the same techniques to offer the other person a chance to agree to conclude (a trip to the buffet table or bar, the need to "get back to work," a chance to speak to the host or guest of honor). Follow with a comment such as "I've really enjoyed talking with you," perhaps adding, "I hope we can talk again soon." If the person responds favorably, it is okay to follow up with a suggested plan for a future meeting; if the interaction is a social one, ask for the person's phone number, or offer yours ("Are you in the book? I'd like to call you sometime," or "My number's in the book. Give me a call if you'd like to get together"). In workplace situations, you might say, "I could use some feedback on my next project. Could we arrange a time that I could run it by you?" If the response is very favorable, you might even suggest a specific time and date to get together.

As you conclude, say the person's name again (if he or she is a new acquaintance), and reiterate with body language and with words that you have enjoyed talking with him or her. Smile and maintain eye contact. Then, give a warm handshake or nod, if it is appropriate, and be on your way.

Don't draw the ending out—a protracted closing to a conversation can be counterproductive. Unlike the beginning of the conversation—where almost anything can serve as an opener—the ending does make a lasting impression, so be sure to end in a friendly, confident, and upbeat manner.

One more thing: Many people find they are intrigued by a person whom they feel they didn't get to talk to long enough. It's much better to leave before you've said everything you could possibly think of to say. That way, there will be more to talk about next time!

MAKING THE CALL

Suppose you had a successful social encounter at a party. Last night went fine. But now you sit by the phone, the person's phone number in hand, afraid to make that call you know you want to make. Maybe the person doesn't really want you to call. (Then why did she give you her phone number?) Maybe she's changed her mind. (There's only one way to find out!) If you have a problem following up, you need to internalize this self-coaching advice: Dread, then *do*.

If you feel anxious, use relaxation techniques to ready yourself to make the call. Then make it. No matter what, you will feel relieved and even proud of yourself once you've done it.

Appropriate follow-up is crucial; otherwise, all the groundwork you've laid in your initial conversation will go to waste. When you call someone on the phone, remember all the skills you've practiced so far. And be sure to call when you say you are going to call. Imagine how you'd feel if someone whose company you'd enjoyed promised to call you on Tuesday and the call didn't come until Friday, if at all. And finally, remember to ask about things the person told you in previous conversation. This is your chance to broaden your new friendship, so make plans and follow through on them soon. (Remember: friendship first. It's okay, especially at this stage, for a woman to initiate a social engagement with a man, whether it leads to romance or not.)

If you would like to follow up with someone in your company or outside it who could become a valuable part of your career network, the procedure is much the same. Stay in touch in whatever ways are appropriate for your workplace. A clipping of a work-related article with a simple note—"Bill: Thought this would interest you," and your name—lets the person know you appreciated his knowledge and insight. If you like, you could follow up on an outside contact with a brief note saying you enjoyed meeting the person, and then call later, perhaps with an invitation for a business lunch or a lecture. Developing contacts inside your workplace and beyond could help you build job opportunities. And feeling connected to the business community in which you work can be fulfilling too. People may soon want to begin networking with you!

As you proceed to Chapter 9, which further explores ways to refine the social skills you are working on, ask yourself whether you have felt that your social skills are at the crux of the problem. Many clients have suggested this on first meeting with me. But to blame your lack of interactive success on poor social skills alone is to deny the presence of social anxiety. The two go hand in hand. In fact, one of my clients, a fifty-one-year-old woman who was getting divorced from her husband after twenty-five years of marriage, initially argued that her interactive skills were rusty because she had been out of the mainstream during her years as a homemaker. As we worked together to identify the issues she was facing, she ultimately realized that she felt a great deal of anxiety about her situation and indeed was afraid of entering the workplace after so many years outside it. Use your self-help techniques to allow you to make forays into the interactive world. Then follow up, using the methods described here. There is very little to lose, and much to gain.

CHAPTER NINE

Applying Your Interactive Skills

You now have the basic components you will need to create your map for change. This chapter explores the ways you can apply your interactive skills to specific areas of your life: your personal life (friendship and dating), your current work environment, the job search, and mixing business and pleasure. Building on the strategies included in the last chapter, this chapter will show you how to create or enhance your social system. When and where should you use the self-help strategies included here? In whatever interactive situations you confront, from the purely casual to the more formal, both in your personal life and at work. The previous chapter detailed the finer points of interaction. This chapter will provide you with strategies to apply what you have learned to these specific areas of your life.

Whether you've lived in your community for decades or just moved there last week, interactive skills are an essential part of developing your own social system. Let's suppose you did just move to an area. How would you begin to look for friends and business contacts? One way would be to define your own interests, and find people who do what you like to do—sports, continuing education, crafts, or other activities, for example. The same holds true for a longtime resident hoping to meet more people. In my practice, I have found so many people who desire friendship that I once thought about creating a formal friendship service. These days, it can be very difficult to meet people, given the stresses of our society. It does take effort, but the rewards are well worth it.

The more you are able to apply these interactive skills in a natural, spontaneous manner, the more success you will achieve. Spontaneity, after all, is a vital part of creating good interactive chemistry between you and the people you encounter. We've talked about chemistry before. Think of chemistry as the energy created by the mutual feeling of being understood and accepted. As you become familiar with the concepts explained in this chapter, you will clarify your own values and gain a heightened understanding of what particular qualities are important to you in your personal and working relationships.

First, let's look at the different types of relationships and the role chemistry plays in them.

YOUR PERSONAL LIFE

Friendship
Friendship can be one of the most fulfilling and important components of your life. Without close friendships, there can be a void. (In fact, a sense of "something missing" is one feeling new clients often cite as a reason for seeking help with social anxiety.) Devising strategies for successful interaction will enable you to enrich the relationships you already have as well as to develop new ones. As you examine your current relationships, ask yourself how many close friends you have. Consider the basic components I use to define quality friendships:

Understanding: Taking the time and effort to get to know who your friend is, and what his or her needs are. He or she should do the same for you.

Empathy: The ability to step into the shoes of your friend and see the world from his or her perspective.

Support: Showing that you care and are available in times of need, and feeling that your friend is someone you can count on as well.

Sharing time: Creating opportunities to allow the friendship to grow. It is possible to develop and maintain friendships over the telephone. But shared time can be a way of bonding and becoming closer.

Sharing common interests, goals, and values: People most often form bonds of friendship when they are interested in the same things and share a common core of basic beliefs. At the very least, you should respect your friend's interests, goals, and values, even if you don't agree. (In fact, good friends may find they strongly disagree on certain things—but closeness means accepting each other's differences and being able to discuss or argue productively.)

Giving and taking: The more sharing, the greater the friendship. Both parties should receive something from the relationship: understanding, empathy, or just good times.

Mutual attraction and opportunities to have fun: You see something in the other person that you admire or can relate to. And you enjoy doing things together or talking about things that interest you.

Levels of Friendship
Friends play many roles in our lives. They are our playmates, our confidantes, our colleagues, and our role models. Most people have a number of friends of varying degrees of closeness. As you consider the friendships in your life, think about the following categories, which describe three different levels of friendship:

Close: This describes one's most intimate friend or friends. Most people have one or two friends who fall into this category. There is good energy between you, and you can have fun together. A close friend is someone you can really count on in times of need; someone who you would do almost anything for, and who would do almost anything for you.

Casual: This describes someone with whom you have a much less intimate relationship. Most people have several casual friendships (though the sky's the limit; you might have many, even dozens, of casual friendships). This is someone you get together with only once in a while and whose company you enjoy; but the depth of your friendship is much less than with a close friend.

Friend with a purpose: This is usually someone with whom you share a common interest. For example, a person you get together with to play cards, play ball, carpool with, or attend business functions. Workplace friends often fall into this category. What characterizes the friend with a purpose is that you meet to perform a given activity, not just to socialize.

Most of us have the opportunity for casual contact with other people throughout the day. How do you tell when there is a possibility for friendship? The following list of characteristics may help. As you adapt the techniques outlined in Chapter 8 to enhance your interactions, use the list below to consider whether a basis exists for a friendship of any type. Of course, it's not necessary to fulfill all of these characteristics, but it's usually true that the more you find, the better the chance of a genuine friendship developing. What you are looking for is a pattern of connections that suggests the basis for further conversations or activity.

1. Common interests
2. Living in close proximity
3. Common values
4. Similar socioeconomic levels
5. Both of you listen equally to each other
6. Similar life goals
7. Involvement in common activities (such as an association, team, gym, etc.)
8. Sharing other friends in common, or can get along with your other friends
9. Good communication—good chemistry

When you are pursuing friendships, age is not the most important ingredient, and friendship can cross age barriers. But a pattern of friendships exclusively outside the peer group bears looking at: It may be symptomatic of a problem, such as underlying issues of competition that you may be avoiding. A healthy balance usually includes several peer relationships.

What about gender? Same-sex friendships are likely to constitute the majority of your relationships. They are valuable because they build closeness based on bonding from shared experiences, and the companionship and fun you can have with same-sex friends will add a lot to your life. But friends of the opposite sex also have an appeal. They can give you the "opposite" perspective on socializing, and may create opportunities for you to meet some of their same-sex friends for the purpose of dating. In fact, Linda, a twenty-nine-year-old lab assistant, told me she especially valued her opposite-sex friendships for just this reason. She had lived in her area for several months and had met few women with whom to form friendships, but she had gotten to know several men in her apartment complex, which had a pool and barbecue area where residents congregated. Linda had dated a few times since moving, but she felt somewhat anxious about meeting new people. The platonic relationships she developed at poolside helped her to feel more comfortable with dating. Her friendships with men became a means for overcoming her anxiety and were actually a good first step toward her being able to forge more intense relationships later. In many cases, there is a useful purpose for the male-female friendship, and positive energy can come from it, provided both parties really do have the same expectations. Of course, I am aware that there is considerable debate as to whether male-female friendships are truly possible, given the potential for underlying sexual tension. But that debate is too complicated to go into here. Think of it as an individual issue: Whatever works for you is okay. If you are comfortable with platonic friends of the opposite sex, by all means include them in your social system.

And don't discount the idea of couples as friends. Many couples enjoy spending time with people whose current situations are different from theirs, and they too may know single friends whom you might be interested to meet. One couple I know enjoy a healthy family life with their three kids but say they find it hard to find other couples to become close to: It's difficult, they say, to have good chemistry with both members of a couple—they might like the company of one member, but not the other. Similarly, a single person might find he or she relates better to one member of a couple than the other. In any case, do consider getting to know the couples you have met. And don't be put off by fear of the stigma of socializing with couples. If you keep the characteristics of potential friendship in mind, you will meet with success.

Friends and Lovers
Sometimes what starts out as a male-female friendship turns into romance. And in fact, there is a lot to be said for taking things slowly. Give yourselves time to pursue common interests, meet each other's friends, and just get to know each other, and the relationship can evolve naturally, without the pressure of any preconceptions. This way, no matter what develops, your expectations are in line with reality, and you may feel less disappointed than you would have if you had pinned all your hopes on romance. Other people want the romance right away. But be clear with yourself about your expectations or objectives. And if the chemistry is not right, or your expectations are different from the other person's, then move on.

But what about romance? When should a friendship turn into a deeper relationship? As in any friendship, compatibility is the key, and where physical intimacy is concerned, only you can assess your comfort level. Love is, as they say, a mysterious thing. But there is an essential element to romance that goes beyond friendship: chemistry. Interactive chemistry is a part of every relationship, and it appears in romantic relationships as a mutual attraction between two people. It's difficult to describe this attraction, but it usually appears as a high degree of interest in each other, almost a craving to be together. When you talk, you may find time passes very quickly, and suddenly it's five hours later. In many cases, this chemistry exists immediately upon meeting—a kind of interactive "love at first sight"—and you simply hit it off right away. In other cases, romance can develop out of friendship and spending time together.

As you continue getting to know the person, you may find that when you're apart, your thoughts drift back to that person—to the time you have spent together or to your future plans.

It is important to note that there is a difference between loving and being in love. Both emotions are valid, but the differences are distinct. Where being in love connotes the intensity described above—a higher degree of energy and passion—loving someone may be described as a steady feeling of contentment and connection. Neither one is necessarily deeper than the other. One of my clients, Melanie, was separated from her husband and living with a boyfriend when she came to see me. She very much wanted to sort out her feelings. She was passionate about the man she lived with, and had a very good sexual relationship with him, but after fourteen years of marriage and two children, she still felt a deep connection to her husband. In the end, she went back to him, having worked through her issues with me. After all, compatibility and caring are a vital part of feeling close to someone. They may, as in this case, even override feelings of attraction or infatuation.

Seven Steps of Relationship Development
For people with social anxiety, dating can be particularly stressful. There are many unknowns: "Does this person share my interest?" "Will it work out?" and so on. Here are a few guidelines to help keep you on track through the initial stages of a potentially romantic relationship:

1. Develop conversation that explores areas of common interest or experience.
2. Make it clear that you like the person, and make plans to meet again.
3. Make a follow-up call to arrange your first date, and plan an interesting or enjoyable time. Be prepared with suggestions, but be flexible.
4. On your first date:

   • Be yourself—and be attentive.
   • Continue exploring areas of mutual interest.

- Determine if there is positive chemistry and if a relationship is worth pursuing. If a potential relationship is developing, both individuals usually drop hints about doing other things together. Each expresses enthusiasm through eye contact, voice qualities, body language, and a developing conversation that expresses a sincere desire to learn more about each other.

5. Continue to see each other and share your feelings. Let the other person know how you are feeling about him or her. The frequency of contact is usually a good indicator of whether a romantic relationship is developing; less intensity is likely to mean it is something more casual.
6. Consider being romantic—sending flowers, having a candle-light dinner, and so on.
7. If the chemistry develops, you may be ready to become involved physically. Take it slowly. Good things are not rushed.

Friends in the Workplace

In our society, there is an increasing pattern of people seeking social contact on the job. This can be quite positive—for all the reasons that friendship is usually positive. But it is important not to let workplace relationships interfere with your ability to get your job done. I can think of several examples in which personal relationships developed among colleagues—some having positive results and some negative.

Frank and Tim started work as bank tellers in the same branch on the same day, and formed a friendship that lasted for years. They became best friends, and supported and helped each other both on and off the job and in later years through many career changes, first to different branches, then to different positions within the executive levels of the organization.

Tom and Maria worked in separate departments at the same company, and met for the first time at the annual Christmas party. They began seeing each other and eventually were married.

Sara was hired as Eric's secretary, and shortly after she began working, Eric asked her out. A relationship developed that made everyone in the office uncomfortable and began to interfere with overall productivity. Eventually, they were both fired.

A married man began to have an affair with a single woman in his department. Although they tried to be discreet, rumors began circulating, and the relationship caused a great deal of internal stress in the department as suspicions of favoritism ran rampant and morale plummeted.

Dating can become a problem most often if the two people involved work closely together. Perhaps the worst situation is when one is a supervisor of the other—or when the relationship affects the social system already in place within the company. For example, one woman at an importing business was a diligent, responsible worker. But when a new executive began going out with the boss, her anger and resentment resulted in reduced productivity. She feared favoritism, and perceived her own work to be of less value than the work of the colleague who was seeing the boss. The anger of this longtime employee caused her to question seriously how much longer she could stay in what had been a pleasant work environment. Again, if you interfere with the way co-workers are accustomed to relating to each other, you risk bad feelings on the part of your colleagues. If you do end up dating someone in your office, here are a few guidelines.

1. Make clear in your mind the difference between your work relationship and your personal relationship.
2. Don't allow a "playing favorites" situation to develop: Don't accept special treatment or give special treatment. Be fair to everyone involved.
3. Get the job done efficiently, and don't use work time for personal pleasure or take yourselves out to lunch on the company.

In general, you will have to go out of your way to make sure that your relationship is not perceived by others as a hindrance to smooth functioning. If you do consider the workplace as a place to meet potential dates, it's important to follow the protocols of the social system. Understand the boundaries with the opposite sex in terms of what is appropriate, and bear in mind that what may seem like friendly banter to you could feel like sexual harassment to someone else. You don't know the nature of the other person's anxiety, so it is better to err on the side of caution when engaging in any kind of flirtation at work. Again, it's important to understand the chemistry.

Stop and Think
Right now, let's do an imagery exercise to make use of the social skills applications we've discussed so far. Sit down in a comfortable chair. Breathe in through your nose and out through your mouth. Feel yourself relaxing. Let your body grow limp and let your mind go. What feelings do you have about your current relationships?

Friendships

_____

_____

_____

_____

Dating relationships

_____

_____

_____

_____

What are your present goals regarding friendships?

_____

_____

_____

_____

What about dating relationships?

_____

_____

_____

_____

Now, formulate a plan for achieving these goals:

Friendships

_____

_____

_____

_____

Dating relationships

_____

_____

_____

_____

If there is a block, examine what it is. Write it down. What self-help strategies could you apply now to help you to get beyond the block and reconsider your friendship and dating goals?

_____

_____

_____

_____

YOUR WORK ENVIRONMENT

Remember the story of the computer genius who couldn't keep a job because of poor social skills? In every workplace, good interactive chemistry is essential, and the basis of good interactive chemistry is *good communication.* Where there is good chemistry, both parties understand each other and perceive a camaraderie that makes them feel like a productive part of a team. This section explores ways to apply your interactive skills in acquiring a job and developing your career once you have a job.

Job Acquisition

The entire job-acquisition process—considering job prospects, your personal and professional preparation, creating a résumé, going on a job interview—depends for success upon possessing social skills and managing anxiety. How you adapt to the stress of this process can play a major role. As with other aspects of interaction, anxiety can often keep you from getting the jobs you really want and would be well suited for. If you allow your anxiety to control you, you may avoid applying for a new position because you fear rejection. Or you may let the fear of failure keep you from accepting a new challenge, no matter how badly you would like to take the job. But let's look first at the job process and consider self-help techniques that will lead to a more rewarding, productive career. For people with social anxiety, low self-esteem is often a stumbling block to fulfillment in their careers: If you feel you are underqualified, you may hesitate to seek challenges, whether in a new company or within your current one.

I have worked with several men who say their self-esteem is low because they are not the stereotype of success: They do not wear a suit, carry a briefcase, or drive the latest-model car. In their minds, this is the most important measure of success. But they themselves are not failures. One of the men I can think of is a successful plumber, another has a telephone sales job, and a third manages a large warehouse. Still, they have doubts about their appeal to women because of their career choices; increasing their self-esteem will help them to see themselves in a new way. Success need not be defined by media standards such as the right clothes or an expensive automobile. Everyone is different. Your personal success can only be measured by your own personal fulfillment and productivity.

The following exercises should help to free you of your fears of self-expression and failure. Do not burden yourself with thoughts of "I can't," or "No one would hire me to . . ." Instead, let your imagination go, and allow yourself the freedom to explore your interests and ambitions. Don't worry about what others will think of your answers. These exercises are just for you.

Your Dream Job

In my clinical experience, I have found that many talented people have allowed anxiety to hamper them from pursuing their aspirations. They may achieve a measure of success but are unable to go as far as they could because they are afraid that acknowledging their goals could lead to embarrassment if those goals aren't met. This results in performance anxiety that hampers their chances of success. It is important to take risks in order to pursue what you really want out of life. In the next exercise, you will use your imagination to expand your potential. As you do this exercise, remember: No one ever succeeded without experiencing some failure along the way.

First, consider what areas you'd like to work in. List the jobs or career fields that interest you. For now, forget about whether you yourself would be qualified for the job. Just think about the jobs that you find most interesting or inspiring. (Even the most outlandish or unusual job—music video director, auctioneer, astronaut—should be listed, so long as it appeals to *you*.)

Now, without assessing whether you would be qualified for these particular jobs, write down the different factors that are important to you in a job. Examples might include: large (or small) organization; close to home; smoke-free environment; a chance to work with others; a chance to work outside.

_____

_____

_____

_____

In doing these exercises, you are exploring your values—the things that are important to you and that you find exciting. While you may not fulfill your grandest dreams, you can begin to look for ways to bring your current career into closer contact with your ideal career field. For example, after examining her dreams and goals, Shana, who had expressed an interest in space exploration, got a job at the Air & Space Museum gift shop in Washington, D.C. It may not get her to the moon, but she enjoys the museum atmosphere and keeps up to date with her favorite topic.

Career Possibilities
Next, let's examine your career prospects. Don't ask yourself what jobs you are qualified for. Instead, consider your skills. Even if you have been out of the work force for a long time, you may have experience managing a household or doing home improvement (handling finances, purchasing and cooking food, repairing plumbing and electricity, repairing your car, landscaping, caring for children, etc.). Take a moment to brainstorm the many things you do know how to do:

_____

_____

_____

_____

Now consider your formal education, training, and experience. Make a list of any relevant background information. You needn't create an actual résumé here. Just list the things you know how to do that are commonly considered job skills (typing, adding machine, carpentry, etc.).

_____

_____

_____

_____

With both your dreams and practical skills in mind, you can begin to create some real goals for yourself. What jobs might suit both your desires and qualifications? It's okay to be creative here. Again, don't allow anxiety or lack of self-esteem to hold you back. In Shana's case, she considered her current job as a bookstore clerk in a D.C.-area mall, her qualifications (cash register and inventory experience), her interest in space, and her own personal desire to work downtown in a place accessible by public transportation. The next time she visited her favorite museum, the idea hit her: Why not make a change that would match her interests and her qualifications?

When seeking a job or developing a career, put yourself in the mind-set of the Adult (your internal "computer"). As you think objectively about your situation, you will realize that there are issues of competition involved in putting yourself on the market. "I don't have enough experience." "The other person is more attractive." "I don't have as much education as the other candidates." Sound familiar? Answer the following questions:

What issues of competition do you feel you will have to face?

_____

_____

_____

_____

What are your feelings about these issues of competition?

_____

_____

_____

_____

What strategies will you apply?

_____

_____

_____

_____

When you are contemplating a job or career change, anxiety can be a large stumbling block. Hand in hand with anxiety goes low self-esteem, which can be especially detrimental during the job search. Employers respond best to those who project a comfortable, confident, and motivated self-image. If your anxiety is uncontrolled, it may mask your underlying confidence and motivation. As you do the exercises in this chapter, consider whether your anxiety is causing you to sell yourself short. If you find it difficult to list your capabilities and skills, you may wish to ask for some objective help from a friend, family member, or professional. And if anxiety is so high that it keeps you from focusing effectively on these exercises, you should try to use the various stress management strategies you have learned thus far in order to approach the project from a perspective of personal calm.

Stop and Think
Again, let's take some time to step and think about the issues in this section. Sit back in a comfortable chair, breathe deeply, allow your

body to grow limp and your mind to let go, and integrate the issues into your thinking. Now, list the ways that anxiety is negatively affecting your career:

_____

_____

_____

_____

What are some strategies for controlling career-related anxiety?

_____

_____

_____

_____

Preparing for the Job Search
The first phase of getting ready for a job search is mental prepara-tion. This is a resolve that you will do what it takes to succeed—even if it means dealing with rejection time and again. *Rejection is a natural part of the job search.* Therefore, it is important for the person with social anxiety to measure motivation. Adapting the motivation exercise from Chapter 5, let's measure your degree of motivation on a scale of 1 to 5, with 1 being the lowest and 5 the highest.

5: *Extremely Motivated.* You recognize your potential for happiness and fulfillment on the job and feel a sense of urgency about remedying the problems that inhibit your career success and thus affect your overall quality of life. You are totally indepen-dent and take responsibility for problem solving. You perse-vere, keeping in mind the old saying, "If at first you don't succeed, try, try again." You haven't given up, and you un-derstand that the route to success has not only ups but downs.

4: *Substantially Motivated.* You understand the importance of resolving problems. You are fairly consistent, and are able to
commit to many of the projects you wish to complete. The job
acquisition process is no exception. You want to create change,
but you sometimes question whether it is worth the effort—
especially when you meet with failure.

3: *Fairly Motivated.* You know *something* is wrong, but you aren't
ready to admit it is the quality of your interactive chemistry in
the workplace. At times you want to change, but you vacillate
over it, saying it's "not worth it," or "things are fine the way
they are," even though deep down you know that it *would* be
worth it and things are *not* fine. You hesitate to take responsibility for your own job satisfaction, refusing to see your role in
the reality of the situation. You may give up on the task at
hand, especially when the anxiety of confronting your fears
increases to the point that you are uncomfortable.

2: *No Real Motivation.* You are considering change, but this is
mainly at the urging of others on whom you are dependent—in
order to avoid conflict with them, you tend to agree, however
halfheartedly, to try harder to be independent, seek new job
challenges, and confront the situations that obstruct your productivity and fulfillment at work. You have succumbed to the
problem—you are allowing your anxiety and fear to control
you. As you see it, there is very little hope. Occasionally,
though, you do have positive feelings, but these are quickly
overwhelmed by feelings of anxiety when you are confronted
with stress.

1: *Nonfunctional.* Motivation is an abstract concept for you—
social anxiety is something that others experience. You maintain that you are content in your current work situation, that
you don't want or need to change, despite a general uneasiness
or lack of interest in what you do. You probably would not
even look at your career situation were it not for the consistent
pressure of others, and even then, you usually remain in an
extreme state of denial. Since you avoid confronting career
issues, it is difficult to point out interactive problems (which

don't come up because you don't examine them), although they are present, totally camouflaged.

What is your current career motivation level? If it is not high enough, why not? What do you need to do to increase your motivation?

THE JOB SEARCH

To be successful in the working world, you must steel yourself against rejection, whether you are a salesman, a grant writer, or even a job candidate. Employers often interview many, many candidates for a given job opening, and you will probably get more no's than yeses. But don't take it personally. That's just part of the process. (Remember the salesman's strategy of thinking that each rejection brings him closer to a sale!) With the right attitude, any rejection you do experience can give you valuable information about the job search process. Practice makes perfect, so look at your interviews as a chance to perfect your interactive skills in the working world. In fact, it is sometimes appropriate to inquire about the possibility of an "informational interview"—in which you are not applying for a job but simply meeting briefly (half an hour or so) with a person whose career field interests you to ask questions and tour the place of business. (This is most appropriate when you are considering a career change.) Either way, if a suitable position is not available but you have made a good contact, you may get a call when an appropriate job does open up. Keep in mind that it is up to you to create opportunities for yourself. Do not wait for them to happen to you!

Listed below are three basic rules that will help you become a successful candidate. Remember, however, that you need not be offered a job in every case to consider yourself successful. Rather, you are successful if you keep the job search process going in a professional manner. In working with countless people in the process of looking for a job, I have concluded that, for those who are currently unemployed, the full-time job should be just that: looking for a job. For those who currently have a job, but are openly seeking

a better position with new challenges or a higher salary, take comfort in knowing you are working from a position of strength; use that
knowledge to add to your self-esteem. In all cases, see yourself from
the employer's point of view. In their eyes, you are a more likely
candidate if you behave professionally before and after the interview
(with appropriate inquiry and follow-up—more on that later) and if
you interact appropriately during the interview itself. As you continue to look for a job, remember the following tips for success:

1. When you call about a job prospect, get as much information
   as you can about the position and the company—including
   the name of the person doing the interviewing. Don't be put
   off by feelings of anxiety—you have a right to "interview"
   them too. If possible, go to the library and research the company. By the time of your interview, you will feel more confident—and less anxious—because you will have resources
   from which to draw during your conversation.
2. If you have time to mail your résumé before your scheduled
   interview, do so. But be sure to include a cover letter as well.
   While the résumé gives background information about you,
   the cover letter explains why you are writing and briefly describes what makes you a good candidate for the job. Don't
   allow low self-esteem to make you afraid to "sell yourself"!
   Only you can say why you would be an asset to the company.
   And one more thing—write the letter to a particular person,
   not "To Whom It May Concern" or "Dear Sir or Madam."
   Most of the time, a prospective employer's receptionist is willing to tell you exactly whom to contact. Use courtesy titles
   ("Dear Ms. Smith"), unless the person is someone you already
   know on a first-name basis.
3. Do follow up. An appropriate measure of assertiveness goes a
   long way. Most employers appreciate someone who is diligent
   and communicates a genuine interest in the position. But
   don't be aggressive. Limit your contact to a follow-up note, a
   phone call two weeks later, and perhaps a third one a few
   weeks after that. Be sure to let them know that if another,

more appropriate, position comes along, you would be interested to learn about it. Again, by communicating properly and creating your own opportunities, you can achieve some control over your own destiny.

The Résumé
Your résumé is like an advertisement for you as a job candidate. It should present you in the best possible light. Consult reference books for appropriate formats. Styles vary, but a résumé should be typewritten or typeset, with your name and address clearly displayed at the top, and your employment history and educational background listed below in an organized fashion. If you wish, you may include a heading for personal interests—this can often be a good ice-breaker during the interview itself.

People with social anxiety often find it very useful to pay for professional assistance in preparing a résumé. Having an objective person categorize your skills and experience can be extremely helpful, especially if you are reentering the work force or are experiencing difficulty putting your background into the appropriate format.

Remember, your résumé is often your first contact with a prospective employer, and it may determine whether you will get an interview in the first place. It is your calling card and should be impeccably professional in appearance and content.

A Professional Image
The image you project begins with the first phone call you make. If you feel some initial anxiety, remind yourself that other people are calling too; you are entitled to inquire as well. Be professional, giving your name and the reason for your call, and then ask the name of the appropriate person to contact. At smaller establishments, the person who answers the phone may well be the person doing the hiring, so you should project a professional image from the outset. Your phone manner, including language, tone of voice, and level of assertiveness, is reflected even in a short telephone conversation. *That first phone call is what may or may not get you in the door for an interview.* If you don't conduct yourself professionally, that

may be as far as it goes. For example, I once received a phone call from someone interested in a position I had advertised. The man who called about the job—who may not have realized that "the boss" himself would answer the phone—was eating as he spoke to me. If he cared so little about the position that he could not make the effort to behave professionally, how would he act on the job? It wasn't worth my time to find out!

To prepare yourself mentally for the initial phone call, determine first of all how you would like to be perceived. This behavior re-hearsal exercise will help to put you in the proper frame of mind for making the call. Sit back in a comfortable chair, close your eyes, take a deep breath . . . let go. Now, use the TV screen in your head to picture yourself making the phone call. See, hear, smell, touch the scene. See yourself being confident, communicating clearly, and receiving a favorable response. Above all, you are relaxed and nat-ural.

As you talk, what aspects of your personality would you like to emphasize?

_____

_____

What do you want the other person to think about you?

_____

_____

It may help you to jot down a few notes to alleviate any fear of becoming tongue-tied—your name, the position or company you are interested in, how you can be reached, any questions you may have. You won't be reading it verbatim, but it may be comforting to refer back to it now and then as your conversation progresses. Know your message clearly. Have a plan for exactly what information you want to convey and what you intend to find out. It helps to visualize your success in the call beforehand, and if you feel anxious, to do relaxation exercises before you get on the phone.

The importance of your image continues with any subsequent contact you make prior to the interview, such as your cover letter and résumé.

The Interview

The largest determining factor in whether you get a job is usually the interview itself. You've made impressions all along—with your telephone call and your cover letter and résumé. Now it is imperative that you create a favorable impression when at last you get a chance to talk in person. This can be the ultimate test for a socially anxious person: After all, you are being evaluated on your performance in the interview situation. Activate your PMA, then build up your energy level. If you have followed this program, you now possess the self-help techniques you need to help you through the situation. *You can prepare yourself for success.*

As with any interaction, good chemistry is important. The prospective employer will think hard about whether you will fit in—both from a production perspective and an interactive one. The employer may think: Will this employee help to increase the bottom line? Will he interact well as part of the team within the social system that already exists here? In fact, your chemistry with the interviewer may be more important than your background and experience.

One twenty-three-year-old woman who held a fairly junior position in an advertising firm nonetheless found a good media position with one of the networks, not only because of her skills and potential, but because of her ability to gauge a situation and react quickly on her feet. What happened? The interviewer began listing the qualifications necessary for the position that was available: "Self-starter, motivated, creative . . ." "Oh," she said, after the executive paused, "you've just read my résumé!" That kind of confidence, and an ability to take risks not only amused the interviewer; it displayed some of the very skills the position required!

The fact that interactive chemistry plays such a large role in getting a job has both positive and negative aspects. The positive side is that a lack of experience doesn't necessarily mean you can't get a particular job. Often, with the right basic education and life skills, you can make a strong enough impression based on who you are and how capable you seem that the employer may feel you are trainable for the job at hand. In my office, for example, we interviewed a number of experienced applicants for a secretarial position, only to choose a woman whose office skills were not as good as several others', but who had the right chemistry, and who we felt would fit best into the existing system in the office. It's often easier to teach or perfect the required skills than it is to try to force an interactive chemistry that just isn't there. The downside of interactive chemistry is that even if you *do* have the required skills, you may be turned down if you don't "click" with the interviewer. (Later, you will learn more about how to develop a positive rapport with an interviewer.)

Now use behavior rehearsal to imagine the interview itself. Sit back in a comfortable chair, close your eyes, breathe deeply . . . let your body grow limp and your mind let go. See the situation very clearly. What are you wearing? What does the office look like? Use all your senses to create the scenario. You are walking into the office. What does the interviewer say to you? How do you respond? See yourself in control—confident, relaxed. Develop this image clearly. Write down what you see:

_____

_____

_____

_____

As you do this exercise, distracting thoughts may come into your mind. Let them pass. Eventually, your mind will drift back to the exercise. Use your deep breathing as a centering technique.

Appearance

Like it or not, appearance counts, especially in the workplace. Dressing appropriately and professionally is a minimum requirement when applying for a job. Do whatever you can do to make a favorable impression. Dressing appropriately is a way to say that you care about the interview, that it is important to you, and that you take it seriously. It also says you will make an effort to behave professionally once you are with the company. Keep in mind that you are owed nothing when you go on an interview. But behaving professionally by following appropriate business etiquette will nearly always gain you the courtesy of professional treatment in return.

The following ideas will help you be prepared to make the best impression possible. In previous exercises, you have examined your self-image. Now, look at yourself and get feedback from others on your overall appearance. Not only must you look neat and well groomed for a job interview, but your overall image should be appropriate to the job, the company, and the industry you are hoping to enter. You can determine the appropriate image by observing the appearance and attitude of those currently in the area you are looking into. But even where casual attire is appropriate for those already in the workplace, clean, pressed clothes and a neat appearance will be appreciated. One young photographer I know of inquired about the style of dress at the newspaper he was interviewing with; informed that most people wore casual clothes, he chose to do the same. At the interview, the editor gently teased him about wearing jeans (she herself was in khaki pants and a sports shirt). "I guess your suit is at the cleaners," she said, chuckling. But her point was made. Making the effort shows that you take the interview seriously.

Second, you should carry yourself as though you are confident and self-assured. Use self-help techniques such as internal coaching to tell yourself you can do it. Focus on your past successes, and hold your body as if you were unstoppable. Breathe deeply, with an abundance of self-confidence. Your goal is to convey an image of being comfortable with yourself in order to make the other person feel comfortable with you.

This time, use behavior rehearsal to focus on the way you will look during an interview. Sit back. Close your eyes. Breathe deeply. Picture yourself with the appropriate appearance for an interview. Imagine your posture. Now, write down a list of the things you might wear for an interview:

_____

_____

_____

Are there things you need to acquire (new shoes, a folio for notes)?

_____

_____

_____

Communication Skills
As most employers will tell you, performance is based upon your ability both to assess and to respond. You need to be able to assess the person you are speaking to in order to understand what his or her needs are, how the person makes decisions, and what he or she finds valuable. Then, you should be able to respond in an appropriate manner, pointing out your assets and how you could benefit the company were you to be hired.

In the workplace, social anxiety can impair a person's memory and therefore communication skills. A pharmaceutical salesman in one of my groups said that when he made sales calls to the doctors in his territory, he would become anxious and find himself at a loss for words. He couldn't communicate well because he was distracted, and he therefore sought to learn self-help strategies that would improve his sales ability.

On the Job
Leaders in business rank communication as the number-one skill needed for success. Once hired, you will use a variety of basic communication skills—the same ones you relied on during the interview process. What can interfere with good communication in

the workplace? Stress. In my experience as a stress management consultant for various corporations, I have identified two primary types of stress issues. One type is exhibited by the person who is doing too much or is "burnt out"—suffering from attitudinal, emotional, or physical exhaustion. The solution? If stress management strategies do not provide significant relief, modifying the requirements of the job or even a new job may be the best answer. The second category is what I call being "understressed." People suffering from this kind of stress usually have had the same job for many years and are no longer able to exert creativity or to feel a sense of challenge. For them, there is no positive energy flow where the job is concerned. Both types of stress are dangerous. *Your stress level is a major component of the quality of your overall health and well-being.*

One person I treated worked for a transit system checking the subway tracks. He made a decent living, but his job was not terribly challenging. He spent most of the time alone in his office, and actually got into the habit of bringing model airplane kits to work to occupy his time. In his case, having too little to do was extremely stressful. His self-esteem suffered, and he began having anxiety attacks on those occasions when he did have to interact. He would drink to calm his nerves, even in preparation for a game of golf—and he was an excellent golfer! In time, this man learned to seek out social contact on the job, and to ask for new challenges that made him feel more valued and productive. By adding to his repertoire of self-help techniques, he was able to get the most out of his interactions both at work and in his personal life.

Use your self-help techniques to get the most out of your workplace interactions and take the risks that will enhance your productivity. Risks? Yes, communication with other people is a risk that all of us engage in every day. The degree of your success boils down to the quality of your communication in the daily business encounters that you choose to risk.

Getting More Out of Your Current Job
In spite of the potential payoffs, perhaps you have allowed interactive anxiety to stand in your way in the past, letting the fear of

rejection on the job or in the business environment hold you back from career success. The suggestions below will provide you with ways to put the various social skills described in preceding chapters to use in helping you succeed in a variety of business situations. In today's competitive climate, good communication skills are an absolutely vital part of getting and keeping a job. Without them, you have almost no chance for upward mobility within a given business structure.

If you would like to stay with your current company but want to move up and to feel comfortable doing so, you must face your anxiety and learn to become part of the interactive system in your workplace. One accountant for a large corporation remained stuck in his middle-management job for several years, worried about what his colleagues might think of him if they got to know him personally. He never had lunch with co-workers, and seldom inquired about them, except to follow up on work-related matters. The result was that four years later, he was exactly where he'd started, but miserable and stress-ridden to boot. Eventually, he left the company and made sure to address his anxiety issues in order to avoid a similar pattern the next time around.

If your anxiety is interfering with your motivation, ask yourself the following questions.

1. What specific payoffs can I get by improving my communication abilities on the job?

   _____

2. How can I overcome any obstacles that may be standing in my way?

   _____

3. What will it cost me financially and emotionally if I don't?

   _____

   In five years? In twenty years?

   _____

4. What will I miss out on in terms of job satisfaction or personal fulfillment?

___

The more you focus on these questions, the greater your motivation will be to stretch beyond your current limits and actually put to use the interactive skills we are discussing.

Communication Skills and Career Success
Many people with social anxiety make the unfortunate mistake of assuming that if they communicate very little, they will be less likely to meet with failure. Exactly the opposite is usually the case. Often, people with significant social anxiety give very little of themselves and are therefore not a part of the effective chemistry necessary for overall productivity and fulfillment. Usually, their reticence is the result of an effort to blend in, but rightly or wrongly, such people are perceived by others as uninteresting and unimportant—the equivalent of death in the workplace. Instead of creating the desired safety net, the persona incognito provides the surest way to be ignored on the job and considered generally ineffective.

PERSONAL PROFILE FOR EFFECTIVE COMMUNICATION

Consider the following list of twelve characteristics that are central to communicating both in an interview and on the job. If you feel you are lacking in a particular category, you can use the explanations and suggestions given to enhance your interactive ability in the workplace.

1. *Activation of PMA.* Use positive thinking techniques such as internal coaching.
2. *Physical appearance.* Make sure to dress appropriately for the event. In most interviews, business attire (a suit or sport coat and tie for men; a suit, dress, or tailored pants for women) is

recommended. What you wear to the interview communicates not only how important the event is to you but your ability to assess a situation and how you should behave in it. Appropriate grooming is essential, both in an interview and on the job.

3. *Posture.* Carry yourself with confidence. Let your posture communicate that you are a winner. Keep your face on a vertical plane, spine straight, shoulders comfortably back. By simply straightening up and using the diaphragmatic breathing you learned in Chapter 6 (which proper posture encourages), you will feel much better about yourself. Others will perceive you in a more positive light as well.

4. *Rate of speech.* Your rate of speech ought to be appropriate for the specific situation and person or persons it is intended for. Too fast is annoying, and too slow is boring. A good way to pace your speech is to speak at close to the rate of the person who is talking to you.

5. *Eye contact.* Absolutely essential for successful communication. Occasionally, you should avert your gaze briefly in order to avoid staring. But try not to look down at your lap or let your eyes wander all around the room as you speak. This suggests a lack of confidence and an inability to stay on track.

6. *Facial expressions.* You gain more credibility when you are open and expressive. The warmer personality will seem stronger and more confident. And perhaps most important, remember to smile in conversation. If you seem interested and enthusiastic, it will enhance the chemistry between you and the interviewer or your supervisor.

You can develop the ability to use facial expressions to your advantage through a kind of biofeedback that makes use of the mirror and continuously experimenting in real life. Look at your reflection for several minutes. Practice being relaxed and create the expressions that are appropriate. Do you look interested? Alert? Motivated? Practice responding to an interviewer. Impress the "muscle memory" of these expressions into your mind.

7. *Energy.* Your degree of personal energy and enthusiasm has a great deal to do with whether or not someone will want to hear the message you are trying to communicate. Believing in what you have to say also helps you to overcome interactive inhibition. If you care passionately about something, your life force will flow naturally, energizing you, and you will be able to focus better on getting the message out to others.

Before entering an interactive situation, try "turning yourself on." Put yourself in a peak state of enthusiasm. This might involve playing a piece of music that makes you feel great or thinking back to a time when you felt absolutely unstoppable. By accessing memories of a time when you felt energetic, you can induce the same state again.

8. *Pitch and tone of voice.* Speaking in a monotone is a quick way to turn off any audience. Practice using a variety of vocal qualities in your speech. Try using a tape recorder to make sure your voice is pleasant to listen to, and that your message matches your tone of voice. People pick up more from the voice tone than from the actual words you use.

9. *Animation and gestures.* Don't be afraid to use your body, especially your hands, to use moderate gestures during conversation. Gestures send signals of enthusiasm and energy. Whenever you speak, you are essentially on stage, and appropriate gesturing helps you to communicate.

10. *Ability to hold interest of others.* In an interview, be prepared to discuss a variety of topics—not just the job you are applying for. And be sure to ask questions (prepare some in advance if necessary).

11. *Commitment.* This attribute has to do with caring passionately—about yourself, the other person, and the message you are trying to convey. If you convey that you can make a positive difference in the prospective workplace, you are much more likely to influence the interviewer and leave him or her with a lasting positive impression of you.

12. *Ability to make others feel comfortable.* In order to make others comfortable, you must first appear comfortable yourself. Prac-

tice looking more comfortable and relaxed by watching yourself in the mirror.

Encouraging others to speak openly and freely also helps them to feel more comfortable and at ease with you. Dominating a conversation makes others feel uncomfortable very quickly. Asking others for their opinions, feelings, and values opens them up to you equally quickly. In an interview situation, it is usually a good idea to let the interviewer do most of the talking. Again, prepare some questions to get a two-way conversation going.

All twelve elements are essential for good communication. They should work together in harmony, and each element should support the overall message you are communicating.

Taking Others In: Learning to Listen and Watch

Any new enterprise requires market research—analyzing the marketplace to determine whether there is a need among the public for a product or service. Similarly, the more you can take in about other people, the better you will be able to provide a message that they will find worth taking in. Listening and watching people allows you to find out more about them before you even say anything, in order to make sure that the message you give is one for which there is a demand, and to ensure that you can communicate successfully.

Up the Career Ladder

Developing your ability as a productive worker others can count on is the best way to move up the career ladder. And the more productive you are—interacting effectively with co-workers, serving as a valuable team member, getting the job done—the more rewarding your work is likely to be. If social anxiety has prevented you from being as productive and fulfilled as you could be, make a commitment to yourself to learn the strategies that will take you beyond interactive inhibition to a new level of success. Just as interactive chemistry is important one on one, group chemistry is important to those who work as part of an organization. What is group chemistry?

In every workplace, there is a social system in place, and to be an effective employee, you need to perfect your skills of decoding and becoming a part of whatever system exists.

Group Chemistry

What happens when an employee fails to participate actively in the social system? Randolph was a fifty-year-old ad executive hired by a major agency to coordinate media issues. One of his colleagues, who was somewhat junior to Randolph according to the formal hierarchy, felt threatened by his superiority, and decided he would do whatever he could to undermine his success. Randolph became aware of this problem almost immediately, and although it would have been entirely within the bounds of office protocol for him to raise the issue, he felt anxious about confronting it. He did nothing about the problem and after a few years it had escalated to the point that Randolph found it necessary to find another job—all this because his lack of assertiveness had allowed the other person to usurp his authority.

Jason is an example of someone who simply didn't grasp the social hierarchy of his work environment quickly enough. Hired to create new programs in a fast-paced social service agency, Jason spent the first two months creating elaborate background materials to assess how everyone fit together in the system. His problem was that he was too analytical about the social hierarchy. As a result he wasn't productive and was soon fired. He was so concerned about the social system that all he did was analyze it; in this way, he avoided actually becoming a part of the system and ultimately was denied the chance to become part of it. Understanding the hierarchy or social system in your workplace takes time and thought, and every workplace is different. But once you see the way things work, it is vital that you participate within the system. Two types of hierarchy are common in business practice.

Formal hierarchy: The formal hierarchy is the structure of power within the organization—titles such as CEO, vice president, administrative assistant, and so on. The formal hierarchy may or may not match the actual structure of power. Ask questions to determine who is granted formal power in the workplace. This will tell you about de jure power, or power as it is formally delegated. But determining who has the most influence and sway may not be possible unless you yourself can observe it from within the organization.

Informal hierarchy: Often there is also an informal hierarchy, whereby individuals without impressive titles have power through their ability to get things done or persuade higher-ups to follow their recommended courses of action. Watch how work gets done in order to determine who has de facto power in the workplace.

Tom is an example of someone who has a good deal of power within the informal hierarchy, though his formal title of administrative assistant to the president is fairly junior in the formal hierarchy. His ability to get the job done is impressive to those who know what is going on in the organization, and his position as right-hand man makes him visible to many of the executives whose opinions matter most in the large corporation where he works. As a result, when an important project comes up, those higher up in the company hierarchy often bypass Tom's boss and go straight to him. After all, it is clear to them that the president delegates most detail-oriented projects to Tom. Hence, Tom is treated with much more respect than other people of his "rank" within the organization.

Similarly, your understanding of the structure of power within the organization you work for will determine who you should go to in order to get particular tasks completed, and how you should interact with them.

And remember not to discount those who appear by formal standards to be your workplace inferiors. There is a story about a politician who learned a memorable lesson about de facto power. One of his speech writers requested a sizable raise, and the politician turned him down in a condescending manner. When the politician delivered his next public speech, he flipped a page mid-sentence, expecting to make an important point. Instead, he found that his speech abruptly ended with the words: "You're on your own now!"

Don't take "underlings" for granted. They are the foundation of most big companies.

BUSINESS AND PLEASURE

Often, people with social anxiety feel comforted by the routine of day-in day-out office work, but informal meetings and gatherings still cause them anxiety. Still, it is better not to forgo them, because they can provide tremendous opportunities for you to move up in your career—and make new friends and associates in the process. "Networking" is the current word in fashion for this activity, which can help to catapult you in your professional aspirations.

Preparing for a Business-Related Social Function

1. Activate your PMA.
2. Take a few minutes alone before the event—in the car, outside the room.
3. Utilize relaxation techniques.
4. Think about your goals for the event.
5. Visualize your success.
6. Think of a series of self-praise phrases that will give you energy and self-confidence. For example: "I am feeling confident and competent, and I will express this to all of those I meet."
7. Boost your personal energy level up.
8. Walk with confidence into the event.
9. Focus on something other than yourself. Find out about other people and look into their concerns and interests. If you find your attention becoming too self-absorbed, see what you can notice about the appearance of others at the event.
10. Continue to initiate and follow up on conversations throughout, using the suggestions in the previous chapter to propel your interactions along.

Introducing Yourself

You're ready to walk in. How can you remain composed and confident, with your social anxiety in check? To take the edge off approaching strangers, try not to think of them as "strangers." Look for things you share in common with them. When you are attending an event or function with a specific purpose, such as a professional association meeting, a little advance planning will help you to determine some interests you share with members of the group. Use your common interests and values as the basis for conversation, following the guidelines in Chapter 8.

Your professional introduction itself should be planned and practiced—though it is a good idea to keep it brief: "Hi, I'm John Smith, from Consolidated Metals," or, "Mary Jones of the *Tarleton News*. Glad to meet you." Don't go into any detail right away. People need time to absorb your name and affiliation. When there are more appropriate details to share, you can follow up with a comment such as "I was recently transferred to this branch from Baltimore," or, "This is my first meeting. How long have you belonged to this association?" The way you introduce yourself should make the other person feel relaxed and at ease with you and offer the opportunity for further conversation. It should be natural and relaxed. Using a business card as a prop is okay, but be sure not to force your card on anyone, or to be the only person handing them out. Watch what others are doing. If it seems appropriate, then go ahead. If there is someone in particular with whom you would like to follow up later on a professional basis, it may be appropriate to ask for their card first; then offer yours.

Breaking In

Often, you walk into a business event, and it seems as if everyone is already engaged in conversation. Don't let that throw you. There is a way to move toward the edge of a conversation without intruding. To avoid interrupting a private conversation, don't approach two people who appear engaged in intense conversation. Instead, approach groups of three or more people. Get close to the group, and watch the key speakers. Maintain eye contact with them without staring, and when you in turn receive eye contact, or they move to include you or otherwise begin directing their comments toward you as well as the rest of the group, you can begin to look for a place to interject a comment and gently move into the conversation. In the meantime, once you seem to have been physically included in the circle, it is appropriate to interact.

Remember that *communication works both ways*, so be sure to include others from the periphery into your conversations as well. They will appreciate your friendliness, and may well seek you out next time.

Breaking Out

When you attend a professional meeting or other gathering, your networking goal is to meet a number of people, so you may want to limit your conversations. If it is appropriate (and genuine), you might say, "I would enjoy hearing more about your company. Could I contact you sometime to discuss it further?" At that point, an exchange of business cards means you've made a new contact. Or you may at some time find yourself in a conversation with someone you'd like to get away from—whether because you are bored or you simply see someone else you've been waiting to meet or follow up with. It is important to know a polite, professional way to end one conversation and move on smoothly to the next. Wait until you have just finished a comment (when you are in control of the conversation), then smile and say something like "It's been nice talking with you," and move on. There's no need for a lengthy explanation. Just head casually for another part of the room.

Putting It All Together

Now more than ever, in today's tough business climate, you need to assemble a practical mix of job skills and interactive know-how in order to succeed in the job market. Being a successful part of your team at work means knowing how to interact effectively and clearly. Social anxiety need not interfere with your quest for career fulfillment. As you work through this self-help program, continue to refer to these exercises to refine the job-related skills you need to work on most. Are you committed to becoming more productive and fulfilled through enhanced understanding of workplace chemistry?

As always, personal fulfillment is more attainable when you have a group of friends and acquaintances you can spend time with away from work. Having fun, pursuing hobbies, talking things over in good times and bad—all of this requires friendship, and true friendship requires quality interaction. With these strategies at hand, you're on your way to a more productive, enriching life.

CHAPTER TEN

Making Community Resources
Work for You

You've begun to master several techniques for controlling your anxiety. You're learning the finer points of interaction and studying ways to apply your interactive skills. The next step is to add community resources—relevant agencies, groups, and organizations—to your self-help program. As you consider your particular needs, look to your own community for ways to enhance your social system: Parks and recreation departments, churches and synagogues, singles groups, self-help groups, clubs, volunteer organizations, business associations—there is an infinite array of resources to choose from. Contact your local chamber of commerce, consult newspapers for upcoming activities, and even inquire at area shops about any clubs or groups that share an interest (for example, ask at a garden center about a garden club, at a bookstore about a book club, and so on). Working through the exercises in this book is merely one component of a total self-help program. To progress from background knowledge to practical application, you must venture beyond your home and workplace (and beyond the confines of the therapist's office, if you are in counseling). For people with social anxiety an outside system of resources is the best place to work on interactive difficulties. Here are three excellent reasons to use community resources:

1. *To facilitate self-help.* Conquering social anxiety necessitates interaction and involvement within the community, which is

your laboratory. Using community resources creates a practical means of refining your skills and so moving forward on your individual map for change.

2. *To diminish loneliness.* Becoming part of the community provides the opportunity to develop personal and professional contacts that can enhance your life in many ways.

3. *To network.* Community involvement will not only give you the chance to improve your interactive skills, but will allow you to promote your academic or work life as well as your social life. Building connections on different levels can be the key. Any setting can provide a good opportunity for networking. In fact, I met the writer who helped me with this book in a fairly unlikely place—on the basketball court! A mutual friend introduced us, and when the subject of our professional interests came up, we saw the opportunity to work together on this project. You never know!

THE GROUP THING

My definition of a group is four or more unrelated people who get together for a common purpose. Group situations are a part of life: Groups make up society and are a component of the social process. If you have interactive difficulties, joining a group can be an important part of overcoming them. Participating in a group takes the stress and anxiety management techniques and interactive skills out of the abstract and into the realm of reality. The practical experience you gain from placing yourself in social situations is every bit as important as the previous steps of identifying your symptoms, learning to control them, and developing and refining interactive skills.

There are many different types of groups: social, recreational, therapeutic, political, educational . . . the possibilities are endless. Make a list of your interests, and then survey your local media— newspapers, radio, magazines, TV—to see whether there might be groups whose interests mesh with your own. In particular, watch for events sections in newspapers and on local cable TV stations. Below are some examples (you might want to make a note of those of particular interest to you):

Book clubs
Self-help groups (Alcoholics Anonymous, Single Parents, Emotions Anonymous, etc.)
Outings clubs (hiking, fishing, travel)
Dance clubs (folk dance, ballroom, swing)
Singing clubs (church choirs, barber shop quartets, etc.)
Volunteer organizations (working with the elderly, the handicapped, children, environmental or other causes, fund-raising, etc.)
Political campaigns
Charities
Religious organizations
Athletic groups

A local newcomers' organization such as Welcome Wagon, or the chamber of commerce, the library, or any other resource center may have a list of area groups, clubs, and other organizations, along with contact people and their phone numbers.

A word of caution: Staying committed to a group is vital to your ultimate success at improving your interactive skills. Give a group a chance before deciding it's not for you. My experience has shown that people with social anxiety tend to be predisposed to reject a group—often as a way of protecting *themselves* from being rejected. I hear excuses such as these all the time: "I don't really understand the purpose of the group." "These people are not like me." If you are having difficulties, you too may try to avoid confronting your anxiety by dismissing the group or its members. But stick with it! Attend meetings a reasonable number of times before you decide whether or not the group is for you.

Identifying your problem is not enough. Group experience is important. If you have trouble interacting, there is simply no substitute for practice. Linda is a twenty-six-year-old woman who lives with her parents and works as a nurse in a city clinic. She does not have trouble meeting people; in fact, she encounters people all day long. But she does have tremendous difficulty moving past the initial stage of a relationship. Her specific social anxiety—fear of closeness—hampers her efforts to develop emotional or physical intimacy. Linda had spent almost ten years in therapy on and off when she came to me. I immediately noticed how resistant to change she was.

As part of my program she participated in a social therapy group, though she strongly resisted joining it. She did attend, but under great protest. Soon, she began dating one of the men in the group. The relationship ended inappropriately, and Linda began to avoid the weekly meetings. Time and again, I explained to her that she had to confront the group and her particular problems. Eventually, she was able to return. As she came to trust the continuity that the group offered, Linda began successfully to confront her problems with intimacy. She developed several close platonic friendships through the group and appears well on her way to achieving a satisfying personal life.

Groups are, in a sense, a microcosm of the real world. In all groups, there are leaders and followers . . . and many people who fall somewhere in between. Some groups are professionally led, and some are self- or volunteer-directed. In every group, there will be people you like and people you don't, people who seek you out, and people who do not. Understanding and joining in the group process and making it work for you is what is important. Experiment with several groups, if you like, to find the ones that you enjoy the most. Strive to find a group in which you think you would feel comfortable expressing yourself or interacting with others and which has an appropriate meaning for you (a self-help group should address your particular issues; a hobby club should focus on something you enjoy). Attend the group a few times to get a sense of how members interact with each other. If the thought of doing so still causes you anxiety, continue working on stress management, and remain fairly passive in the group until you feel more comfortable.

In my own social therapy group program, our purpose is to help individuals learn how to control social anxiety and refine their interactive skills. Social anxiety is a people-oriented problem, which makes group experience important both theoretically and practically. Some traditional therapists have called my program unorthodox because it encourages patients to talk to and learn from each other—as opposed to the isolation and protection offered by many of the more conservative therapies. But I say that social interaction is something you learn by doing. My groups are places to practice, make mistakes, and experience success in a supportive yet challenging environment.

Of course, even in such a supportive setting, resistance still arises. In a "friendly" forum, stressors can be explored and confronted more easily, however, and I have found that the degree to which a person uses the group is often a good indicator of how well he or she is progressing therapeutically. Good attendance shows effort and commitment; poor attendance indicates that a person is giving in to anxiety. I've heard all the excuses and manipulations—canceling plans is typical of people with avoidance problems related to social anxiety. (I'm sometimes tempted to open a garage to repair all those cars that break down on group night!) Yet often, after overcoming the initial stage of anxiety, many participants enjoy the process.

As you consider the option of incorporating various kinds of groups in your community into your self-help program, remember that groups can be a very important component of your map for change. Groups can provide you with the opportunity to practice the skills that are crucial to your success. Make sure that your expectations are realistic and that you understand the purpose and the limitations of whatever group you join.

THERAPEUTIC GROUPS

Individual therapists, mental health clinics, counseling centers, hospitals, and in some cases community centers and schools are all places that may offer therapeutic groups. There are two basic types of therapy groups: those composed of people with common objectives such as weight loss or controlling an alcohol or drug problem, and those that are heterogeneous and include people with many different types of issues.

Unfortunately, our research has shown that there are currently few groups designed specifically for individuals with social anxiety. Those that are available tend to be short term. My interpretation of this finding is that the therapists and agencies who are offering the programs have trouble holding a group together for very long because of the specific nature of the clientele. In our program, once a group has started, we keep it going (though naturally some people come and go).

Because of the limited amount of research available, with very few clinical programs combining individual and group therapy geared specifically toward the socially anxious, it will be difficult to find a group that addresses all the issues that pertain to you. Nevertheless, finding a group that addresses at least some of your issues and fears can be extremely beneficial. You can adapt the principles and techniques set down in this book in combination with group therapy. My experience has clearly demonstrated that many individuals of all ages who are looking for help with their social anxiety can have a difficult time asserting themselves productively in a group setting. Individual therapy may then be warranted for backup support and encouragement. *The most important thing you can do for yourself is to be committed and assertive.* Bring specific issues into the group. That's what it's for.

SELF-HELP GROUPS

In recent times, we have seen a proliferation of self-help groups for all kinds of ills. Self-help groups, which rely on the dynamic of group support and guidance rather than on the expertise of trained professionals, are available in most communities across the United States. Check your local newspaper for listings and meeting times, and look into the local possibilities through sources at libraries, hospitals, perhaps your chamber of commerce. Most groups are open to the public and welcome one-time visitors.

There are pros and cons to self-help groups, and you should weigh them carefully:

Pro	Con
You can relate to others who have similar issues.	Sometimes, a group can allow you to become too involved merely in
You can get support.	ventilation—talking about what's
You may get good advice and insight.	bothering you without helping you to confront the issue. You may
The group provides interactive opportunities and a chance to practice self-help strategies.	receive understanding without making any real progress.

SOCIAL AND RECREATIONAL GROUPS

Churches, synagogues, YMCAs, YMHAs, and other community centers offer a variety of social and recreational programs for people of all ages, backgrounds, and with varied interests. Choose an organization that appeals to you, and don't be afraid to experiment to find a group that is right for you. Often, these agencies and organizations are staffed by professionals who would be sensitive to your needs. For example, at one point in my career, I worked in a community center where there were trained social workers and other professionals who worked with singles groups, children's groups, and so on. Explore your area and find out what is available.

SPECIAL INTEREST GROUPS

These days, there are special interest groups of all kinds: sports clubs, outdoor clubs, singles activities, political groups, cooking clubs, travel groups, and many more. You can join any of these groups as a way of experimenting with your social self. The people there need never know you wrestle with social anxiety. If you seem quiet or reserved at first, that's natural. If you need to, you can apply your self-help strategies to make it easier for you to interact.

DATING SERVICES

Dating services can be very helpful if you enlist them for the right reasons and with the right expectations. Think of the dating service

the same way you think of the social group: another place to practice being social. Tom, thirty-six, lived at home with his parents
and had very little social experience aside from day-to-day encounters at the insurance company where he worked. He had gone on
very few dates in the recent past, and the longest relationship he
had ever had lasted just two months. I referred him to a dating
service, thinking it would provide him with the opportunities he
lacked. His "luck" with the service was mixed: Some of the women
they put him in contact with chose not to return his calls. But he
did go out with two or three women, and one of the relationships
lasted six months. When it ended, Tom naturally felt disappointed,
but I encouraged him to see the relationship in terms other than
failure. It was an important learning experience, I told him, and he
had certainly enjoyed some aspects of it.

Philip, forty-two, was aware of the dating service option: His
sister had married a man she met through a dating service. When
Philip asked me whether I thought he should join, I encouraged him
to do so. After Philip had worked through his initial anxiety about
making contact with women, he did arrange a number of dates. His
strategy was the same each time: Meet her for coffee, have a conversation, and then decide whether he was interested in pursuing
anything further. Philip did meet several women through the service, he often came back with reports of "too fat" or "too ugly"
or "too cold." But as we talked about the way Philip handled himself, it became clear that he too had his faults. He worked too hard
on a date; there was no sense of play, which resulted in too much
stress. After seven first dates, with no interest in any seconds, Philip
had to reassess his expectations and examine the role he played in
making sure they weren't met. While he may not have met with
success from the dating perspective, however, the experience did
provide material for him to examine and learn from in refining his
attitude and social ability.

Sometimes, well-meaning relatives sign their lonely brothers, sis-
ters, or cousins up with dating services. That's okay as long as it is
with the individual's consent; without this consent, relatives' un-
reasonable expectations increase the potential for failure. But never
allow yourself to get in a situation where a relative is making your

social calls for you. One of my clients had an overzealous father who did exactly that, and the consequences were disastrous. Take responsibility for your own social life!

When considering a dating service, follow these guidelines:

1. Above all, have realistic expectations. Joining a dating service does not guarantee success in terms of dating, developing a relationship, or marriage.
2. Realize that a certain amount of energy has to be put into the process: Making the calls, returning phone calls, spending money on dates, dealing with rejection, and so on.
3. Be aware of what they're charging you for. Dating services have legal limits regarding the amount of money they can charge. Often, there is an attempt to get around these limits by charging for additional activities or services. Be clear on what they are before you get charged for them!
4. Find out how long the service has been in business. One survey we conducted in the New York City area showed that a substantial number of services went out of business after a short time. Buyer beware!
5. Be clear about your objectives:

   - Are you interested in just casual dating?
   - Are you interested in a serious relationship?
   - Are you looking to get married?
   - How will you handle rejection if it occurs?
   - Are you ready to handle the positive stress of a relationship if one develops?
   - Do you accept that any interactive experience is a valuable part of your self-help program?

6. Individuals with handicaps may have a hard time finding success with dating services. Some dating services have specialized in a handicapped clientele but have appeared and disappeared. Still, a void exists that could be filled by the right service.

PERSONAL ADS

Like dating services, personal ads can be a valuable part of creating a social network as long as your expectations are realistic. In today's society, it can be very difficult to meet people—whether you have social anxiety or not. I approve of any vehicle that makes this process easier.

Again, be realistic about your expectations. There are success stories, but then again, there are success stories involving more conventional means as well.

Nancy, a forty-eight-year-old therapist I know, had a lot going for her, but a few years after her divorce, she still hadn't met anyone she wanted to date. She was attractive, intelligent, and self-aware. She hesitated to run a personal ad, but got a number of responses once she did. Unfortunately, she found that her background was quite a bit different in terms of interest and income level from that of the men who responded to her ad. Finally, she met someone in a hiking group for singles with whom she developed a good relationship.

There are more serious concerns to be aware of as well. One female client met a man through a personal ad, only to discover that he became overaggressive when they went out on the date. Fortunately, despite a great deal of anxiety, the woman was able to extricate herself safely from the situation, but this points up two safety precautions to bear in mind:

- Talk to potential dates on the phone a few times to get to know them. Make sure that a rapport develops before you progress further.
- Set your first few meetings in a public place, and agree to meet there.

Don't let your fears steer you away from personal ads. Sometimes they work out well, as they did for Will, who was twenty-seven by the time he finished college. A straight A student, Will had struggled through not because of academics but because his social anxieties and depression were often debilitating. After college, Will got a job as an accountant and made plans to apply for law school the following year. Feeling that at last he was better able to manage his anxiety, and looking forward to the plans he had made, Will decided he was ready to pursue a romantic relationship for the first time since high school. He placed a personal ad in the local newspaper, and went on dates with a few women who called. He started seeing one of them regularly. They saw each other for more than a year and eventually got married. Of course, not all personal ad stories end so successfully, but it's nice to hear a happy ending once in a while.

Don't be held back by the stigma surrounding personal ads. They have worked for thousands of people and they may well work for you. Be sure to keep an open mind and to temper your expectations with reality. Use the following guidelines to make your experience as productive as possible:

1. Choose a reputable publication. Try to determine the nature of the personal ads the publication runs—some cater to those in search of strictly sexual relationships. Also be aware of the types of people who are attracted to the particular publications. For example, a literary review might attract a fairly intellectual advertiser and respondent; a glossy magazine with expensive advertising rates might attract a wealthier clientele.

2. Be aware of the pros and cons of responding by voice mail. On the one hand, it adds a more intimate dimension: People can hear the friendliness in your voice. On the other, a problem could arise: One of my clients, an attractive, likable, wealthy young man, got absolutely no response to voice mail because the women who listened to his ad were turned off by his slight lisp.

3. Understand that people who use personals (as well as dating services) are in essence shopping for a relationship. They have an agenda of their own and will be assessing you to see if you fit into it, just as you are assessing them. You may meet

several people through these services, but the contact may not go beyond the initial meeting. Don't take it personally!

4. Be honest. There are many workshops and materials designed for the purpose of teaching you to write a personal ad. But your best bet is to tell the truth about who you are, what you look like, what you like to do, and what you are looking for. This lessens the chances of false expectations, frustrations, and failure later. One of my clients, a fifty-year-old man from a very overprotective family, got into trouble after his well-meaning parents placed an ad on his behalf. Unfortunately, they exaggerated his social skills, describing him as a sophisticated, attractive man. In fact, he had a long way to go before this could be said about him, and he suffered a lot of needless rejection as a result.

5. Write your own ad rather than merely responding to someone else's. This gives you more control over whom you might reach.

6. Be realistic about the number of responses you expect. And don't think every person who writes is the right person for you. It's okay for *you* to be shopping around too.

7. As with dating services, bear in mind that simply placing the ad does not mean you will ultimately be successful.

8. Do not give out information such as your home address until after you have met the person and decided you feel comfortable with him or her.

9. As I said earlier, meet for the first time in a public place for coffee or a drink. If you are having drinks, limit the amount of alcohol you drink (if any). This gives you more control of yourself and ensures that your perceptions will be more accurate.

10. Not all people are serious. Don't take it personally if the person whose ad you respond to never calls. Just move on. (One of my clients' mothers placed an ad for her. She collected more than sixty responses from men in all walks of life and read them aloud for her own amusement. But she never contacted any of the men who wrote her.)

PARTY LINES

Our advanced technological age has made it possible for you to "attend" a party and "meet" new people without ever leaving your house. The 900-number Party Lines advertised on television allow an individual to hook into an ongoing conversation with any number of other people who want to make friends, establish relationships, or just have fun. As with anything else, this method of introduction has its pros and cons.

Numerous clients have admitted an addiction to these talk lines—an expensive habit, considering that some cost as much as $5 per minute! Those who become addicted end up hiding the fact from family members or roommates, but the addiction becomes obvious when the hundreds of dollars in phone charges come due. How do these addictions develop? As one client said, "On the Party Line, no one could see me and I could be anyone I wanted to be." This client, a college sophomore named Ethan, actually racked up a bill of thousands of dollars in one month. He would stay on the Party Line for eight and nine hours at a time, experimenting with different personalities, including female ones. Because he could get a quick fix of companionship through the Party Line, Ethan could continue to avoid interacting with his peers. But once his mother received the $2,300 phone bill, the game was up, and she brought him to me for help. Eventually, Ethan was able to resolve some of the issues that were causing his anxiety and to use self-help techniques to facilitate real live interaction with real live peers.

Dishonesty and exaggeration will get you nowhere. If you must use Party Lines to develop your conversational skills, make the following deal with yourself:

1. I will limit the number of minutes I talk on the line to the dollar amount I can afford. (Use a timer to remind you.)
2. I will use the Party Line as a way to practice my conversational skills. I will tell the truth and respond honestly to those I talk to.

3. I will protect myself by concealing my identity (most Party Lines prohibit callers from giving identifying details such as addresses and phone numbers).
4. I will not use the Party Line as a quick fix for loneliness, or as a way to avoid more stressful social environments.

Again, be careful! The Party Line has some benefits, but there are risks to watch out for.

WHEN TO SEEK HELP FROM A THERAPIST

When and why should you seek professional help? This subject recently came up during a supervisory session with a staff therapist who had joined us right out of graduate school. "Why do you think people come to therapy?" I asked her. "Because they need someone to talk to," she said. But there's much more to it than that, as I explained to her that day. People enter therapy because they want or need to make a major change in their lives. Therapists can help clients to make genuine, lasting change.

This book is designed to be used as a program of self-help. Ideally, you would like to follow the program independently, without professional help. But sometimes, it is appropriate to seek counseling as part of your overall program. Because social anxiety is a people-oriented problem, individual therapy cannot substitute for practice in interacting. Nevertheless, an efficient therapist can help you develop and use interactive approaches in one-to-one therapy and can serve as a base of support and insight as you begin to make use of community resources. Therapy can also help you clarify certain issues, facilitate change, and provide support and insight as you experiment interactively.

When should you seek a therapist's help? If you have worked through the various steps in this program but feel stuck or frustrated because you are not yet experiencing a positive result, it may be time to consider therapy. If you are unable to activate your PMA and feel mired in a negative attitude, that is another strong sign that therapy may be advisable. You started this self-help program to improve your quality of life, and it is my personal goal in creating this program to make it possible for you to overcome your difficulties and have satisfying personal relationships. If underlying psychological or emotional issues are getting in the way, then I urge you to seek professional counseling. In deciding whether to seek therapy, consider the following:

1. Have you tried to make progress or solve the problem on your own by following the self-help program in this book?
2. How successful have you been?
3. If you have not yet been successful, do you have ideas as to why not?
4. Is the situation getting worse?
5. If the situation is in fact getting better, is it a temporary improvement or has the improvement been consistent?

A Note for Parents

If you are a parent and are concerned that your son or daughter with social problems is stuck or has not made much progress with this program, consider the following:

1. How long has there been a problem?
2. Do you feel that your son or daughter will grow out of it?
3. If the answer is yes, about how long should that take?
4. Do both parents agree about the situation?
5. Is the situation better, worse, or about the same as it was when you began working with this book?
6. Have you tried to solve the problem within the family by using this book?
7. If so, how much success have you observed?
8. Do you truly believe therapy is needed but hesitate to take action because you fear your child's "temper tantrum" (behavior designed to manipulate and control)?

HOW TO SELECT A THERAPIST

Not every person with social anxiety needs a therapist. And not every therapist is right for every person. Especially where interactive issues are the primary concern, it is essential for the therapist-client relationship to be comfortable and relaxed; yet the therapist must be willing to confront the client's resistance and denial in a direct manner. Therapy is an investment—of time, money, and energy—and it is perfectly appropriate to shop around to find an investment that is right for you.

Traditional Freudian psychoanalysis—with sessions spent on the couch facing away from the analyst, who focuses only on what the patient volunteers to say—is of little use to the person with social anxiety. Focusing on the past without also looking at the present is a very ineffective way to treat social anxiety. A blended approach that includes trying to understand how the problem developed and also changing the way the individual responds to anxiety is essential. And remember that the past does not equal the future.

Again, practice is everything, and face-to-face discussion is truly a vital component of the necessary therapeutic process. The establishment of a strong, trusting relationship between client and therapist is absolutely imperative for success. I shudder to think of one of my clients, who came to me after seeing two different therapists over a period of two or three months. What did I find so disturbing? My new client couldn't even remember these therapists' names! A good therapeutic relationship requires interaction and intimacy.

Some psychotherapists have called my practice unorthodox, but that's fine with me. What matters to me is success—and the thousands of people who have worked through my program have persuaded me that a confrontational, open therapeutic environment is most conducive to change for socially anxious individuals. I remember early in my practice, when I was sharing office space with several other therapists, one of them expressed annoyance that my clients would chat with one another in the waiting room, rather than sitting in total silence like his own patients. But many of my clients attended group therapy together and found support in talking to each other. "Quite frankly," I told my colleague, "I encourage them to get to know each other—after all, interaction is really at the heart of what I'm trying to do here."

There are millions of people of all ages who are in some form of therapy now because of problems with social anxiety. Their diagnoses may differ—avoidant personality disorder, dependent personality disorder, anxiety and stress disorder—but the basic problem is the same: fear of social interaction. Because the diagnoses and treatments may vary so widely, since no comprehensive treatment program has existed until now, these people may languish for years in individual counseling without ever having the chance to experiment with and improve their interactive skills. The broad spectrum of psychotherapy offers many different therapeutic orientations, philosophies, clinical approaches, and specialties. The guidelines below should assist you in finding the right therapist for your problems of social anxiety:

1. There are numerous professional disciplines in psychotherapy, including psychiatry, psychology, social work, nursing, pastoral counseling, and the creative arts (such as art therapy and drama therapy). Make sure the therapist you choose is certified in his or her discipline.

2. Do not be afraid to interview your potential therapist. Ask questions. Let the therapist know that you would like to find the best person to help you with your particular problem—social anxiety. If you detect that the therapist is uncomfortable answering questions, chances are this therapist is not for you.

3. Find out if the therapist has had specific experience in working with social anxiety and social phobia, and with what results. (One of my clients, virtually housebound with anxiety, had tried hard with ten therapists, but to no avail. It seemed none of these therapists understood the degree of anxiety that was present, and therefore none was equipped to treat it.) Ask what the therapist's feelings are about stress management and social skills approaches. Again, this is a revolutionary combi-

nation, but if you can find out what the therapist would advise you to do to perfect your social skills, you will get a sense of how cooperative, supportive, and innovative the professional is.

4. Find out what the clinical orientation of the therapist is. The socially anxious individual will benefit most from pragmatic (or practical) clinical approaches—treatment that helps you deal with your symptoms and with present-day issues, rather than focusing on the past. Although it is important to develop insight into the development of your social anxiety, most of your initial work should focus on practical insight and productive support, as well as therapeutic strategies designed to help you move forward.

5. Does the therapist offer a practical approach to stress management and anxiety control? Many therapists say they are stress management experts, but in fact stress management is an abstract concept to them. One of my clients reported seeing several therapists over a period of several years in an attempt to learn to control his panic attacks and manage his social fears. He was extremely frustrated by these professionals. "I would ask them what to do when I have an anxiety attack," he said, "and they would just say I had to 'work my way through it.' But how? They never gave me a game plan." Without a structured approach, confusion and frustration are the order of the day.

6. Does the therapist offer groups? If not, can he or she refer you to a group to supplement your treatment? Does the therapist know how to utilize community resources and does he or she believe in making them a component of treatment? My practice includes many telephone clients from other states, and so community resources are an essential backup. One of my therapists worked on the phone with a client from Chicago. While there were no therapy groups for social anxiety there, we did some research and located an assertiveness training group that we integrated into his overall therapy. Again, social anxiety is a people-oriented problem, and access to a group treatment

option is an important part of your overall map for change.
7. Does the therapist give "homework"? Productive therapy in-cludes carryover from the session to outside the office.
8. If as a parent you seek help for your son or daughter of any age, does the therapist believe in involving the parents? Remem-ber, given the nature of this problem and the fact that there may be related dependency issues, you need to be sure that family issues will be addressed—and therapy will include help-ing the parents to develop a map for change. Confidentiality should of course be maintained, but the treatment strategy should include you. If there are substantial dependency issues and the parents are not part of the process, the result could very well be a frustrating waste of time, energy, and money.

A FINAL NOTE

This chapter suggests many options for making use of a social sys-tem. In turning to your community for resources, you are embracing interaction. When you feel anxious about pursuing these self-help components, look back to your stress management and relaxation techniques to help you to control your anxiety. Of course you will feel anxious or inhibited about joining a new group. But remember: *Dread, then do!* You'll be glad you did.

CHAPTER ELEVEN

"Shyness" and Society: Issues and Patterns

Research has confirmed that millions of people have identified themselves as "shy" at some point in their lives. Why, then, has there been so little research on the subject, and so few programs available to help those in need? "Shyness," it seems, has been considered an unchangeable part of the personality, a benignly pervasive fact of life that society simply takes for granted. How unfortunate, though, for those whose social anxiety prevents them from leading the rewarding, fulfilling lives they would like to lead.

I wrote this book to offer a means of changing the supposedly unchangeable trait of "shyness." It is my goal to replace the concept of "shyness" with a new, far more accurate term: *social anxiety*. As I've explained, anxiety is a learned response, and therefore it can be unlearned. To think of "shyness" as a bad habit that can be broken is to free yourself from social anxiety, and allow yourself to take responsibility for your own responses—indeed, you must—and work toward a healthier interactive self. Of course, the benefits include not only interactive success and higher-quality relationships, but also *better physical health and longer life*. There is no magic pill that a physician can prescribe to take away anxiety symptoms and their underlying cause. This self-help program is a new way of life, a new way of looking at oneself and one's world.

During the thirteen years my program has existed, I have observed certain trends that I would like to mention here as a way of putting social anxiety into perspective.

DENIAL

Perhaps the single greatest obstacle I encounter is denial. Unquestionably, this is the biggest issue for society as a whole, and one that we are just beginning to tackle. In cases of social anxiety, denial is pervasive. The mother of a ten-year-old girl who had participated successfully in my program recently called me to say how grateful she was for the results we had brought her. "I have so many parents of elementary-age children to refer to you," she said. "But the problem is, none of them will come. They won't admit there's any problem at all!"

Breaking through denial is an essential part of beginning to treat social anxiety. As I have pointed out, denial has many faces. It is very easy for a person with social anxiety to deny that a problem exists. Given the nature of social anxiety—that it is caused by a fear of humiliation, embarrassment, and scrutiny—it is obvious why a socially anxious person would come to avoid what makes him or her anxious. But to deny the problem is to enable it to continue. Parents are often actively in denial, even though their child's patterns of social anxiety are striking. Typically, parents of young children or teens will respond in the following way: The mother is sure there is a problem, while the father says simply, "I was shy as a child too, and I grew out of it." Or one parent won't even acknowledge the problem exists at all. The reality, however, is that the child or adolescent is truly suffering from anxiety. *The sooner intervention and self-help strategies are put into place, the better the prognosis.* Later in life, anxiety can be too old a habit to break, which is a tragedy for all concerned.

To help yourself overcome denial, use the "Adult"—the objective computer part of your personality—to gain perspective on your situation. Do not allow yourself to confuse denial with strength of character. The first step toward controlling anxiety is to abandon your denial. Make a commitment to yourself to improve the situation that exists. Your success graph will have its ups and downs. But stay with the program. In order to move toward self-actualization— fulfillment on a personal and professional level—you must adopt a work ethic. Self-help requires discipline. There are no instant answers. But a concentrated effort will reward you time and time again.

MEN AND WOMEN

About 65 percent of the calls I receive from around the country are from men or from parents concerned about their adolescent or adult sons. Does this mean that most of the people who suffer from social anxiety are men? Are women for the most part immune to social anxiety? My more informal research says no. My theory—not to be sexist—is that society expects more from men, despite recent gains in equality for women. Men are under far more pressure to succeed, both in their careers and in their social lives, than women are. Women can be considered "shy," "demure," "quiet"—all stereotypically feminine characteristics and all characteristics that can mask social anxiety, which can perpetuate overprotective and enabling behavior.

LEARNING DISABILITIES

I have found that there is a strong correlation between social anxiety, difficulty with social skills, and learning disabilities. Learning disabilities—problems with taking in, storing, and retrieving information from the brain—are considered a hidden handicap. Despite difficulty processing information, a learning-disabled person may go undiagnosed throughout his or her formative years. Learning disabilities are not the mark of an unintelligent person; on the contrary, many learning-disabled people are of above-average intelligence, and, with help, can become highly successful in their careers and their personal lives. Functioning level is determined not totally by the disability but also by the available compensation strategies.

Again, there is a wide range within the category of "learning disabled." Consider: William, a forty-seven-year-old married father of two, is the head of a venture-capital firm that has yearly transactions totaling millions of dollars. He suffers from dyslexia, but has clearly been able to overcome his disability and achieve success. Matt, age thirty-one, suffers from more pervasive developmental problems; he was in special education throughout school, and secured a job with the parks department upon graduating. His salary is $14,000 a year, and he lives at home with his parents. Both men have learning disabilities, but their functioning levels are vastly different. It is important not to stigmatize the learning disabled.

Unfortunately, although there is much new research to draw upon, little has been documented about the connection between learning disabilities and interactive difficulties. But in my thirteen years of clinical practice, several things have become clear. The high correlation between learning disabilities, social anxiety, and poor interactive skills stems from two things. First, the person with a learning disability is more susceptible to mistakes and failure, and at an earlier age, and may have more trouble picking up on the normal social cues that guide the rest of us through a social encounter. This lack of skill leads to anxiety and confusion, which leads to avoidance—a pattern similar to the one described in Chapter 1. But here, the confusion starts with the learning disability.

The second component that may cause a learning-disabled person to withdraw is low self-esteem. As we've discussed, low self-esteem is pervasive among those with social anxiety. In the case of the learning disabled, a poor self-image may result from years of being frustrated in school and among peers. If you suspect that you have learning disabilities (or that your socially anxious son or daughter does), seek testing from a qualified professional. The best way to cope with learning disabilities is to understand the limitations they cause and to explore new ways of compensating for them. NOTE: The connection between interactive abilities and learning disabilities could be the subject of a book in itself. What is presented here is merely a synopsis.

ELECTIVE MUTISM

Social anxiety appears in many forms, some of which are only now coming to light. Socially anxious children, for example, are usually thought of as quiet and reserved and of course "shy." But some children, though they function fairly well in their home environment, have great difficulty talking in social situations. Donny was one such child. At fourteen, he managed quite well at home, but never talked to his peers. His parents encouraged him to join in group activities, and even sent him off to an overnight camp. But he remained silent, even when he became lost in the woods. The child was alone for several hours; dusk was approaching, and he began to get cold, but he still could not bring himself to call out. The counselors were near enough for him to attract their attention and yet he remained mute.

Alarm bells went off for Melanie when she noticed that her daughter at age three had trouble talking with people outside their home. When the little girl went to see Santa Claus, and he asked her what she wanted for Christmas, she became hysterical and couldn't respond verbally. And the problem continued: She would speak only with the immediate family, and never to peers or potential playmates.

Elective mutism is a very specific symptom of social anxiety. Fear turns into panic which inhibits speech; the elective mute is capable—physically—of speaking to outsiders, but anxiety prevents him or her from speaking. Only recently has there been any media attention paid to this syndrome, and research in this area has just begun. After an article appeared in a New York–area newspaper, however, someone who had expressed interest in starting a self-help group for elective mutes was besieged with phone calls from desperate relatives, eager to get help for their silent family members. I have worked with people of all ages who suffer from varying degrees of elective mutism. From my perspective, elective mutism is treatable relatively easily in childhood or early adolescence. But treating the adult is very difficult because of the pervasive progression of the problem.

TECHNOLOGICAL BREAKTHROUGHS?

The tremendous technological advances our society has enjoyed in the latter part of this century have created numerous new ways to reinforce socially anxious behavior. Children come home to their televisions, computers, Nintendo games, with no need to seek each other out for companionship and social experimentation. Adults use 900-number Party and porno lines as a substitute for dating, and do their shopping from the Home Shopping Network in their living rooms. This technology is not destructive in and of itself, but when it becomes a substitute for peer relationships and healthy interaction, it can be extremely unhealthy. Teenagers are especially susceptible. Johnny, age fifteen, came home every day to his best friends: Nintendo and computer games. He never did things with his peers, though he told his parents he had lots of friends at school. He isolated himself totally from kids his own age. The recent cases of teenage computer bandits throughout the country are another example of an antisocial personality; no doubt in some cases social anxiety and poor interactive skills have contributed to those young people's outlook.

On the other hand, technology can become a valuable part of social success. Craig was a twenty-four-year-old college graduate who worked as a computer programmer and lived at home with his mother. He had one friend he considered close but very limited experience with the opposite sex. He would spend most of his time after work experimenting with his computer. He hooked up a national bulletin board which created the opportunity to begin communicating with people from all over the country. He made contact with a woman who lived in Florida and developed a relationship with her that eventually led to his moving to Florida, where he got a job and lived with her.

ALCOHOL

The inappropriate use of alcohol to compensate for social anxiety is at epidemic proportions. Unfortunately, many people who feel anxious in social situations turn to alcohol to calm their nerves and make them more relaxed. Usually, alcohol in moderation is not dangerous. But for the socially anxious, it can become habit-forming. Larry is a fifty-two-year-old postal worker who, after being divorced, tried the singles scene as a way of meeting people. But whenever he managed to attend an event, he drank four or five shots of whiskey to "take the edge off" his social anxiety. Larry swore he was not an alcoholic—after all, he only drank a few times a month, the same few times he socialized. But because he was dependent on alcohol to enable himself to cope socially, I do consider him an alcoholic.

Terry, a twenty-six-year-old telephone operator, was very good at his job and set a record for handling information requests each day. He was promoted to manager, which necessitated his having to give group presentations. The result? High anxiety, which he dealt with by having "a few beers" before his talk.

Elliot, twenty-nine, tried desperately for companionship. His relationships with women had not been successful, and although he did have a few male friends, he often went out alone. He began going to a neighborhood disco, where he would have a couple of drinks, maybe dance a little. Before long, he was going there seven nights a week and drinking heavily. In a sense, alcohol had become his lover, his substitute for companionship. He didn't want to give it up.

All three men were self-medicating with alcohol. Their social anxiety led to alcohol abuse, a secondary problem. Alcohol is not the answer. It temporarily masks the problem but ultimately makes it worse.

DEPRESSION

Many of the individuals in my program have pointed to a level of depression as an initial symptom. Depression—pervasive, overwhelming feelings of sadness and hopelessness—is a natural result of social anxiety. Anyone who has been inhibited by anxiety and fear will experience less success, less pleasure, less gratification, and ultimately, lower self-esteem. The more pervasive this pattern, the more frustration and anger build. The result can be a reactive depression, caused by the situation the individual finds himself in. Other forms of depression—indigenous or biological depression—have a chemical basis. But some degree of reactive depression is common among socially anxious people, and many mental health professionals erroneously identify depression as the overwhelming problem (in fact, social anxiety is at the root, and has caused the depression). With this kind of depression, decreasing social anxiety and promoting healthy interaction is the long-term answer.

PATTERNS OF THE "SHY"

What else is common among people who identify themselves as "shy"? Below are the results of a survey that was administered to 150 of my program's participants. The results of this informal survey reveal certain facts and attitudes common among the socially anxious. Let me point out that these are the subjective answers of the clients themselves—not the professional opinions of the therapists. The average length of time in the program for all who responded was eight months. The average age was twenty-eight. (Some of the answers are based on a scale of 1 to 5, 1 being the lowest.)

- Most clients considered shyness to be a serious problem at some point in their lives. Almost everyone rated the seriousness of their problem at level 5, which makes sense, considering that all who responded were seeking help for their problem.
- 60 percent of the respondents said that "shyness" first became enough of a problem that it held them back from things they wanted during adolescence; 35 percent reported the problem began in childhood; and 5 percent said not until adulthood. This answer reveals when clients were first aware of social anxiety as an inhibiting force.
- The respondents perceived the average degree of "sociability" of their parents was a 2.7, which translates to "fair"; 60 percent of the respondents reported that no other member of the family

had a problem with "shyness"; and 40 percent said there was at least one other family member who had a problem with "shyness."

- 50 percent were aware of rejection by their peers during childhood.
- 66 percent had physical symptoms of discomfort during social interaction that they believed were related to social anxiety.
- 55 percent reported that they had experienced panic attacks.
- 85 percent do not use any medication for anxiety; 15 percent do.
- 90 percent said they avoid opportunities to meet new people; 75 percent acknowledged that they often stay home because of social fears, rather than going out.
- 80 percent identified feelings of depression that they connected to social fears.
- 70 percent said they had difficulty with social skills.
- 75 percent felt that before they started the program it was impossible to control their social fears; 80 percent said they now believed it was possible to control their fears.
- 50 percent said they believed they might have a learning disability.
- 70 percent felt that they were "too dependent on their parents"; 75 percent felt their parents were overprotective; 50 percent reported that they would not have sought professional help if not for their parents' urging.
- 10 percent of respondents were the only child in their families; 40 percent had one sibling; 30 percent had two siblings; 10 percent had three; and 10 percent had four or more.

Experts can play many games with statistics. Of importance here are the general attitudes and patterns of a population of socially anxious individuals who were in a therapy program designed to combat their problem. Of primary significance is the high percentage of people who first thought that "shyness" was uncontrollable, but then later changed their minds, once they realized that anxiety is a habit that can be broken—without medication. Also significant is that 50 percent of the participants recognized that their parents were the catalyst for their seeking help. Consider these statistics and think about where you fit into them. Do you identify with this profile? Look back on it in the coming months and examine the ways in which your sociability changes. Give yourself credit for successful breakthroughs, and keep in mind that you are not alone!

CURRENT RESEARCH

In the past few years, research has been conducted for the first time on social anxiety and social phobia. Most of this research, however, includes medication as a component of treatment. In fact, the National Institute of Mental Health has announced that a combination of medication with cognitive-behavioral therapy is the most effective. Yet as of this writing, there is no systematic psychotherapy protocol for treating social anxiety. This book is based on my own protocol, which has been developed over more than a decade. It is also important to note once more that the correlation between learning disabilities and interactive issues has yet to be studied in a comprehensive way; yet perhaps 50 percent of those with social anxiety do also suffer from learning disabilities.

A CHANGING SOCIETY

What does today's high incidence of social anxiety tell us about modern society? As we've seen, social anxiety is connected to a person's drive for self-preservation and a feeling of safety. It is natural to withdraw from situations that we expect will lead to pain. Avoidance—while not necessarily healthy—is logical. Because the negative social experience of a growing number of people has caused them emotional pain and suffering, the number of individuals who choose to avoid socializing is increasing at an alarming rate. The sometimes wide distance among family members these days only adds to isolation. And the anonymity of large cities creates a vacuum in which many lonely people co-exist, often leading solitary lives in which they pursue their interests and activities alone.

We live in a society in which social fears are perhaps not unjustified. As cities become denser, isolation seems to be the best way to counter urban decay. Consider the dangers of the outside world: Crime rates are soaring. Caution—and its companion, fear—are in the air. As the twentieth century draws to a close, we find ourselves in a society where meeting people can be difficult.

These larger forces can combine to create a further sense of distance among people. Particularly significant is the change that has taken place as the social organization of the smaller-scale community gives way to that of the larger, increasingly fragmented city. In a "hometown" setting, the character of daily life is largely composed of face-to-face relations with friends, neighbors, co-workers, and family members. But in the hustle and bustle of today's cities, whose urban sprawls extend to what author Joel Garreau has called *Edge Cities*—creating light industrial suburbs even larger than the cities they surround—the individual can get lost. It is common in these areas for people to focus solely on themselves, seldom getting to know their neighbors, and rarely living close to family. We may call these places home, but they are a far cry from the definition of that word as we knew it when we were children.

Today's cities are hotbeds of competition on all levels, from the professional to the social. It often seems as if only the most sophisticated "win." To be ready for this constant challenge, you have to be able to manage in a stressful environment, relying on a whole repertoire of social skills just to stay afloat. This competitive environment can be terrifying for the socially anxious person.

The 1980s were a consumer decade in which picture-perfect images on television and in magazines caused many of us to cast our lots with either the haves or the have-nots. Pressure to succeed grew to an all-time high. For those who felt they could not measure up, the challenge seemed daunting. I think the escalating crime rate in today's urban centers—drugs, burglary, rape, and murder—ties into this trend and society's response to the pressure. In looking at the forces that influence the social context of modern life, it is clear that feelings of frustration at not "making it" socially and financially are a component in many people's choosing a life of crime. Interactive ability determines success in establishing a rewarding career, in experiencing relationships. Without these prospects, crime can appear to be a quick fix for a lifelong problem.

So what good is to be found in today's metropolitan areas, amidst all the alienation, the anonymity, and the lack of cohesiveness that characterize the life-style there? Along with separation and disintegration comes specialization—and therefore excellent opportunities to socialize and utilize a vast interactive system involving the many special interest groups discussed in the previous chapter. Opportunities are there for the taking: in social and academic areas, in business and career fulfillment, for personal and financial growth. Opportunities for self-actualization abound. In the years to come, there will be increasingly more chances to socialize with like-minded peers, in environments never before conceived. These opportunities, when viewed as a testing ground for the self-help program described in this book, can become the basis for tremendous interactive success, no matter what your past experience has been. Change is in the offing, both for you and the ever-changing society in which you live.

CHAPTER TWELVE

Go for It! Some Final Words
of Encouragement

The average life span of a man in our society is about seventy-seven years, and that of a woman slightly higher. If you or a member of your family is struggling with problems of social anxiety, it is to your benefit to approach the situation with a practical sense of urgency. Remember: Time is not elastic. It cannot be stretched or manipulated. You get one chance. Life, as they say, is not a dress rehearsal. You owe it to yourself to do all you can to get the most out of it right now!

Social anxiety can be controlled, and even cured, if you develop a combination of strategies that work for you. This self-help program could well mean the difference between a healthy, happy, productive life and a life of loneliness, negative limitations, and real debilitation. The choice is yours. Even if you live to be one hundred years old, life is too short not to get what you want. The person who is inhibited by social anxiety will not get what he or she wants. That is a shame, because social anxiety is a very manageable dynamic!

By now, you understand that fear of interacting with people has at its roots a fear of humiliation, embarrassment, scrutiny, and judgment by others. Don't let anxiety keep you from having the kind of life you want. You don't have to. Make PMA—positive mental attitude—a part of your personality. Tell yourself that things will get better; integrate these self-help strategies into your daily life;

and discover in yourself the confident, fulfilled, productive person you want to be.

Still afraid of failure? That's natural. Embarking on a course of major personal change can be daunting at times. But remember, any rejection you encounter along the way, while disappointing, will not be devastating. Consider: What is the worst thing that can happen if you fail in an interactive situation? Usually, it's embarrassment, which happens to all of us. What does embarrassment mean to you? Write down your thoughts on humiliation and embarrassment. Let me ask you these questions:

1. What is the worst thing that can happen to you if you are embarrassed?
2. Does embarrassment say anything significant about your character?
3. If you "lose control," what happens? Is it a temporary feeling?
4. What is the worst thing that can happen if your anxiety really goes up? Will it pass?
5. Are you aware that people usually cannot tell you are in an anxiety state? That they cannot read your mind?
6. Considering that life is short, doesn't risking embarrassment or failure in order to have fulfilling interactions seem worth it?

Now, use mental imagery to imagine yourself feeling embarrassed. Take a deep breath, sit in a comfortable chair, use your mind's eye to picture the interactive situation clearly. Now see yourself interacting, having a conversation. What do you say? Picture excusing yourself from the situation and moving on to another conversation. How do you feel? If you need time, visualize getting some refreshments or leafing through a magazine until you've used your relaxation techniques to bring yourself under control. See yourself applying stress management techniques. See yourself in control. How does it feel? What would make it better?

Now go back and do the exercise again. See yourself making it even better and more successful. As you've worked through this self-help program, you've gained the skills to get through a stressful or potentially embarrassing situation. You can do it, and you won't be devastated.

NOTE: If, after attempting to follow this self-help program, you are still unable to take the necessary risks, refer back to the section on getting professional help.

YOU CANNOT HAVE SUCCESS WITHOUT FAILURE

No one ever became successful at anything without experiencing some measure of failure first. In anything, there is trial and error. Babe Ruth hit 714 home runs, but he struck out a lot more than that. For each new invention, there are numerous abandoned prototypes. For each business success, there are usually months and months in the red. There must also be a long investment period for interactive success. Stay committed to your program. *See it through.* A lot depends on it.

Remember your motivation, remember why you're doing it! Everyone experiences ups and downs, and these ups and downs will continue even after your social system is established and thriving. Make sure you keep your expectations realistic, and remember what your graph of social success is expected to look like:

You have your map for change. I have included in this book all the information and know-how that you need to conquer your social anxiety. The rest is up to you. Apply what you know. There will be roadblocks along the road to success, but you will be able to maneuver around them effectively using the skills and strategies you have learned. Rely on your PMA. Continue to nurture yourself, keeping in mind that one of the most helpful aspects of *nurturing is helping yourself to confront difficulties rather than avoid them.*

After following this self-help program for twenty-one days, complete the physical symptoms and recurring thought patterns profiles again.

What does your body do when you feel anxious or nervous?

Frequency	Severity	Social Life Interference
1 = Never	1 = No problem at all	1 = Not at all
2 = 2 times a month or less	2 = Minor discomfort but you can manage it	2 = A little
3 = 1 or 2 times a week	3 = Noticeably uncomfortable	3 = Moderately
4 = 3 times a week but not daily	4 = Severe	4 = Significantly
5 = 1 or more times daily	5 = Absolute panic; feels out of control	5 = Severe to the point of incapacity

a) Shortness of breath
b) Accelerated heartbeat
c) Sweating
d) Dizziness or faintness
e) Nausea or abdominal stress
f) Choking
g) Depersonalization—feeling of unreality, being "outside yourself"
h) Tingling or numbness

i) Flushes or chills
j) Voice quivering or shaking
k) Sweaty palms
l) Cold hands
m) Your mind going blank
n) Twitches, tics, or spasms
o) Lump in throat
p) Stuttering
q) Difficulty concentrating
r) Other

Total Scores:

What thoughts recur when you are anxious or nervous?

Frequency	Severity	Social Life Interference
1 = Never	1 = No problem at all	1 = Not at all
2 = 2 times a month or less	2 = Minor discomfort but you can manage it	2 = A little
3 = 1 or 2 times a week		3 = Moderately
4 = 3 times a week but not daily	3 = Noticeably uncomfortable	4 = Significantly
5 = 1 or more times daily	4 = Severe	5 = Severe to the point of incapacity
	5 = Absolute panic; feels out of control	

a) What will people think of me?
b) Am I good enough?
c) Am I dressed okay?
d) How do I look?
e) I'm going to embarrass myself.
f) People can tell I'm nervous.
g) People can tell what I'm thinking.
h) I'm going to lose control.
i) I'm going to have to run from the room.
j) What will I say?
k) I'm ugly.
l) If they knew me, they wouldn't like me.
m) I always do the wrong thing.
n) They can see I'm different.
o) They can see I'm lonely.
p) They can see I don't belong.
q) I can't.
r) They all have more than I do.
s) I always screw up.
t) I don't know what to say.
u) Other

Total Scores:

Now, refer back to Chapter 1, where you first used these indexes to chart your current situation.

What has changed?

_____

_____

_____

_____

What would you like to improve?

_____

_____

_____

_____

What steps will you take to try to improve these categories?

_____

_____

_____

_____

In three months, complete the profiles again. *Continue to incorporate these self-help strategies into your life-style.* Refer back to the book for the techniques that will enable you to make progress. When you are ready for a progress check at three months, complete the profiles below, and compare your answers at the beginning of the book with the answers 21 days into the program and your answers today.

What does your body do when you feel anxious or nervous?

Frequency	Severity	Social Life Interference
1 = Never	1 = No problem at all	1 = Not at all
2 = 2 times a month or less	2 = Minor discomfort but you can manage it	2 = A little
3 = 1 or 2 times a week	3 = Noticeably uncomfortable	3 = Moderately
4 = 3 times a week but not daily	4 = Severe	4 = Significantly
5 = 1 or more times daily	5 = Absolute panic; feels out of control	5 = Severe to the point of incapacity

a) Shortness of breath
b) Accelerated heartbeat
c) Sweating
d) Dizziness or faintness
e) Nausea or abdominal stress
f) Choking
g) Depersonalization—feeling of
   unreality, being "outside
   yourself"
h) Tingling or numbness

i) Flushes or chills
j) Voice quivering or shaking
k) Sweaty palms
l) Cold hands
m) Your mind going blank
n) Twitches, tics, or spasms
o) Lump in throat
p) Stuttering
q) Difficulty concentrating
r) Other

Total Scores:

What thoughts recur when you are anxious or nervous?

Frequency	Severity	Social Life Interference
1 = Never	1 = No problem at all	1 = Not at all
2 = 2 times a month or less	2 = Minor discomfort but you can manage it	2 = A little
3 = 1 or 2 times a week	3 = Noticeably uncomfortable	3 = Moderately
4 = 3 times a week but not daily	4 = Severe	4 = Significantly
5 = 1 or more times daily	5 = Absolute panic; feels out of control	5 = Severe to the point of incapacity

a) What will people think of me?
b) Am I good enough?
c) Am I dressed okay?
d) How do I look?
e) I'm going to embarrass myself.
f) People can tell I'm nervous.
g) People can tell what I'm thinking.
h) I'm going to lose control.
i) I'm going to have to run from the room.
j) What will I say?

k) I'm ugly.
l) If they knew me, they wouldn't like me.
m) I always do the wrong thing.
n) They can see I'm different.
o) They can see I'm lonely.
p) They can see I don't belong.
q) I can't.
r) They all have more than I do.
s) I always screw up.
t) I don't know what to say.
u) Other

Total Scores:

What has changed?

_____

_____

_____

_____

What would you like to improve?

_____

_____

_____

_____

What steps will you take to try to improve these categories?

_____

_____

_____

_____

By now, you are aware of the ways in which your past social experience has shaped your social self. And you have completed a number of personality profiles to help you to understand what your present situation is. You've set some short- and long-term goals to work toward. Let's take a moment now to look into the distant future.

What do you want your life to be like five years from now?

1. Where do you expect to be living?
2. With whom?
3. How much money will you be making?
4. What will your social life be like?

5. What kind of work will you be doing?
6. What will you be doing for fun and enjoyment?
7. If you don't control your social anxiety, will you be able to reach these goals?

You can reach these goals if you take responsibility for controlling your anxiety.

When Adam, the anxiety-prone student I introduced you to in Chapter 1, was sixteen, he would spend his free time in his room, playing a home computer baseball game. He had no friends. He stopped going to school. He didn't know there was any other way to live. His anxiety was controlling him. But Adam was able to regain control, and he eventually graduated from high school and went on to college, where he made many friends of both sexes. Today, not only does he have a steady girlfriend, but he is pursuing a Ph.D. in computer sciences. And most important, the anxious, miserably unhappy sixteen-year-old is now an outgoing, well-adjusted, and happy twenty-one-year-old. It can be done!

Charlie, from Chapter 2, who had been interested in the "hot" young woman with the sports car, eventually developed realistic social expectations. By working on his interactive ability, Charlie developed a higher opinion of himself as a companion. With increased confidence, he was able to venture into the social world. As his self-esteem increased, he started to make more of an effort with his appearance. In time, he was able to develop dating relationships with several women. Career success followed, too, and he is now a fulfilled, productive person.

There are countless examples of individuals of all ages with varying levels of problems who are able to make improvements big and small that lead them forward on the path to self-actualization. Remember, 85 percent of people I surveyed who at one time thought change was not possible now believe it is!

The point is, you are capable of change! Life is what you make of it! Use this self-help program to make it all you want it to be. Don't spend your life waiting for your luck to change. Make your own good luck by changing the way you respond. Go for it! The rewards are immeasurable.

Index